GREECE

Frontispiece. RELIEF OF ARCHELAUS OF PRIENE:
THE APOTHEOSIS OF HOMER

Zeus and the Muses are shown in the upper part of the relief upon
a mountain side, and Apollo stands in a cave. Beside him is the
omphalos or sacred stone of Delphi. On the right is a statue of a
poet with a tripod. In the lowest row Homer is enthroned between
figures of Iliad and Odyssey. He is crowned by Time and the World;
figures of Myth, History, Poetry, Tragedy, Comedy, and other per-
sonifications are making an offering.

The relief was probably dedicated by a poet who had won a tripod
in a contest, and had derived his inspiration from Homer. It is inscribed with the names of the sculptor Archelaus, son of Apollonios
of Priene. 3rd century B.C. British Museum.

M. ROSTOVTZEFF

GREECE

Translated from the Russian by J. D. Duff

ELIAS J. BICKERMAN
Editor, Paperback Edition

OXFORD UNIVERSITY PRESS
London   Oxford   New York

© Oxford University Press, Inc., 1963
Library of Congress Catalogue Card Number: 63-9628

First published by the Clarendon Press as follows:
A History of the Ancient World, first edition,
Volume I: The Orient and Greece, 1926, second edition, 1930;
Volume II: Rome, 1927, second corrected impression, 1928

Greece first issued as an Oxford University Press paperback, 1963

printing, last digit: 29 28 27 26 25

Printed in the United States of America

PREFACE TO THE PAPERBACK EDITION

This volume contains all of the material on Greece included in Rostovtzeff's A *History of the Ancient World*; that is, Chapters XII through XXVI and parts of Chapters VI and VII. It also seemed advisable to reprint here the two introductory chapters (I and II) of Rostovtzeff's work.

Here and there small changes were made to keep the book abreast of new discoveries. A page was added at the beginning of the book to give some idea of the earliest civilization in Greece, a period which was hardly known at the time of the Second Edition (1930). But the editor never forgot that this was the work of his teacher, and not his own. He deleted statements made doubtful by new evidence but avoided introducing new views or judgments. For the same reason, he partly rewrote Chapters XXI–XXVI (now XIV–XVII) to bring them into agreement with Rostovtzeff's *Social and Economic History of the Hellenistic World*, published in 1941.

Mrs. M. Rostovtzeff kindly helped to choose illustrations from the plates of the Second Edition. Some illustrations have been added, the bibliography has been compiled anew, and the chronology revised. The redrawn maps now exhibit almost all the geographical names mentioned in the text, and only those names.

May 1962   E. J. B.

PREFACE TO THE FIRST EDITION

This book was planned and written between 1921 and 1923 at Madison (Wisconsin). It is a course of lectures on Ancient History which I gave yearly for nearly five years to the Freshmen of Wisconsin University, and which I am now giving, in a slightly altered form, to the Sophomores of Yale University. For publication in the shape of a book, these lectures of course have been revised, corrected, and supplemented.

My 'Outline of Ancient History' was not written merely as a text-book for the use of students. My chief object was to collect therein those fundamental ideas and views, concerning the main problems of ancient history, which I had gained from long years spent on the study of the subject. To give to this work a strictly scientific form would have required too much time, and also too great sacrifices on the part of the publishers. And further, it is too late for me to think now of a large and complicated work of the kind. I consider it more useful to devote what remains to me of life to work of a more specialist nature. For this reason I publish my book without scientific apparatus, endeavouring merely to make the exposition as simple and clear as possible. Published in such a shape, my book may serve as a text-book for students beginning the subject, and also may be read by those who wish to acquaint themselves with the general course of development in the ancient world.

In composing a brief outline of the subject, the chief difficulty was the selection and distribution of the matter. We know, of course, much more about the ancient world than is here set forth. It was difficult, also, to assign the right space to each epoch in the development of antiquity, and to each aspect of that development. My own interests and studies have been directed, and are still directed, to certain subjects in particular—the East, the Hellenistic Age, and the Roman Empire—and to the problems connected with the history of those periods, whether economic or social or cultural. But I have done all I could to prevent the matters in which I am specially interested from being too prominent, and have tried to allot due space to the history of the Greek cities and republican Rome, as also to the political and military history of the ancient world in general. How far I have been successful in this attempt, it is not for me to judge.

This 'Outline', as has been said already, does not contain references either to the ancient sources or to the works of modern scholars. This limitation was made necessary for me by the nature of my book. In general, I only refer to sources where the course of my narrative seems to require it. The most important modern works on the subject are enumerated in a short bibliography appended to the book; and there I mention also such English books as give a good summary of our knowledge in an easily accessible form. I have given this preference to English books, because my own book, in its English version, is intended mainly for English and American readers and students.

I recognize the very great importance of good maps for historical works. But unfortunately I am not a specialist in historical cartography or cartography generally, and I cannot myself make maps. I have been obliged therefore to be content with certain maps borrowed from other works—such maps as I considered most necessary to explain the narrative.

An archaeologist myself, I recognize the immense power of archaeological material to throw light upon antiquity. I have therefore devoted much time and pains to the selection of such material for the illustration of my book. I have been much helped in this matter by my friends Mr. B. Ashmole, Mr. J. D. Beazley, and Mr. H. Mattingly; the last has helped me specially with coins. In the choice of these illustrations, my object has not been merely to amuse and entertain my readers.

The soul of a people is just as clearly reflected in its literature as in its art. I have endeavoured to make due use of ancient literature in the course of my text; but extracts can give no idea of its real character and real greatness. Mere quotations from any great literary work are lifeless things, and therefore I abstain from them. If any reader of my book wishes to understand the soul of the ancient world, he must read at the same time the great works of ancient literature either in the originals or in translations. If other teachers do me the honour of recommending my work as a text-book to their students, they must insist on this point—that the chief monuments of the literature, Eastern, Greek, and Roman, be read, in their entirety and not in extracts, at the same time.

With regard to the plastic arts my position was different. In this case it is possible to give a selection of the noblest productions of ancient art, and to give it in the same book in which this material is used by the historian. Moreover, each of these monuments not only throws light upon various aspects of the ancient mind, but brings before the eyes either the great characters of the age in portraits which are often remarkable, or separate scenes from life, as they were represented in the fancy of the ancient sculptors and painters. These considerations account for the large space allotted in my book to the monuments of ancient art. For the benefit of the reader I have given short descriptions of the separate monuments, but without references to modern publications of them. Some such references the reader will find in the bibliography.

Lastly, an immemorial custom allows an author, when concluding his preface, to thank those whose assistance has lightened the composition and publication of his book. Unfortunately, I cannot enumerate all those who have contributed to the illustration by sending me photographs or permitting me to use monuments already published: a list of the names would probably fill more than one page. One acknowledgement, however, must not be omitted. My requests, which were often not too modest, did not meet with a single refusal from any European country or any institution in the United States. This is one more proof of the rapid restoration of international scientific relations, which the war seemed at one time to have shattered irrevocably. I must make a further exception and record the friendly assistance of my pupil, Miss T. S. Varsher, who spent much trouble and time in collecting photographs for my use in Rome and Italy.

My book appeared first at Berlin in the Russian language. I had not myself the time to make an English version of it; but fortune sent me an ideal translator in the person of Mr. J. D. Duff. Mr. Duff, who combines an exact knowledge of Russian with the training of a classical scholar, did not decline the thankless task of translating the work of an author who was too modest to translate it himself. I permit myself to offer him here my sincere and warm acknowledgements.

I must also mention here, not for the first time, my great obligations to the Clarendon Press and its conductors. It is due entirely to their courtesy that the book is provided with so large a number of excellent illustrations; and, further, I feel bound to acknowledge the assistance of the Oxford Press, both in the choice of a translator, and in procuring originals for illustration, and in the distribution of these illustrations upon the plates. A better publisher for my book I could not possibly have found.

I dedicate the book to the University of Wisconsin. In the darkest hour of my life the University of Wisconsin made it possible for me to resume my learned studies and carry them on without interruption. During five years which I spent there I met with constant kindness from my colleagues, and unvarying consideration, on the part of the University authorities, for my requests and my scientific occupations. Nor can I recall without a feeling of gratitude the sympathy of the students. Such an atmosphere lightened the toil of writing this book; and it was addressed in the first instance to the students of Wisconsin.

Vade felix libelle.

New Haven, Conn.,   M. R.

Sept. 25, 1925.

PREFACE TO THE SECOND EDITION

Since the publication of the first edition of this book four years ago a great deal of work has been done in the field of ancient history. Especially important are the new discoveries in the history of the Orient. Excavations in Egypt, in Mesopotamia, in Syria, and in Asia Minor have brought to light so much new material that it was impossible to leave the text and plates which deal with this period as they were compiled in 1925. The new edition, however, has been mainly printed from the stereo plates of the first edition (corrected for the purpose), and for that reason, and also because my publisher was obliged to call upon me for my corrections at short notice, I have been able to make fewer changes than I should have wished. In the sections dealing with Greece no changes have been made. To the plates of this section two new plates have been added, reproducing some archaic and hellenistic terra-cottas which bear on Greek life in the corresponding periods. The bibliography has been revised as far as it was possible in the short time at my disposal.

Oxford,   M. R.
October, 1929.

CONTENTS

FIGURES IN THE TEXT

LIST OF PLATES

GREECE

I

HISTORY: ITS AIMS AND METHODS

There are many different theories concerning the business of history as a science, but on one main point they all agree: it is evidently the business of the historian to reveal the past of humanity, and to reproduce the life of mankind in all its variety and trace its development from the most ancient times down to our own day.

History owes its origin to the same characteristic of man's nature which has created the other departments of learning: I mean the desire for knowledge innate in humanity. The object of this knowledge is the world in its entirety and, above all, man himself. In this desire to learn about the world and mankind and those powers which work in nature and human life, an important part is played by our inborn desire to know about our own past and the past of the world. From the earliest times man has endeavoured to record the prominent incidents of his own personal life, of the life of his family, clan, and country, and, eventually, of the life of humanity as a whole.

In this, as in other departments of knowledge, practical problems have moved side by side with this innate desire. Man learns by experience, and experience lies in the past. Many of our rights and claims are founded on incidents which took place in past times; and hence the desire to record these incidents and to preserve them from the possibility of being at any time forgotten.

But the memory of man is short, and his imagination is fertile. Facts in their actual form are easily forgotten and soon covered over by the accretions of imagination. Religion and reality overlap in human life; and therefore historical incidents easily assume the form of fairy-tales and legends, and are mixed up with man's belief in higher powers which direct his life. For this reason many historical facts, in the course of oral or even of written transmission, assume the form of myths, or tales which describe the interference in human life of divine and superhuman powers.

As soon as man devised the means of perpetuating the incidents of his life in writing, it became possible for the first time to record exactly what had happened, and written historical tradition began. With the development of civilization man's interest in his own past increased, a number of facts known to him concerning that past were accumulated, and methods were contrived for putting these facts together and combining them into a connected narrative dealing with the past of this or that group of men or of all mankind in general. Just as in other fields of knowledge, a disorderly accumulation of separate observations was followed by a period when these observations were reduced to order and system, and this again by a period when they were utilized by means of a series of methods intended to clear up these two questions: What are the laws which operate in man's life and control him? Is it possible to learn these laws from the facts of history and, having learnt them, not only to understand the past but to foretell the future?

Different methods have been invented by man in order to learn about his own past. The first duty of history is to collect facts about that past. Incidents which aroused the interest of men were sometimes recorded by them immediately, at the moment of their occurrence, and sometimes, in a less exact form, later and from memory. But much was never recorded at all, and merely reflected in this or that form assumed by the outward and inward life of man; and therefore it is obviously the business of the historian to collect not only the written records of man's past but also the material relics of his existence at different periods of his development. For the former purpose all written memorials of the past are collected in archives, libraries, and museums; these are read, and the most important are published, and thus there is created the skeleton of history— a series of facts recorded by man in writing. To accomplish this task, the historian must be a philologer: in other words, he must know the languages in which historical documents are written, and also the gradual development of those languages, that is, the form which they possessed at different periods in the existence of this or that nation. Again, since the symbols which were and are used by man to denote the sounds, syllables, and words of language are unlike, and since this has given rise to an infinite variety in systems of writing, therefore the historian must be a palaeographer; that is, he must know the development of these systems and their peculiarities.

The unwritten monuments of man's history which bear witness to his gradual advance in civilization are studied by specialists known as archaeologists. The results and methods of this specialist study must be completely known by the historian, because many eras of human life have left no written monuments. For it must be remembered that the first written symbols were invented not earlier than the fourth millennium B.C., and therefore have not existed more than 6,000 years, whereas the years of man's life on earth are reckoned by tens of thousands. It must also be remembered that the peoples of Europe, for the most part, were decidedly later than the peoples of the East in making use of written symbols—later by some millenniums— and that the earliest written monuments left by the Greeks, the pioneers of European civilization, are not older than the eighth century B.C. For the period that precedes writing, the material and, in part, the spiritual life of man must be ascertained almost wholly by a single method—by collecting and studying the records of his life left by him in the ruins of his dwellings and in his tombs. This period in the life of man in general and in the life of separate nations in particular is commonly called the prehistoric period.

When the historian has collected facts concerning the life of this or that nation, and wishes to make use of them to reproduce the past, he must, first of all, settle the sequence of these incidents and define which was earlier and which later; he must, that is, make clear their relative chronology. His next business is to define more precisely the time when this or that incident took place, and the interval that divides it from his own age; this we call the determination of absolute chronology. For this purpose, the historian must study and master the different methods of reckoning time which were devised by man in different places and at different epochs. These methods are infinitely different and very complicated; and all of them, including those which we now use, are exceedingly imperfect. We must not forget that our year is shorter than the astronomical year, and that our reckoning from the Birth of Christ is merely provisional, because we do not know the year in which Christ was born. Hence it is one of the fundamental problems of the historian to be able to calculate, precisely or approximately, by means of a series of observations and comparisons, the date of a given event or epoch in the life of a people.

In order to understand the events of history and estimate them aright, it is not enough to know what happened and when it happened: we must know also where it happened; that is, we must be able to connect the event with a definite place and have exact knowledge of the peculiarities of that place. Not only must man and his manner of life be known but also the sphere of his activity—the earth, with its different parts, with their geological and climatic differences, with their flora and fauna. In short, it is necessary to know the conditions of man's life in different places and at different epochs of his existence. The study of the earth is the business of the geographer. But this is not enough for the historian: he must know not merely the present appearance of the earth but also its changes and its history. He must know, too, the changes that have taken place in the distribution of mankind upon the globe, the location of this or that people, and the main centres of the life of separate nations and of the different kingdoms and empires. The history of the earth is taught us by physical geography, while historical geography deals with the relations of man to the earth which he inhabits.

The fact that a man belongs to this or that clan, to this or that race, is of vast importance in human history. Clans and races differ from one another in physical peculiarities, and in peculiarities of habit and language. To explain these differences is the business of anthropology, which studies man, as a part of the animal world, in his historical development. Closely connected with this are two other sciences—ethnography, which studies the peculiarities of separate nations, and comparative philology. The historian must be acquainted with the methods and conclusions of all these sciences.

The facts collected by the historian, when arranged in order of time and definitely assigned to the places and peoples concerned, form only the skeleton of history. These facts, especially such as are recorded in written and oral tradition, require verification. I have said already that man has not only a strong impulse to learn truth but an equally strong impulse to mutilate it, consciously and unconsciously. Man's tendency to poetic creation and the fertility of his imagination cause him often to restate facts till they are unrecognizable; he fills up gaps where he is ignorant and alters what he knows; he mixes up the region of religious and fabulous conceptions with the sphere of actual events. Myth and legend are inseparable from history, and even in our own time grow up round great historical events and, even more, round great historical persons. Together with this process, facts are also deliberately distorted under the influence of various motives—material advantage, or the endeavour to defend the reputation of the narrator or his friend, or the tendency to support a particular point of view or political theory. The influence of patriotism is active here: the writer wishes to prove that the nation to which he belongs is superior to all others, that it is always in the right and its adversaries always in the wrong. We must never forget that historical events were not recorded by machinery but by men, distinct personalities with definite characteristics of their own. Few of them have kept free from prejudice while recording historical events which, in one way or another, touched themselves nearly. Hence the historian, while collecting facts, must at the same time verify them and convince himself that they correspond to reality. This is a complicated and difficult problem: it requires great caution and familiarity with various methods of verification. This part of the historian's work we call historical criticism.

When the historian has collected and verified his facts, he then proceeds to set them forth. But, while methods have been developed and perfected for dealing with facts, in order to collect and comprehend them, to date them and arrive at a critical estimate of them, there has arisen at the same time a different view of the historian's task, that is, of the immediate object of his labours. The number of historical facts is infinite, and they bear reference to different sides of the infinite variety of human life. Which among this multitude of facts are most valuable and important? What sides of life deserve study more than others? For long, history was mainly political history, and historical narrative was confined to an account of the most important crises in political life, or to an account of wars and great generals. But even the Greeks realized that if these facts, the incidents of man's history in politics and war, are important, it is still more important to ascertain the causes of these incidents and their connexion with one another and with the other phenomena of the life of communities. It has become clear that war, in spite of the profound impression it produces, is only one phase of man's life, and not the most important phase, and that the origin and course of wars are closely connected with the development of economic, social, and religious life and civilization. From this point of view politics and war have not become less interesting and important in the history of the separate groups of mankind; but men's eyes have been opened to the immense importance of studying the conditions of human development during periods that were not disturbed by war. From another side, a more thoughtful attitude to historical events has shown the very great importance of personality in the history of man's development; hence the historian endeavours to explain the psychology of the most prominent individuals in history, and to throw light on their character and the conditions which created it. And gradually another fact has come to light—that, if the psychology of individuals has an important influence upon the course of historical development, history is affected not less, and perhaps even more, by the psychology of separate groups of men, the 'psychology of the herd', which finds its expression both in the organization of small groups of men, the family, for instance, and in the peculiar ordering of larger units—the clan, country, and nation. Lastly, it became clear how strongly this 'psychology of the herd' has affected acute crises in the life of the community, such as find expression in wars and revolutions.

In the endeavour to comprehend the complicated structure of man's social life, history works hand in hand with the departments of scientific inquiry which have gradually become separate both from history and from philosophy: these are the economic sciences, sociology, political and juristic science, psychology, and such branches of knowledge as literature and art, which bear upon man's spiritual life and the special products of his civilization.

In close connexion with other departments of human knowledge, history tends to become more and more a science, whose end is to define the laws under which the life of man develops, and the regular process by which one type of communal life is displaced by another. Nevertheless, history still remains a branch of literature, because the narrative of events and the lively and picturesque transmission of them, together with the truthful and artistic delineation of important historical characters, will always remain one of the historian's chief tasks, a task of a purely literary and artistic nature. While becoming more and more a department of exact science, history cannot and must not lose its literary, and therefore individual, character.

II

ANCIENT HISTORY:
ITS PROBLEMS AND IMPORTANCE

Ancient history is the history of man's development in the earliest period of his existence: it tells how at that period he created and developed the civilization from which the culture of all nations now existing is derived. By civilization I understand the creation of those forms of political, communal, economic, and cultural life which distinguish us from the savage. The savage continues to live in those primitive conditions which assimilate his life to that of the animal and distinguish it from the life of civilized man.

This ancient civilization, which spread by degrees over the world, was first developed in the Near East, and chiefly in Egypt, Mesopotamia, and Central Asia, in the islands of the Aegean Sea, and in the Balkan peninsula. From the Near East it passed into the West, beginning with Italy; and from Italy it conquered all western Europe and some regions in the centre of that continent. In this civilization there were successive epochs of high development—a series of creative periods which produced inestimable treasures not only of a material kind but also in the intellectual region of culture; and there were also periods of temporary stagnation and decline, when the creative powers of this or that part of the ancient world were for the time enfeebled. The zenith of cultural creation was attained by Egypt and Babylonia in the third millennium B.C.; by Egypt again in the second millennium and, at the same time, by Asia Minor and part of Greece; by Assyria, Babylonia, and Persia in the eighth, seventh, and sixth centuries B.C.; next by Greece from the sixth century B.C. to the second, and by Italy in the first century B.C. and the first century A.D. From the second century A.D. a general stagnation in creative power is observable in the whole of the ancient world; and from the third century an almost complete cessation of this power and a gradual reversion to more and more primitive conditions of life. But the foundations of culture still survived and were maintained—in the West by Italy and the provinces of the Roman Empire in western Europe, in the East by the Byzantine Empire, i.e. in the Balkan peninsula and Asia Minor. These foundations were taken over by new centres of government, which arose in the West in consequence of the conquest by German tribes of successive parts of the western Roman Empire, and in the East by the Slavonic kingdoms in the Balkan peninsula and in Russia, and by the great Mussulman powers, first Arabian and then Turkish. Thus taken over, they served as a basis of culture and enabled the peoples of Europe to start their creative civilization, not from the lowest stratum of prehistoric life but from the comparatively high level bequeathed to posterity by the ancient world.

Therefore it cannot be said that ancient civilization finally disappeared at any time: it still lives, as the foundation of all the chief manifestations of modern culture; but its creative period lasted, approximately, from the beginning of the third millennium B.C. to the second century A.D., or more than three thousand years, a period twice as long as that during which contemporary European culture has been developed.

From a geographical point of view, ancient civilization belongs to a single part of the world and not a large part: it was confined to a small part of Western and Central Asia and of the Mediterranean coast. It reached its highest development on the shores of the Mediterranean and may therefore be called 'Mediterranean civilization'. It was not confined to one people or one race:

a series of nations took an active part in creating it. The first pioneers were the Sumerians in Babylonia and the earliest inhabitants of Egypt, probably of African descent; next came the Semites of Western Asia and the Aryans originally of Central Asia; the natives of the Caucasus and Asia Minor; the Iranians in Persia and Central Asia; and, finally, the Greeks in Asia Minor and the Balkans, and the Italians and Celts in Italy. Among all these nations the Greeks were especially remarkable for the power of their creative spirit, and to them we are principally indebted for the foundations of our civilized life.

But it must be remembered that the lofty creation of Greece was developed from the culture attained by the ancient East; that Greek civilization only became world-wide as the result of a fresh and prolonged contact with the Eastern cultures, after the conquest of the East by Alexander the Great; and that it became the property of the West, that is, of modern Europe, simply because it was taken over in its entirety by Italy. We must also remember that Italy alone made it accessible, in its Roman form, to all those parts of the ancient world which Italy united for the purpose of civilized life. If the civilization of the East and of Greece was not confined to the eastern part of the ancient world but became the foundation of culture for the West and for modern Europe, for this Europe is indebted to Italy and to Rome. Hence, if ancient civilization is to have any ethnographical label, it should properly be called Graeco-Roman.

The study of this ancient Graeco-Roman civilization is of immense importance to every intelligent sharer in modern culture, and ought to form one of the main subjects of higher education.

The creation of a uniform world-wide civilization and of similar social and economic conditions is now going on before our eyes over the whole expanse of the civilized world. This process is complicated, and it is often difficult to clear up our minds about it. We ought therefore to keep in view that this condition in which we are living is not new, and that the ancient world also lived, for a series of centuries, a life which was uniform in culture and politics, in social and economic conditions. The modern development, in this sense, differs from the ancient only in quantity and not in quality. The ancient world witnessed the creation of a world-wide trade and the growth of industry on a large scale; it lived through a period of scientific agriculture and through the development of strife between the different classes of the population, between capital and labour. It also witnessed a period, when each discovery became at once the property of all civilized humanity, when the nations and peoples, over the enormous expanse embraced by the Roman Empire, came into daily and constant contact, and when men began to realize that there is something higher than local and national interests, namely, the interest of all mankind.

In a word, the ancient world experienced, on a smaller scale, the same process of development which we are experiencing now. If we study the successive stages of that development, we shall realize how nearly and closely we are connected with that world. For instance, the ancient world created the three main forms of government which are still preserved in our own political life. These are, first, the monarchical form, where the country is ruled by a central bureaucracy and all the threads of government are united in the hands of the monarch alone; secondly, the self-ruling free state, where all are politically equal and power resides in the sovereign people and its chosen representatives; and, lastly, the federal system, which combines in one political alliance a number of free and self-governing political units. To this day we have never got beyond these three fundamental forms of government; to this day we are struggling with the master problem of political organization—how to combine personal freedom and self-government of the separate parts with a single strong and intelligent controlling power.

Our dependence on antiquity is just as great in the sphere of science and art. Modern exact science has been built up entirely on the method of experiment, and this was first applied to the natural sciences by the Greek thinkers of the fourth and third centuries B.C. Our philosophy and morals are still founded on the scientific methods of abstract thought first hammered out by the ancient philosophers, and especially by Plato and Aristotle. In literature and the plastic arts we merely build on foundations laid by the genius of the ancient writers and artists; we re-fashion the same literary ideas and the same artistic themes which they originally created. Finally, in the sphere of religion, a great part, if not the whole, of modern mankind lives by virtue of beliefs which were first made their own by men of the East and of the West in the age of classical antiquity. We must not forget that Christ lived in the time of Augustus and Tiberius; that the Jewish religion is one of the religions of the Semitic East; and that the Mussulman creed grew up among the Arabian Semites who were strongly influenced by Greek civilization. These few indications are sufficient to prove that the study of antiquity is of immense importance to ourselves; for no one can understand the present, unless he has a clear conception of the evolution of government and civilization in the ancient world.

III

GREECE AND THE AEGEAN KINGDOMS

The beginnings of civilization, that is, of settled life, are as early in Greek lands as in Egypt and Mesopotamia. The villagers, who mostly settled in Thessaly, Cyprus, and other places where the alluvial soil was easy to cultivate with the most primitive tools, grew cereals and bred livestock. Men of this prehistoric (neolithic) period used tools and weapons of stone, and although they still did not know how to make pottery, the statuette of a woman (pl. I) from Lerna to our eyes foreshadows Greek art. The Acropolis of Athens, the future site of Corinth, and the hill of Troy were already occupied in the third millennium B.C.

We do not know what race it was or even whether it was a single people who originally inhabited the western coasts of Asia Minor, the Aegean islands, and the southern part of the Balkan peninsula that was one day to be Greece. For simplicity, we shall speak of them as Aegeans. The Greeks preserved no memory of the migration of their ancestors from a distant land, although they remembered that peoples who spoke no Greek (*Pelasgians* and *Leleges*) had once inhabited their country. We do not know how or when men speaking Indo-European tongues entered Greece and imposed what, in the course of time, evolved into the Greek language with all its dialects. An earlier dialectal form of Greek is now known from the tablets written in the fifteenth century B.C.

Thanks to the excavations of Schliemann and his successors

in Asia Minor and Greece, of Sir Arthur Evans and others in Crete, and of a succession of archaeologists in Cyprus, we now know something of the political and social activity of the Aegeans in the second millennium B.C. By that time, with the use of the metals copper and bronze, the Aegeans had developed a more complex, urban civilization.

For this later period we have, for the first time, written sources to supplement archaeological evidence. Some documents found in the archives of the Hittite kings, which date from about the middle of the fourteenth century to the end of the twelfth century, occasionally refer to the kings and the land of Ahhiyawa; that is, in all probability, to the Achaeans. They appear to have been a great seapower and their kings maintained relations with the Hittite Empire. In addition, more than four thousand inscribed clay tablets have been discovered at Cnossus, in Crete, and at Pylus and Mycenae in the Peloponnesus. Michael Ventris (1922–56) succeeded in deciphering the script ('The Linear B') in 1952. The language of these tablets is an earlier form of Greek grammatically akin to the later Achaean dialect and written in about ninety syllabic signs. As far as deciphered, the tablets record business transactions (accounts, payments, inventories). When thoroughly studied, they should throw a new light on the social and economic life of the pre-Homeric Greeks.

The most important centre in the earlier times was the island of Crete—that barrier between the Aegean and the part of the Mediterranean connected with Egypt and Syria, that great island, one of whose sides faces towards Egypt and Asia, whilst another looks northward to the Archipelago, Greece, and Asia Minor. Early relations with Egypt and proximity to Cyprus, whose mineral wealth (copper) was coveted in early times by Egypt and Babylonia, enabled Crete to develop an extensive culture in the late Neolithic Age. Later, when she had learned to work metal and invented a system of writing, she went rapidly ahead, organizing a civilization of her own and adapting what she could borrow from the East. One after another, great cities

1. CLAY MODEL OF A SACRED ENCLOSURE

Plate I AEGEAN ART OF THE NEOLITHIC PERIOD

1. Clay model of a sacred enclosure. Found in a grave in Cyprus. Participants of a sacred ceremony are standing or seated on benches in the attitude of prayer (hands at the chest). A figure larger than the rest is sitting on a throne. At the left of the entrance a figure carries an infant. Bulls in pens may be seen along the enclosure wall. (A bull's skeleton was found in the same tomb.) A figure (the dead man?) is climbing over the wall. End of the 3rd century B.C. Nicosia Museum.

2. Terracotta statue. Height preserved about 7 inches. Found in a room of a house at Lerna (Argolis). About 3000 B.C. Argos Museum.

2. TERRACOTTA STATUE

Fɪɢ. 1. Clay tablet from Cnossus *c.* 1400 in Mycenaean Script deciphered as follows: a-ta-na-po-ti-ni-ja I . . . e-nu-wa-ri-jo I pa-ja-wo (ne? I) po-se-do (o-ne I?) 'To Mistress Athena . . . to Enyalios, to Paian, to Poseidon' (from A. Evans, *Scripta Minoa*, vol. ii, Clarendon Press)

grew up in the bays of the island—Cnossus, Phaestus, Mallia, Tylissus, and others (the ancient Aegean names of these cities, except Cnossus, are unknown). They were not fortified, as there was apparently no danger of attack on land; their life was connected mainly with the sea, from which the rulers and their subjects drew their chief revenue. The cities lived at peace with one another, having probably quickly contrived a kind of federal government for the whole island. United Crete acquired by degrees great authority with the inhabitants of the neighbouring islands, who were, like the Cretans, traders, pirates, and colonizers; and some sort of alliance, under the leadership of Crete, may have been formed. About 1600 ʙ.ᴄ. some great catastrophe occurred, possibly an earthquake, a foreign invasion, or internal revolution; we know at least that the palaces of Cnossus and Phaestus were destroyed at this period; but recovery soon followed, and her most palmy days were in the sixteenth century ʙ.ᴄ.

It is difficult to say how far this culture owed its brilliant development in the age of metals to the influence of Egypt and Babylonia. Knowledge of the metals and greater use of the sea lie at the root of Aegean civilization. We do not yet know how or whence the metals first appeared in that region. As regards seafaring, from very ancient times Aegean ships differed in ap-

Fig. 2. Warrior-vase from Mycenae, showing fore-and-aft helmet, small shield, and thrusting spear. (from Hammond, *A History of Greece to 322 B.C.*)

pearance from both Egyptian and Phoenician craft. Perhaps the Aegeans borrowed writing, or the rudiments of writing, from the East; but they developed it independently; and possibly they owed the potter's wheel to the same quarter. The influence of Egypt asserts itself later also; but it is a mutual influence, as Egypt helps herself in turn from the treasures of Aegean genius. Though the connexion with Babylonia was looser and more fitful, the system of weights and measures may have been taken from there.

A similar type of civilization was simultaneously developed on the eastern coasts of the Aegean sea, in Asia Minor, Syria, and Phoenicia. But, for want of investigation of the sites, the exact estimate of progress, which is now possible in the case of Crete, is beyond our reach here. Only one site on the western coast of Asia Minor is well known to us—that of Troy. Troy, like Cnossus in Crete, was the head of an alliance between towns and tribes in the north-west of Asia Minor; but her position was more difficult, as she was liable to be attacked on land by powerful neighbours. She was therefore always a strong fortress, protected by formidable walls. I do not doubt that excavation will reveal to us in the near future similar political centres of the Aegean type, on the coast (the future Ionia) and in the centre of Asia Minor, and also on the coast of Lycia and Cilicia to the south-west.

In Greece we find just the same phenomena. In the second millennium B.C. fortified towns spring up everywhere near the sea-coast; each has stone walls, with a royal palace, temples, warehouses, storehouses, and barracks inside the walls, and dwellings for the subjects outside. All these towns grow larger and richer; and their culture gradually assumes the same Aegean type as in Crete. Our knowledge of these towns is confined chiefly to Tiryns, Mycenae, and Argos in eastern Peloponnesus, Pylus on the west coast, Orchomenus, Thebes, and Thisbe in Boeotia, and Athens in Attica; and the first two of these are the best known.

As far as we can judge from the excavations carried out of late years in the chief centres of this culture, and from the evidence preserved in the ancient Greek epics—the *Iliad* and *Odyssey* cannot, indeed, be placed earlier than the close of the second millennium B.C., but they abound in recollections of the glorious past of the Aegean kingdoms—the Aegean world consisted, as we have said already, of a number of city-states, ruled by kings and the royal troops. Both kings and soldiers led an active and eventful life. They were chiefly employed in marine trading, which was in that unruly age hardly distinguishable from piracy. The king and his retainers lived in a great palace containing hundreds of rooms; in Crete the palace was unfortified, on the mainland it was protected by strong walls. The subject population, who tilled the land and bred cattle, were scattered over the king's territory. Traders, artisans, and sailors settled close to the palace or fortified citadel of the king, inside or outside its walls. Close ties of friendship and kinship united the king and fighting men of one city with those of another in the neighbourhood, and they formed, as it were, one large family. They exchange frequent visits, feast and make merry together, and unite to take a share in the sacrifice of victims and in religious games. They make rich presents to one another and exchange compliments. But quarrels also are frequent, over spoil or beautiful women, or arising out of the mysterious and tragic crimes of a palace.

It is a striking feature of this culture that, though profoundly different from others, it was never self-centred or exclusive. It was active, enterprising, and various, as one might expect from traders, warriors, and pirates. It was probably not associated with any definite nationality. To me it presents itself as not national at all: it seems to have been created by the conditions of life on the shores of the Aegean and in the narrow valleys of the islands and the mainland. A land that was comparatively poor and cramped forced the population to sail away to the nearest islands or even to the world of the Eastern monarchies, in search of what was denied them by their own somewhat grudging soil. Hence it is highly probable that the representatives of Aegean civilization on the islands differed in race from the representatives on the mainland of Greece; but their civilization was essentially the same with important local modifications.

In general, two varieties of it may be distinguished. The first and more ancient belongs to the south and is called Cretan; the second belongs to the north and is called Mycenaean, from Mycenae in the Peloponnese, which has been investigated more thoroughly than other Aegean sites. The difference between the two is revealed most clearly by the plan followed in the construction of their houses and settlements. The Cretan house consists of a number of rooms grouped round a courtyard; the Mycenaean house consists of walls erected round a hearth which forms the centre of the dwelling; the house has a roof and a door but only one room, and its object is to make full use of the warmth diffused by the central hearth. There is an equal unlikeness in their settlements. The Cretans, being islanders and sailors, were content with the protection of their fleet and hardly fortified their cities at all; but the dwellers on the mainland stood always in fear of their neighbours, and therefore built strong thick walls round the palace of the king and his retainers, and sometimes round the whole city. The general trend of life is equally different in Crete and in Greece. The Cretans are mostly sailors and traders. They neglect war and indulge in more pacific arts. Life in Greece is centred round war, sieges and battles.

But both types of settlements have this feature in common, that the settlement grows into a town which quickly assumes an orderly and civilized appearance. It has paved streets, houses of several storeys, drains and other sanitary contrivances, which were unknown to the East, with its huge village-like settlements grouped round a palace and temple. The Aegean way of life was more compact and thus created that kind of settlement which we call 'urban'. Such compactness was natural to men who from early times were chiefly engaged in trade and industry, and natural in a country where there were no fertile alluvial valleys for the population to spread in, and where the comparative poverty of the soil made concentration impossible except in towns not dependent entirely upon agriculture. Another peculiarity of Aegean towns is that they have no temples like those of the East, none of those huge palaces built for the gods. It appears that they worshipped mainly the powers of nature, personified in the Great Goddess, mother of gods and men. Her shrines were generally caves, or groves of consecrated trees, or small chapels forming part of palaces. Another form of worship was paid to dead heroes. The Aegeans did not build pyramids in their honour; yet their beehive tombs with a cupola roof and a long passage for entrance, hidden under mounds of earth, are not inferior to the Pyramids and the rock-cut tombs of Egypt in originality of artistic conception.

Lastly, it was a peculiarity of the Aegeans that they never sought to create anything imposing by mere size; the buildings they preferred were of moderate proportions, adorned with colour, and pleasing to the eye. Their sculptors carved no colossal

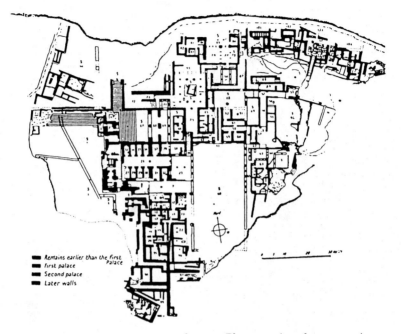

Remains earlier than the first Palace
First palace
Second palace
Later walls

FIG. 3. Plan of the Minoan palace at Phaestus (modern name) as excavated by an Italian expedition. The palace shows the same general features as the plan of the larger and more gorgeous palace of Cnossus.

shapes of gods or men; their architects did not task themselves to build a pyramid, or a row of columns in a temple—columns of such a size that a hundred men could find standing-room on the capital of each. The palaces of Cnossus, Phaestus, Mycenae, and Tiryns do indeed cover a large space: they are extensive and contain a number of small rooms and a number of courts. But the reason for this is that a number of people lived there together—the king, his court, and his retainers. The palace courts are extensive, because they were always filled by a crowd of men seeking air and light, and served as a public resort for the inhabitants of the palace, for divine worship or games or military reviews. In fact the palace is large because it is a whole town

25

1. STORE-ROOMS   2. A STATE ROOM

Plate II THE PALACE OF CNOSSUS

1. The store-rooms of the Palace of Cnossus with the big oil-jars.

2. One of the state rooms of the palace as restored by Sir Arthur
Evans on the spot. Note the peculiar columns growing wider above,
and the capitals, prototypes of the later Doric capitals of Greece.

3. THE THRONE ROOM

3. The so-called throne room in the palace. The central place is occupied by a monumental stone chair, and around the walls are stone benches. The walls are covered with stucco and the stucco painted. Part of this decoration has been restored from fragments by Sir Arthur Evans. It shows an eagle-griffin lying in a flower garden. There must have been a similar figure on the other side of the throne. (The throne in the palace at Pylus, which dates to the thirteenth century, is flanked by pairs of lions and griffins.) Here and elsewhere (see Lion Gate, Pl. VI) beasts are guardians of a divine symbol. The incised decorations on the sides of the throne are also probably symbolic. Whether the throne was used by the king when presiding at the state council or acting as the supreme judge while the other members sat on the benches, or the throne was supposed to be occupied by the invisible Great Goddess, is uncertain. Religious and state life were closely connected in the Minoan Age. Late Minoan. About 1450 B.C.

with a large and motley population, but it is not colossal. The only part of it that strikes one by its dimensions is the courtyard intended for religious ceremonies and shows connected with them—the earliest attempt to create a theatre.

All these peculiarities go to prove that the manner of life among the Aegeans was unlike that of the East—it was more akin to the type subsequently created by Greece, more democratic. Men lived in a swarm, with one of themselves for chief, like the queen-bee in a hive, but their life was identical with his. In the East the king was divine and lived in magnificent isolation, an object of reverence and worship. The life of the Aegean king was more human. He had neither the will nor the power to separate himself from his comrades in war and partners in trading ventures; to them and their wives he was not, and could not be, a deity. But after death, as the best and strongest and bravest, he became a hero and his tomb became a temple.

Aegean art, so live and sparkling, is all full of humanity and individuality; it is free from the oppressive magnificence and majesty of the god-king, before whom his subjects are pitiable grains of desert sand before the sun; it bubbles like a fountain with vivacity and merriment; it thirsts for life and delights in life; it is intoxicated with sea and sun, trees and flowers, sport and war. These men reproduce life on their household utensils, on the walls of their houses, and in works of art; their fancy is not for separate figures or portraits—no portraits have been bequeathed to us by them—but for groups; and these groups are not rows of identical figures but related to one another and full of movement. The ornament is lively, impersonal, capricious, and infinitely various, finding models everywhere, both in the elegance of the geometric spiral and in natural objects, such as flowers and marine animals, and the odder these are, the better —cuttle-fish, flying fish, sea-shells.

This is why the productions of Aegean art, sometimes sketchy and impressionistic, often childish in their simplicity, impress us so strongly after the splendid monuments of the East—the refinement of Egypt and the dramatic power of Babylon. On palace walls, utensils, and ornaments these artists represent by preference scenes from the life of the spacious palace courts: young men running and jumping in honour of the god; athletes leaping over the back of maddened oxen and clutching them by the horns; women dancing with wild ecstasy in honour of the Great Goddess; peasants returning home in procession and singing hymns to the great earth-goddess; the hero-king reviewing his soldiers. But Aegean art carries us beyond the limits of the palace, and shows us other lively pictures: bulls caught with nets in the forest; the attack on a fortress by enemies who come from the sea; the ship carrying a statue of a horse (it recalls the horse of Troy); a funeral procession and rites performed at the grave. There is not a trace of conventionality or tradition throughout, and there is hardly any repetition. The brightness and variety of the colours is surprising; they are laid, one on another or one beside another, in the most unexpected combinations, with a constant endeavour to get novel tints.

The Aegeans, particularly the Cretans, gradually extended their political and commercial influence. In the sixteenth century they exported their wares to Syria and Egypt, and settled at Miletus about 1600 B.C. In the fourteenth century B.C. the hegemony of Crete suffered a crushing blow: at the highest point of its development Cnossus was destroyed, probably by an alliance of Aegean city-states in Europe. This event is probably connected with the natural development of the European kingdoms of Aegean civilization which from the very beginning were Greek, that is Achaean. It is certain that these kingdoms with their centres at Mycenae in the Argolis, at Thebes and Orchomenus in Boeotia, and at Athens in Attica, not to speak of minor states with the same civilization, were rich and powerful as early as in the seventeenth century B.C. and developed their own version of the Aegean civilization. By the fourteenth century a large Mycenaean Empire had been formed. The kings of Mycenae appeared in this empire as suzerains of a host of minor feudal lords.

1. STONE VESSEL FROM ISOPATA   2. POT OF KAMARES STYLE

Plate III MINOAN POTTERY

1. Stone vessel from Isopata near Cnossus. The upper part has rows of symmetrically placed circular holes, inlaid with shell. Late Middle Minoan. About 1700 B.C. Museum of Candia (Crete).

2. Beautiful pot of the so-called Kamares style, with white, orange, and pink floral ornaments on a black ground. Middle Minoan. 1800-1700 B.C. Museum of Candia (Crete).

3. Minoan jug with figures painted dark on a light ground, found at Pseira. It shows dolphins swimming—one straight up, the next straight down, amid honeycombed rocks and seaweed. Early Late Minoan. About 1600 B.C. Ashmolean Museum, Oxford.

4. Minoan amphora with papyrus ornament from Isopata near Cnossus. Late Minoan. About 1500 B.C. Ashmolean Museum, Oxford.

5. Minoan jug with dark figures painted on a light ground: from Hagia Triada. Octopuses are shown amid stylized rocks. Late Minoan. About 1500 B.C. Ashmolean Museum, Oxford.

The figures show the condition of the potter's art in Crete at its highest development when the Cretan Empire was in its prime. Note the skilful use of polychromy and the beautiful stylization of plants and animals for decorative purposes without any rigidity but with full understanding of the principles of decorative art.

3. MINOAN JUG FROM PSEIRA

4. MINOAN AMPHORA FROM NEAR CNOSSUS

5. MINOAN JUG

1. STEATITE VASE FROM HAGIA TRIADA

Plate IV LIFE IN THE MINOAN WORLD

1. Steatite vase. Found at Hagia Triada. A religious procession of agriculturalists is represented (each man carries an agricultural implement, decorated with reeds). The men are moving in the rhythmic step of a sacred dance. They sing a hymn in honour of the Great Goddess. A priest, very like an Egyptian priest, with three attendants, is shaking an Egyptian musical instrument, the 'sistrum', sacred to Isis. The leader (a priestess) wears a peculiar dress like scale armour. Early Late Minoan (about 1600 B.C.). Museum of Candia (Crete).

2. Steatite vase. Found at Hagia Triada near Phaestus. An officer at the head of three soldiers is reporting to the king or the royal prince. Late Middle Minoan or Early Late Minoan. 1700-1550 B.C. Museum of Candia (Crete).

3. Gold ring-bezel. Found at Mycenae in one of the graves of the early Mycenaean kings on the Acropolis. Two groups of two warriors each are engaged in fierce battle. One of the warriors is wounded. Another has sunk on his right knee and is lifting his long sword while the hero of the scene is aiming at him with his short dagger.

2. STEATITE VASE. MINOAN KING AND OFFICER

3. GOLD RING-BEZEL

4. GOLD AND ENAMELED
SCEPTRE

A fourth man tries to reach the hero with his long spear from behind his large shield. Note the pathos and the ruthless realism of the
scene. The hero and his rival with the shield and spear wear scale-
helmets, and are probably two kings or princes. The scene on the
ring excellently illustrates many descriptions of battles in the *Iliad*.
Late Minoan. 1550–1400 B.C. National Museum, Athens.

4. Gold and enameled sceptre. Found at Curium (Cyprus). A tube
which was originally mounted on a staff. On the top is a sphere on
which stand two hawks. Cf. Agamemnon's ancestral sceptre 'for-
ever imperishable' (Hom. *Il.* II, 46). 11th century (P. Dikaios).
Nicosia Museum.

33

Many wars were waged by the Mycenaean kings. Greek tradition preserved the record of two of them: a war of Mycenae against Thebes and the war of the Mycenaean coalition of Achaeans against Troy, celebrated by Homer in his *Iliad*. The cultural influence of the Mycenaean Empire was also spread far and wide by means of an extensive commerce. It reached the route of the amber trade in the North, Sicily and Italy in the West, the northern shore of the Black Sea and the Caucasus in the East, and Asia Minor, Cyprus, and Syria in the South. The art of Phoenicia for instance shows very strong Mycenaean influences.

In the thirteenth century B.C., the Mycenaean world was in a state of confusion, caused no doubt by an important movement of peoples in the northern part of the Balkan peninsula. Our historical tradition speaks of attacks of 'sea-peoples' on Egypt first under Merenpta and later under Ramses III. In the later attack Philistines took an active part, and settled down a little later on the Palestinian shore. All these events must be connected with the dismemberment of the Mycenaean Empire under the pressure of conquerors from the North.

What exactly happened in Greece at the end of the second millennium B.C. and the beginning of the first we do not know. There are many questions to which science so far can give no positive answer. The key to their solution lies in exploration by archaeologists in Greece and Asia Minor. At present we must be content with surmises. It seems that folk-movements in the north of the Balkan peninsula drove the stocks belonging to Northern Greece southward towards the centres of Aegean-Greek civilization. The division of that quarter into a number of independent kingdoms perpetually at war with one another made it impossible for any of them to resist the invaders, who were not inferior to the Aegeans in military equipment and used the same bronze weapons of highly developed forms. The appearance in Greece of these Greek conquerors drove out many inhabitants, especially the ruling classes, of the Aegean-Greek kingdoms from their old abodes towards the east and south.

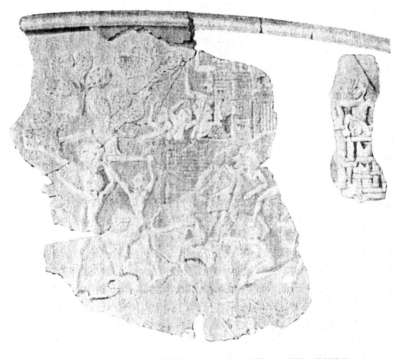

Plate V   A CITY ON THE MAINLAND ATTACKED
BY ENEMIES WHO COME FROM THE SEA

Fragments of a silver drinking horn from the fourth shaft-grave on
the Acropolis of Mycenae. The bas-relief shows a fortified city. The
inhabitants come out to meet the enemies who have just landed and
are moving towards the city. The upper part of one of the attacking
warriors with a helmet adorned with a crest is seen in our figure on
the right, below; some others are seen on some fragments not reproduced in our figure. We may recognize equally some ships which
brought the besiegers to the land. The men from the city are armed
with bows and slings. The women, greatly excited, are watching the
battle from the walls of the city and exhorting the men to courage.
The city is situated on a hill and surrounded by trees (olive-trees?).
The scene is a beautiful illustration of the well-known description of
the battle between Hector and Achilles in the *Iliad*. It must be
noticed that such a vivid scene of battle was a novelty at that time.
1700–1550 B.C. After Sir Arthur Evans. National Museum, Athens.

There conditions were in their favour. In Asia Minor the Hittite empire had been destroyed by the invasion of 'sea-peoples'. Hence, the exiles, Aegeans and Graeco-Aegeans, seized the opportunity to establish themselves on the rich coast of Asia Minor, driving out the old inhabitants, who had their own comparatively high culture, akin to that of the Aegeans. These in their turn sought new abodes in Syria, Phoenicia, Palestine, Egypt, Sicily, Italy, by routes which had long before been opened up by Aegean trade. It is therefore quite probable that the Philistines were a part of the Graeco-Aegean population expelled from Crete, or inhabitants of the south coast of Asia Minor who were forced to migrate. The Etruscans also, who appeared in Italy not earlier than the end of the second millennium B.C. or the beginning of the first, probably came from Asia Minor.

In Greece these new Greek stocks, moving forward to the coast and finding their way from there as far as Asia Minor, inherited from their predecessors their cities, the boundaries of their kingdoms, and a part of their technical skill. How many waves of population succeeded one another on these coasts we do not know; but there was certainly more than one. By degrees, however, when the Dorians had appeared in southern Greece and large numbers of them had settled in the Peloponnese, the troubled sea began to calm down, more permanent national kingdoms began to take shape, and once more the beginnings were developed of a peculiar culture—like that of the East, and therefore of higher quality, in Asia Minor, and more primitive in Greece itself.

The political organization of Greece was dictated by the geographical and economic conditions. Nature had divided her into small economic units, and she was incapable of creating large political systems. So it had been during the prevalence of the Aegean culture, and so it still remained. Each valley was self-centred, and its inhabitants jealously guarded their pasture and arable land. The best parts of the country, especially its rich valleys, are open to the sea and shut in by land—separated from

Fɪɢ. 4. Reconstruction of the north-western angle of the courtyard of the palace of Mycenae. The architecture and the decoration (ornamental friezes) were very like those of the later parts of the palace of Cnossus in Crete. After A. J. B. Wace and W. Lamb.

the central high valleys and plateaux by formidable barriers. They are more in touch with those neighbours from whom the sea divides them than with those whom the land brings near them. It is easier for them to exchange goods and ideas by sea than by land. Hence civilization develops quickly on the coast but slowly in the centre of the country.

The type of life, however, is the same in all parts. Stocks, and portions of stocks, form petty political units which keep jealous guard of their independence. To protect themselves and their property against attack, they build fortified refuges on the hill-tops, and these by degrees are converted into cities, which offer a market for their produce, a centre of religious life, and a residence for their kings, leaders in war, and priests. The city becomes the focus of a larger or smaller territory, inhabited by farmers and shepherds who live either in detached houses and

1. LATE MYCENEAN VASE

2. GOLDEN MASK FROM MYCENAE

3. LION GATE OF MYCENAE

Plate VI   LIFE IN MYCENAEAN GREECE

1. Late Mycenaean vase showing two sphinxes facing a geometrized tree in an heraldic position. About 1300 B.C. British Museum.

2. Golden mask from Mycenae. Some men, probably kings or princes, whose graves were discovered at Mycenae, wore golden masks over their faces. These gold masks have hooks which were used to fasten the mask behind the ears. Such death masks perpetuated the person of the deceased. Their use is attested from Siberia to Rome. At Mycenae, each mask is individual, but all have distinguishing features in common, such as a straight nose, small lips, and a beard. The Mycenaean masks help us to visualize the Homeric heroes. National Museum, Athens.

3. Lion Gate of Mycenae. The Lion Gate was the entrance to the citadel of Mycenae. A door, probably made of wood, closed the gate. Sockets in the side posts served to hold a beam which closed and opened the door. Over the lintel two lions guard a column which may symbolize the royal palace. Mycenae. 13th century B.C.

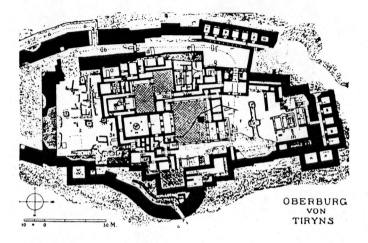

OBERBURG
VON
TIRYNS

Fɪɢ. 5. Plan of the fortified palace of Tiryns. The palace is surrounded by powerful 'cyclopean' walls (see pl. VII, 2). The centre of
the palace consists of a large northern house (megaron) with a
spacious forecourt and a tower gate which led to the court. This
central building is surrounded, in the Minoan fashion, by an irregu-
lar complex of halls, chambers, and passages.

cottages scattered over the country, or together in villages
(demes). Such city-states steadily increase in number. Among
them there always existed groups united by the tie of a common
language, or, more strictly speaking, a common dialect of the one
Greek language. The distribution of these dialects in Greece,
the islands, and Asia Minor, throws light on the process by which
the resettlement of Greece by Greek stocks took place. Three
dialects are sharply distinguished. The oldest of these is the
Achaean group (Aeolic and Arcadian) already attested in the
fifteenth century (fig. 1); the Ionian comes next; and the Dorian
is probably the third and last. The three groups divided the
whole Greek world between them. Thessaly in northern Greece
was Achaean-Aeolic from time immemorial; and also central
Greece, except Attica, became so, and all the north-west of
Peloponnese. The Arcadian dialect belonged to central Pelo-

ponnese and the island of Cyprus. Ionic dialects prevailed in Attica, Euboea, and most of the Aegean islands, especially the largest of them—Imbros, Lemnos, Chios, Samos, and Naxos. The Dorians were firmly established in the south and east of Peloponnese, Aetolia, and the southern islands of the Aegean, Crete and Rhodes being the largest and richest of these; they left a permanent impression also upon Boeotia and Thessaly. There was a similar distribution of these groups in Asia Minor. The northern coast of the Aegean and that of the Black Sea were Aeolic; the central coast, closely connected with the islands, was Ionian; and a small district to the south, connected with Rhodes and Crete, was Dorian. Thus the Ionians cut in like a wedge between the other two groups, and their chief centre was not in Greece but in the islands and Asia Minor.

Some of the districts which were independent and wealthy kingdoms in the Aegean and Mycenaean ages still remained the centres where civilization and political life were most vigorous. Such were Sparta in the south of Peloponnese, Argos in the north-east, perhaps Olympia in the north-west; Corinth and Megara on the Isthmus; while in central Greece there were Delphi in Phocis, Thebes in Boeotia, and Athens in Attica; in northern Greece there was Larissa in Thessaly. The same rule applies, even more generally, to Asia Minor. The most ancient and important cities were all older than the Greeks: Miletus, Ephesus, Smyrna were centres of economic, political, and religious life long before the appearance of Greeks in the country. And the same thing is observable in Crete and in Rhodes.

The system, economic, social, and political, of these ancient Greek communities is described in the Homeric poems—the *Iliad* and the *Odyssey*, which probably were put together and assumed the form in which the Greeks knew them and in which they have come down to us, not earlier than the ninth or eighth century B.C. These poems describe the past, not the present: they refer to the time when the redistribution of Greek stocks was everywhere going on, and when not a few features of the Aegean

41

2. VAULTED CORRIDOR AT TIRYNS

Plate VII   LIFE IN MYCENAEAN GREECE

1. General view of the ruins of the fortified Palace of Tiryns in the northeastern part of the Peloponnese in Greece. Tiryns was first excavated by Schliemann. A typical example of the Mycenaean fortresses which were scattered all over the southern and central part of Greece, and which reached the highest point of their development after 1400 B.C.

3. TREASURY OF ATREUS

2. The vaulted corridor (which probably served as a store-house) inside the fortification walls of Tiryns. Huge blocks of stone were used for building the walls. The later Greeks ascribed this type of building to the mythical Cyclopes. It is probable that the wall existed on the hill of Tiryns before the palace of the Minoan type (see fig. 5) was built on the top of the hill.

3. The Treasury of Atreus. The so-called Treasury of Atreus (also called the Tomb of Agamemnon) is the greatest of the *tholoi*, that is, of the vaulted tombs discovered at Mycenae. It is a vaulted chamber of beehive shape built of large hammer-dressed blocks. The chamber is over 43 feet high and over 46 feet wide. It is hewn in the hill and is approached by a long passage. Mycenae. 14th century B.C.

past were noticeable in the life of the aristocracy. It is likely that separate legends concerning the heroes of the *Iliad* and *Odyssey* who took part in the conquest of Troy—legends which served as material for Homer—appeared in Aeolian Thessaly as early as the Graeco-Aegean period. They were worked over later in Aeolian Asia Minor and assumed their final form in one of the Ionian cities there. But in spite of the complicated origin of the poems, it is possible for us to pick out what is characteristic of the life of these Greek stocks in the earliest period of their existence.

We observe in them all nearly identical institutions, economic, social, and political—institutions connected in one way or another with the Aegean stage which the different parts of Greece passed through. The ruling element in all Greek cities of the Homeric Age is the aristocracy, embodied in certain families which play the leading part in the life of each clan. Each of these families traces its descent to a single founder—a god or hero; and to one of them belongs the king who directs the clan in war and peace. Each family is subdivided into groups—*phratries* or brotherhoods—mainly of a military and religious nature. Next to these families comes the general population, divided from one another by occupation, place of residence, and social position. Some members of this plebeian class or *demos* own land, others, as tenants or serfs, till the land of their masters, others hire out their labour to employers, and others live in the city as artisans. There are also slaves, as is natural in a society where war is constant and clans are for ever shifting from place to place.

How this social system grew up we do not know. Greek tradition regards these ruling families as descended from heroes who came to Greece, some from the north and some from the east, and were closely connected with the most ancient myths about the gods and heroes. A considerable part of these myths was inherited by the Greeks from the Aegeans and Graeco-Aegeans who preceded them. This suggests that the aristocracy of Homeric Greece was composite—consisting partly of the military chiefs who led their clans to conquer Greece, and partly of the ruling families in the conquered kingdoms. So the lower classes also belonged partly to the conquering stock, and partly to the original population of the conquered country.

The system of land-ownership in ancient Greece corresponded with this division in the origin of the population. In some districts the conquerors probably found a large number of cultivators who had long been in serfdom to a group of the directing and ruling families; and this system they maintained. The origin of the system is unknown; but to the inhabitants of some districts, e.g. the Thessalians, Cretans, and Spartans, it seemed immemorial and was long kept among them. Elsewhere, as in Attica and Boeotia, there were probably no serfs at the time of the conquest; and there the land was divided between the conquerors and the conquered, though no doubt the former, and especially the leading families, claimed the lion's share. The conditions on which the conquerors owned the land are not quite clear. In the Homeric poems we find joint ownership by a whole family existing side by side with individual ownership. Perhaps the former system is older, and the division of the clan into families was universal among the conquerors and only by degrees became a privilege of the aristocracy, to the exclusion of the population generally. In that case private ownership was probably a development of the earlier system. Persons expelled from the family for delinquencies and crimes, younger sons in a large family, or free men working for wages, could retire to the edge of the cultivated territory, and there clear away forest and drain marshes, till they made farms which belonged to them personally and to their families.

The farming of the Homeric Greeks consists mainly of agriculture and stock-raising; but horticulture, especially the growing of vines and olive-trees, is also developed by degrees. The last industry, however, is only in its early stages; Greece is still a land of cornfields and flocks. Cattle, swine, sheep, and goats are the common animals; to own horses is a privilege of rich and noble families. The stock owned by such families is sometimes very numerous, and a man's wealth is measured by his head of cattle. Little buying is done, and that unwillingly: most necessaries are produced at home. Domestic manufacture supplies not only food but also clothes, furniture, agricultural implements, and foot-gear. The whole family works: the men plough, sow, plant trees, reap, mow, look after the cattle, milk the cows and goats, make butter and cheese, go out hunting; the women spin, weave, embroider, wash linen and clothes, cook the food. Hard work is no humiliation and is not considered burdensome or oppressive. Odysseus boasts that he had no superior in reaping and mowing, that he could build a ship and his own bed and adorn it with cunning patterns. His old father Laertes enjoys working in the garden. Penelope, a queen, weaves every day in the palace with her maidens. Nausicaa, a king's daughter, washes the linen and clothes of her brothers. Work is done in the house by all the members of the household. The slaves and houseless hired servants form a part of the household as a social and productive unit. Though the hardest and most repulsive labour falls to their lot, yet they are neither machines nor animals. Like the other members of the family they come under the patronage and protection of the household gods, and humane treatment is secured to them by religion and custom.

Only the more difficult work is done by professional craftsmen who are paid for their labour. To build a ship or a good house or strong walls for a town is not a job that any one can do; and therefore the specialist is called in. Ther merchants play a conspicuous part. The mysterious knowledge of prophets, priests, and physicians is highly prized; so is the loud voice of the herald and the skill of the singer and musician.

Commerce, so brilliantly developed in the Aegean age, was not brought to a standstill even by political anarchy and the constant shifting of population. The Greeks were helpless without metals and could not get on without them; and they prized the fine productions of Eastern industry and art, so strikingly superior to the primitive objects that issued from their own workshops. The old routes to the sources of this wealth were never forgotten: the Greeks inherited this knowledge from the Aegeans. From the same source they learned the art of navigation, the tradition of which had never died out in that sea. But their way of life was primitive, and what they could offer by way of exchange was not specially attractive. Their wealth was confined to slaves and a certain amount of raw produce. Hence their expeditions in search of what they needed were more like piratical inroads than commercial ventures. Plunder, not purchase, was the purpose that carried them to Asia Minor, Egypt, the coasts of the Black Sea and of Italy. But these descents were dangerous and not always profitable, while their need of metals was urgent. Thus trade was not entirely squeezed out by piracy, and the Phoenician merchants were welcome guests in Greece. Articles of Eastern production, whether stolen or received in the way of trade, were imitated locally; thus local industries were improved, and a profitable trade in such goods, either imported or produced locally, sprang up between the inhabitants of the coast and their neighbours who had no access to the sea.

The political system of Greece probably remained much the same as it had been in the Aegean age. The separate kingdoms were still ruled by a king, who relied upon the armed force of the clan and especially upon the richest and strongest of his companions in arms. The royal power was exercised by the man who was stronger, more ready-witted and intelligent, richer and better armed, than the rest. Wealth, knowledge, and the power to rule he inherited from his ancestors, as they had from the god; for all royal families, and noble families in general, traced their descent from heaven. But, for all his divine origin, the king was no eastern despot: not a god himself nor the master of his subjects, he was the head and leader of his clan and the chief of his heaven-descended family.

Round him are ranged other similar heads of old and distinguished families, who are his regular advisers and his brothers-in-arms. This small group has considerable wealth, and owes that wealth to their enterprise, activity, and excellent bodily training for warfare on land or sea. All the members of such families are well armed: each has a breastplate, a helmet and greaves, a good sword and spear, and a bow that carries to a distance. They drive into battle in chariots. They are perfectly skilled in all the niceties of single combat, by which battles are often decided. Hence the aristocracy are indispensable to the clan and kingdom, and their high position is secure. But the members of this group are all equals; they are all descended from Zeus just as the kings are; they are necessary to the king, as he is to them, and therefore are not merely his obedient servants.

So the plebian members of the clan are not the slaves of the king and aristocracy. They acknowledge the superiority of their leaders; but their leader and king is not their owner, and they are not his slaves. An unsuccessful or degenerate king cannot reckon upon the support of the clan; and it is easy for some one else, richer and stronger, more intelligent and successful, to take his place. The life of a king is by no means a bed of roses, but full of danger. He reigns while he fights, and he fights with his own hands. If he is rich, it is because he knows where and how to direct the arms of the clan, and how to organize its economic and military life. He is surrounded by envy and hostility. Greek tragedy tells us of more than one sinister episode from the lives of these primitive kings. Horrible crimes and bloody revenges, murders and revolutions, were common in the kingdoms of the Homeric Age.

IV

ANATOLIAN GREECE. ECONOMIC REVOLUTION IN GREECE IN CENTURIES VIII—VI B.C.

It is one of the most notable features of the migratory epoch in Greece, that the redistribution of population at the end of the second millennium B.C. and beginning of the first drove out a number of clans, and parts of clans, first to the islands and then to Asia Minor. There is no doubt that the emigrants were exceptionally active, enterprising, and ambitious. Some of them, belonging to the old population of Greece, had been unable to defend their kingdoms against the new-comers, and preferred to emigrate rather than come to terms and submit to new masters. Others belonged to the invading clans and looked on Greece as merely a temporary halting-place in the course of their instinctive march to the south and east, whose wealth was well known to them. Both alike brought with them from Greece the habits of civilized existence which had grown up there, either from the continuous influence of Aegean culture, or from the independent development of that culture by the Graeco-Aegean population of southern and central Hellas.

The emigrants established themselves in Asia Minor by force of arms and seized the choicest parts of the coast, especially the fertile valleys at the mouths of the chief rivers—the Granicus, the Scamander, the Caicus, the Hermus, the Maeander—and lying near to the most convenient harbours. They found here conditions of life not very different from what they had left behind.

1. CLAY FIGURES FROM A SANCTUARY

Plate VIII EARLY GREEK RELIGION

1. A group of clay figures from a sanctuary. About 2000 such figures were found at Ayia Irini (Cyprus) around the altar. Their size varies from some inches to life size. They represent worshippers. Note the terracottas of war-chariots and armed men. 7th or 6th century B.C. Cyprus Museum (Nicosia).

2. Ivory statuette of the overseer of the temple of the Great Goddess of Ephesus found under the ruins of the early temple of Ephesus. The overseer (*megabyzos*) is apparently a eunuch. He wears a high tiara, a long embroidered robe with a belt and a string of beads on the neck. Just like the megabyzos described by Xenophon in the *Anabasis*. Greek work under strong Oriental influence. 8th–7th centuries B.C. Museum, Constantinople.

3. Ivory statuette of a priestess of the Great Ephesian Goddess found at Ephesus under the ruins of the early temple. The priestess is represented in a long dress with heavy gold ear-rings. She holds in her hands a jug and a dish. On her head is a long pole with a bird at the top. 8th–7th centuries B.C. Museum, Constantinople.

50

2. IVORY STATUETTE FROM EPHESUS.
HIGH PRIEST

3. IVORY STATUETTE FROM
EPHESUS. PRIESTESS

4. COLOSSAL ATHENIAN VASE

4. A colossal Athenian vase. Vases such as this one served as vessels
from which to make drink offerings to the dead below. For this reason these pots generally have an opening at the bottom for the pouring of libations. In the 9th–7th centuries, these very large painted
vases were used as grave monuments. The ornamentation consists of
a series of geometric motives in various combinations. The figure-
scenes are treated in the same geometric spirit and are very primitive. They represent a funeral with the deceased laid out on a bier,
surrounded by his wife and children and by mourning women tear-
ing their hair. The lower frieze shows warriors on foot and in chariots, some carrying large shields. Found near the Dipylon Gate of
Athens. 8th century B.C. Metropolitan Museum of Art, New York.

The Anatolian coast had long been civilized: it kept up regular communications with the East and was familiar with the routes of maritime trade in the Straits, the Sea of Marmora, and the Black Sea. Hence when the Greeks had established themselves in Asia Minor, they could not help inheriting Anatolian traditions. The Late Aegean culture which they brought with them was bound to blend with the form which culture had already taken on the spot; Graeco-Aegean religion took over many Anatolian religious ideas; and, finally, a mixture of blood between the immigrants and the local aristocracy was inevitable.

The system, social, economic, and political, which prevailed in these Anatolian kingdoms before the Greek invasion, is somewhat obscure. But from survivals of that system and from the picture of Troy drawn by Homer we must suppose the existence of fortified cities as the centres of political life. The king's palace was in the city, and his retainers lived there. The form of later institutions makes it probable that the chief sanctuary was habitually placed close to the city—a sanctuary consecrated to one of the many Anatolian Mother-Goddesses, who continued to be, in later times, the chief objects of religious worship in that country. The worship of the goddess was performed by a numerous class of priests, whose head was perhaps king of the city and adjacent territory. It is possible, however, that even at that early time there was a special chief priest, distinct from the king: we know that in some cults of the Great Mother the chief priest was bound to be a eunuch. Below this aristocracy of priests and warriors came the general population, who tilled the soil for their superiors. Peasants who lived on temple lands were counted as slaves of the god; and so were the numerous workmen employed in shops belonging to the temple. The inhabitants of land not owned by the temple were, in all probability, serfs belonging to the king, his favourites, and his warriors. We must suppose that these relations were formed during the existence of the great Hittite Empire. It is probable that the fortified towns were built then, and that the aristocracy of the conquer-

2. BEZEL OF A GOLD RING

3. PAINTED FAIENCE
STATUETTE

Plate IX MINOAN RELIGION

1. Bezel of a gold ring. Found at Mycenae. The Great Goddess is
represented seated on a rocky ground beneath her sacred tree. Above
her in the heaven, symbolized by the sun and the moon, are divine
emblems: the double-axe and a small figure protected by the double
shield—the shield goddess. Left is a row of lion-heads. Near her
are seated two little handmaids; one is offering her a spray, the other
plucks fruit for her from the tree. Two women votaries present
flowers: to one of them the goddess presents three poppy-heads, the
other holds some lilies. The scene represents no doubt the epiphany
of the divine world to her worshippers. Late Minoan. About 1500
B.C. Athens, National Museum.

2. Bezel of a gold ring. Found at Mycenae. A shrine of the Great
Goddess is represented standing perhaps on the top of a mountain.
The doors of the forecourt, which is surrounded by a wall and con-
sists of three terraces, stand wide open. A paved road leads to the

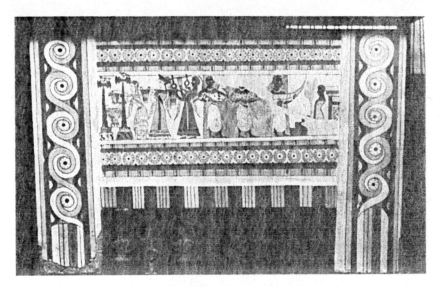

4. PAINTED SARCOPHAGUS FROM HAGIA TRIADA

cult-room of which the front is represented. Behind the front grow
two trees. Two other trees grow outside the walls of the forecourt.
Before the shrine two priestesses are worshipping the invisible Goddess by performing a sacred dance. Similar shrines are known at
Paphos in Cyprus and at Byblos in Phoenicia. Late Minoan. About
1500 B.C. Athens, National Museum.

3. Faience statuette, painted. Found in the Palace of Cnossus
among other sacred objects in a temple-depot. The figure represents
either the Snake-goddess herself or her priestess. Her arms, her waist,
her tiara are surrounded by snakes. Snake-goddesses are familiar
figures in Oriental religions. Middle Minoan. About 1700 B.C. Museum of Candia (Crete).

4. Painted sarcophagus. Found at Hagia Triada. Cult of the gods
and of the dead. The right half of the fresco is occupied by the
mummified figure of the dead man standing before his grave-monu-
ment. Three male-priests bring him gifts: the first, a ship for his last
voyage, the others, animals. The left half represents a sacrifice (of
blood and wine) by two ladies at the double-axe shrine of the Great
Goddess. On the axes are two doves, the birds of the Great Mother.
Between the axes is a large krater for the liquid offerings. Behind
the offering ladies a priestess is playing the lyre and singing the
praise of the Goddess. After 1400 B.C. Museum of Candia (Crete).

55

ing Hittites settled down in them. But the temples and temple lands were older than the Hittites. Before the Hittites came, the king and the chief priest were probably identical.

When groups of emigrants from Greece conquered one of these kingdoms after another, their first business, no doubt, was to establish their power, define their relations to the local inhabitants, adapt themselves to new conditions, and defend their possessions against fresh swarms of invaders from the west. They were few in number and the place was strange. Hence the difficulty of their position dictated a policy of agreement in their dealings both with the local population and with subsequent colonists. It is certain that the Greeks spared the rich and powerful temples on the Anatolian coast. The cult of the Great Goddess had been familiar to them even in Greece. Hence their first object was to secure for themselves the protection of the local goddess; and they secured it by maintaining her temple and the immunities of the temple. This is why we find later a large and wealthy temple of some local deity with a Greek name standing near most Greek cities in Asia Minor. If the deity was male, he was called Zeus or Apollo by the Greeks, and every goddess became Artemis. Some of the Greek names, indeed, had been taken over by the Greeks in their own country from the Aegeans or from the pre-Greek population of Hellas. This policy of agreement can be traced at Ephesus, for instance, with its famous temple of Artemis. In all probability the Greeks and the ruling aristocracy of the conquered cities combined to form a single dominating class, with the local population of tillers and herdsmen to work for them. It is probable that the Greeks seldom came into armed collision with fresh groups of settlers. Generally they admitted such freely to their kingdom, and sometimes guided them to districts in the neighbourhood that were ripe for the spoiler.

This conciliatory policy was the necessary result of the political situation, already described in Chapter III, in the eastern world at the beginning of the first millennium B.C. After the disruption of the Hittite Empire its place was filled by the Phrygian kingdom, whose power and wealth were very well known to the Greeks—a fact sufficiently proved by the stories current among them of Midas, the great King of Phrygia who 'bathed in gold'. When Phrygia was broken by an invasion of Cimmerians, Lydia by degrees took its place. Lydia had withstood the pressure of these devastating marauders, who spread as far as the Greek cities in Asia Minor and destroyed some of them early in the seventh century B.C. The kingdoms of Phrygia and Lydia had both kept up constant relations with Greece. Carrying on an extensive trade with the East, they resented the interposition of the Greeks between themselves and the sea, and therefore strove to add these Greek cities to their own dominions. The settlers had to exert themselves to the utmost to defend their independence. Under these conditions, every addition to the population of the Greek cities increased their power of resistance; and the better their relations with the native inhabitants, the less likely they were to be betrayed by them. In spite of all, they were unable to maintain their freedom against the last kings of Lydia, or against Persia, when she took the place of Lydia in Asia Minor. They were all obliged to submit to Cyrus and his successors. Their internal life went on unchanged; for the Persians did not interfere with the institutions of the cities.

These institutions were partly brought from European Greece by the settlers and partly taken over from their predecessors in Asia Minor. The form of government in most of the communities was not monarchical. It is probable that the conquest of the Anatolian coast was effected under the rule of kings; but our historical tradition, at least, refers almost exclusively to a contest between different forms of popular government—aristocracy, or government by a few rich and noble families, and democracy, or government by the whole people. The aristocracy probably consisted of those descended from the original conquerors, who had shared among themselves the conquered land and the serfs connected with it. The lower classes would probably include later settlers, who lived chiefly by industry and trade; some of these would be rich and influential citizens, while others would be plain artisans, small traders, and labourers.

The economic life of the settlers was based mainly on agriculture and stock-raising. Further, the culture of the vine and olive was successfully carried on both in the Aegean islands and on the Anatolian mainland. The production of wine became a Greek speciality, notably in the islands, some of which, such as Lesbos, Chios, and Samos, are really inseparable from the mainland. The soil of these islands, less suitable for agriculture, is excellent for vines, which supply splendid wine, sweet, fragrant, and strong—exactly the qualities prized by the inhabitants of Hither Asia, where viticulture was unsuccessful and the produce of the grapes indifferent. A kindred industry was the production of olive oil, which gradually became, throughout Greece and in parts of the East, essential for diet, health, and illumination. Olive oil drives out butter; olive oil drives out lighted brands and torches, just as paraffin drove out tallow candles and has now given place to electricity. Thanks to her wine and oil, Greece, and especially Anatolian Greece, was able to produce wares which earned respect for her in the world's markets. The revolution in cultivation, caused by the development of these two industries, had a notable influence upon the life of the whole Greek world. The islands and European Greece were soon able to compete successfully with Asia Minor, especially in the production of oil, and captured the markets in the east, south, and north.

Nevertheless, Asia Minor did not lose her predominance in the economic life of the Aegean coast. In districts occupied by Greece since the time of the Hittite dominion industry as well as agriculture was firmly established. The technical skill of Aegeans and Egyptians, of Mesopotamia and Phoenicia, found a refuge in the Anatolian temples, which were not merely religious centres, but also important centres of art and the scene of animated fairs. The conditions were specially favourable for the textile industry, and for work in wood and leather. The central plateau of Anatolia fed enormous flocks of sheep, which had long been famous for the exceptionally fine quality of their wool. The country was rich in minerals, and in the materials for vegetable dyes that could match the Tyrian purple extracted from marine shells. In metallurgy Anatolia was not inferior to the Transcaucasian kingdom of Van: gold she produced herself; and silver, copper, and iron were shipped to her along the coast from the land of the Chalybes on the southern shore of the Black Sea. This route had been familiar to the Carians even before the Greeks set foot in Asia. The natural wealth of the country had long been known, and to it was due the prosperity of the Hittite empire.

The Lydians, as the heirs of the Hittites, raised the industry and trade of the country to an unprecedented height. Nor were the Greeks on the coast left behind in the race. They soon acquired from the native inhabitants technical skill in the manufacture of textiles, and bettered the instruction. They learned to work in wood and leather, and to make fine jewellery of Anatolian gold after Lydian patterns. They brought with them into the country the ancient speciality of the Aegeans—the manufacture of excellent vessels of clay for oil and wine, and of lamps for illumination. They took full advantage of the high quality of Greek clay, especially clay from the islands; and their natural taste made these objects masterpieces of decorative art, as unique in their kind as the Aegean vases. Their woven fabrics, leather and wood manufactures, gems, weapons, and metal articles for household use and furniture, were bartered for wine and oil from the islands and from Greece; and these, together with wine and oil of their own production, were exported to east and west. Thus the foreign trade of the Anatolian Greeks became very extensive, including Lydia, Greece, and the Greek communities now springing up in the west, in Italy and Sicily, and in the east, along the Straits, the Sea of Marmora, and the Black Sea. For the purposes of this trade, Lydia and the Anatolian cities now

1. CLAY STATUETTE FOUND AT TANAGRA IN BOEOTIA

2. CLAY STATUETTE FOUND AT TANAGRA IN BOEOTIA

3. and 4. TWO CLAY STATUETTES FOUND AT THEBES IN BOEOTIA

Plate X GREEK LIFE IN THE 6TH AND 5TH
CENTURIES B.C.

1. Clay statuette found at Tanagra in Boeotia. The statuette represents a Boeotian peasant ploughing his field. The workmanship, though primitive (note the almost geometric oxen), is unusually good. The group is full of life. Note the primitive plough, of which all the parts as we know them from literary sources (e.g. Hesiod) are perfectly recognizable. 6th century B.C. Paris, Louvre (*Bull. de corresp. hell.* xvii, 1893).

2. Clay statuette found at Tanagra in Boeotia. A street cook seated on a square stone, before him his transportable stove. He is cooking meat or pastry. Probably early 6th century B.C. Berlin, Lapiquarium.

3. and 4. Two clay statuettes found at Thebes in Boeotia. One represents a man playing the lyre with five strings. In his right hand he holds the 'plectrum', with his left he moves the strings. The second represents a man writing on a diptych, i.e. a double wooden tablet covered with wax. In his right hand the 'style'. Greek letters (three lines) are seen on the tablet. The letters give no sense. Is the musician a Homerist, and the writer a poet or a modest scribe? Early 6th century B.C. Paris, Louvre.

began, for the first time, to make use of coined money—gold, electrum (pale gold), and silver.

Trade and commerce became even more active when Persia took the place of Lydia in Asia Minor. The existence of the world-empire of Persia, together with the construction of roads, assisted the growth of trade in the Persian monarchy generally. The Greeks made full use of all these advantages. Their merchants steadily squeezed the Phoenicians out of the Aegean world and drove them to the western part of the Mediterranean. In the eighth century the Greeks established trade posts in Syria (modern Al Mina, by the mouth of the Orontes River) and on the Phoenician coast. From that time all the attention of the Phoenicians was given to the western district of the north African coast, where their colonies of Utica and Carthage prospered greatly; to the south coast of Spain, with its rich mines of silver, copper, and tin, including Tartessus, a wealthy centre of trade and industry; and to the north-west coast of Italy, where the Etruscans were always faithful allies and regular partners in business, and where there was a considerable supply of metals—copper and iron.

This commercial prosperity of the Greeks in Asia Minor affected their social and political life as well. In consequence of it their cities take the lead in the life of the country. Their growth is irresistible, and adventurers in search of gain crowd into them. A new aristocracy—the great merchants, the owners of vineyards and olive groves and of large factories—grows up beside the old landowning aristocracy and acquires a considerable part of the land. They own whole fleets of merchant vessels. Slave labour begins more and more to displace free labour in mercantile business. Slaves work in the vineyards and factories, and serve as rowers on the ships.

The growth of trade makes it necessary to seek new markets for produce; and the growth of urban population makes it impossible for each small community to find food for itself from its own territory. Therefore the new markets must provide not

Fig. 6. Paintings of a black-figured cup showing the hoeing and ploughing of the field, transportation of big jars (oil or wine), and other scenes of rustic life. Like others of this period the pictures are full of life and humour. 6th cent. B.C. Paris, Louvre. After Perrot and Chipiez.

merely raw products for industry and more slaves, but foodstuffs as well. Corn, above all, is needed. Flocks and herds are too small to provide meat for every one; beasts are no longer bred for the butcher but for their milk and wool and their use in agriculture. Fish becomes a substitute for meat. The leading speculators therefore look out for districts where fish can be caught in great numbers for salting. These conditions stimulate colonization in all places suitable either for the extensive production of cereals or for a fishing industry. The places which prove most suitable are—the shores and seaside valleys of Italy and Sicily; the coasts of the Balkan peninsula, the Straits, the Sea of Marmora, and the Black Sea; there was an inexhaustible supply of tunny-fish in that region, and of fresh-water fish at the mouths of the Danube, the Dniester, the Bug, the Dnieper, and the Don. These coasts, known to the Greeks at an earlier date, were now populated by crowds of new Greek colonists—tillers of the soil and fishermen, not working for themselves alone, but also for an extensive and steadily growing market.

The economic revolution, beginning in the eastern part of the Greek world, soon made itself felt in the west also, and especially along the line of the coast. Here the disruption of the family had long been going on, and small separate holdings had been

FIG. 7. An excellent black-figured cup signed by the painter Theozotos. It shows a herd of goats with the shepherds and the dogs. 6th
cent. B.C. Paris, Louvre. After Morin-Jean.

formed on the territory of each community. In some places this
process resulted in a division of the land between the families
of the predominating stock, who finally reduced the conquered
native population to a state of serfdom. This was apparently the
origin of the system in Sparta, Thessaly, and Crete. But in most
of the other communities—we know more about Attica and
Boeotia than about other countries—the disruption of the family
resulted in the creation of two classes, a number of smallholders
and a group of large landowners, members of the royal house
and other great families. The life of the poor farmer, driven by
the pressure of great neighbours to the hills and marshes, is excellently drawn for us in the poetry of Hesiod, a Boeotian peasant. He depicts a hard life on a little patch of land, with no
brightness in the present, constant care for the morrow, and
no hope for the future.

At this time the economic revolution already mentioned began. The demand for wine and oil forced the large owners to give
up the production of cereals and take to vineyards and olive-
trees. This industry is suitable for slave-labour, because it requires a number of hands directed by a single owner. The result
was a great increase in the number of slaves. In the cities, as,

F<small>IG</small>. 8. One of the votive plaques of which scores were found in a sanctuary of Poseidon, near Corinth, the great centre of commerce and industry of Greece in the 6th cent. Our plaque represents miners working in a pit. 6th cent. B.C. Berlin Museum. From 'Antike Denkmäler'.

for instance, in Athens and Corinth, trade and industry began to grow. Each city tried to produce for the market something individual and unknown to other cities; they improved their methods of production and the quality of their goods. Money now made its appearance. At first it was very dear, and it was possible to buy a quantity of goods for a small sum.

This economic advance did nothing to improve the position of the smallholder. Holdings became smaller and smaller. That vines and olive-trees were lucrative was proved by the example of the large landowners; but capital was needed for this new enterprise, and capital was all in the hands of the merchants and manufacturers in the city. Money was dear, and high interest had to be paid for loans. It was necessary to borrow money for other purposes—to keep the farm going in bad seasons, to divide an inheritance and form new holdings, to clear away forest and drain marshes. All this tended to the wide development of the money-lender's business and the growth of debt among the smallholders. They were exposed to a terrible risk: if they could not pay, the debtor himself and his family became the property of the creditor.

In the meantime, this expansion of industry, trade, and navigation opened up wide possibilities for ambition both within the city and beyond the borders of the country. Cities became crowded and new colonies were formed. All the Greek coasts took an active part in colonizing the west, north, and east. Miletus throws off swarm after swarm; and colonists in considerable numbers go forth from Euboea and other islands and from the Peloponnese. Certain cities of European Greece come to the front in the world's markets. Thus the city of Chalcis in Euboea begins to work its copper mines intensively and to flood the market with the metal; Aegina takes advantage of its position between Asia Minor and Greece to become a great exchange for the barter of goods, and in the seventh century begins to coin silver in abundance. Corinth, situated on the Isthmus between the Peloponnese and Greece, becomes the centre of exchange with Italy: it pays better to break cargo at the Isthmus than to sail round the stormy coasts of the Peloponnese. Corinth stirs up the Ionian islands and colonizes on the routes westward (Ambracia, Syracuse) and in the peninsula of Chalcidice. Much the same part is played by Megara, a centre for the production of fine fabrics, and by Sicyon in Achaia, the best harbour in the north of the Peloponnese.

To the economic development of this age we must ascribe the Greek colonization of all sites on the Mediterranean coast that offered a prospect of reasonable prosperity for the settler. Italy and Sicily were soon covered with colonies, till the southern coast of Italy and the eastern half of Sicily were densely populated with Greeks. Tarentum, Sybaris, Croton, Epizephyrian Locri, Rhegium, Elea, Cumae, and Naples, in Italy; Agrigentum, Gela, Syracuse, Tauromenium, and Messana, in Sicily—all these

FIG. 9. One of the votive plaques from Corinth (see fig. 8). The picture shows an oven for making pottery, one of the specialities of Corinthian industrial life. 6th cent. B.C. Berlin Museum. From 'Antike Denkmäler'.

cities gained wealth and power. Central Italy was in the hands of the Etruscans, who were themselves enterprising merchants and skilled agriculturists, and therefore barred their coast against the Greeks. The Phoenicians had seized western Sicily, and there the influence of Carthage predominated. When the Greeks had occupied the east coast, they were forced to begin a long and obstinate struggle against the Cathaginians, who were supported by the Etruscans. The east coast of Italy was peopled by Illyrian settlers coming from what is now Dalmatia, on the east of the Adriatic. These Illyrians were bold navigators and pirates who defended the Adriatic against Greek penetration. In Gaul things were different: that country had not yet been occupied by the Indo-European stock of Celts from the north, and its native inhabitants—Ligurians and Iberians, the first conquerors of southern Gaul—welcomed the Greeks gladly. Massilia became the centre of Greek colonization on the south coast, and was sup-

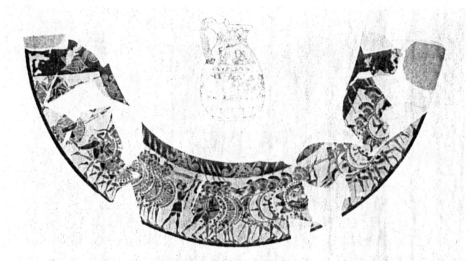

1. PROTO-CORINTHIAN JUG. GREEK WARRIORS

Plate XI   GREEK VASES. 7TH–6TH CENTURIES B.C.

1. Proto-Corinthian jug (made at Corinth or Sicyon) divided into
four friezes. One of them is shown in our figure. It represents two
armies of hoplites clashing in battle. The shields of one army which
are seen from the front side show the various armorial devices of the
warriors. A flute-player between two rows of soldiers plays a military
tune (remember the war-songs of Tyrtaeus). 7th century B.C. Villa
Giulia, Rome. After *Antike Denkmäler.*

2. Archaic polychrome hydria (water pot) from Caere in Etruria.
The vases of this type were probably made somewhere in Ionia. The
picture on the hydria represents the Greek legend of how Heracles
came to Egypt, was captured by the Egyptian King Busiris, was
brought to an altar and here broke loose and knocked down Busiris
and his Egyptians. Some negroes are running to the scene of action
to help their king. The scene is full of life and humour. 6th century
B.C. Oesterreichisches Museum, Vienna. After Furtwängler-Reichhold.

68

2. ARCHAIC HYDRIA FROM CAERE. HERACLES AND BUSIRIS

ported against Phoenicians and Etruscans first by the local population and then by the Celts. The Greeks managed also to establish themselves here and there on the south coast of Spain.

In the east the same process went on as widely. Here the
Greeks began by occupying all the eastern shore in the north of
the Balkan peninsula, with both banks of the Straits and the
Sea of Marmora. The peninsula of Chalcidice, with its rich
mines, was covered with Greek cities. A number of large settlements grew up on the banks of the Straits and the Sea of Marmora. Conspicuous among these were Cyzicus on the south of
the Sea of Marmora, and Byzantium and Chalcedon on the
European and Asiatic sides of the Bosphorus. Here began a perfect network of Greek stations for trade and the fishing industry
—Heraclea, Amisus, Sinope, and Trapezus, south of the Black
Sea; next, on the west, north, and east coasts all the best fishing-
stations at the mouths of the Balkan and Russian rivers; a number of harbours in the Crimea, along the Caucasian and Crimean
coasts of the Cimmerian Bosphorus, and on the Caucasian coast.
The chief settlements on the western shore of the Black Sea
were Apollonia, Mesembria, Tomi, and Ister. Tyras stood at the
mouth of the Dniester, Olbia at the mouth of the Bug and
Dnieper, Cercinites, Chersonesus, and Theodosia, on the Crimean coast; Panticapaeum and Phanagoria on the shore of the
Cimmerian Bosphorus; Tanais at the mouth of the Don; Dioscurias and Phasis on the Caucasian shore. Behind these coast-
towns, the Balkan peninsula and Asia Minor were inhabited by
Thracian tribes of Indo-European origin, who tilled the soil and
raised cattle. In the steppes of south Russia, a powerful kingdom of nomad Scythians (another branch of the same Iranian
stock to which the Persians belonged) had destroyed the Cimmerian kingdom and taken its place; and the same relations
existed between them and the Greek colonies on the Black Sea
as between Persia and the Greek cities in Asia Minor.

The wider the extension of Greek colonization on the shores
of the Mediterranean and the Black Sea, the more fierce became

commercial activity in Greece itself and Asia Minor. One new market after another was opened for trade and industry. The wealth of Greece increased by leaps and bounds. But this growing wealth brought with it changes in political and social life. Classes grew up, and with them class hatred and class contests. The aristocracy of birth found their superiority contested by the aristocracy of the purse; and both were threatened by the numbers of the labouring population. The lavish expenditure of the minority, the luxury with which they surrounded themselves, their exploitation of the masses, and the increasing number of slaves, were not passively endured: they begot active jealousy and hatred, which broke out in the shape of a cruel, and often inhuman, struggle between classes. Thus at Miletus the people were at first victorious and murdered the wives and children of the aristocrats; then the aristocrats prevailed and burned their opponents alive, lighting up the open spaces of the city with live torches. Read the verses of Theognis, and you will understand the intense hatred and mutual contempt which the opponents in this unending struggle felt for one another.

V

SPARTA: HER SOCIAL, ECONOMIC, AND POLITICAL SYSTEM

From the eighth to the sixth century B.C. the political and social development of Greece kept pace with her economic growth. As the chief feature in this development we must reckon the gradual formation and establishment of that peculiar Greek institution, the city-state. This process was not everywhere simultaneous or identical. Some parts of Greece retained for centuries the clan system of government and all the peculiarities of the Homeric Age; among these were Arcadia in the Peloponnese, the Aetolians in the north-west of central Greece, their neighbours, the Acarnanians, and the inhabitants of Epirus. Others developed urban institutions, proceeding from stage to stage in the course of this development. The essential peculiarity of the latter system is this—that political life is concentrated in one place. This place is the city: it is the religious, political, and economic centre of the district united round it and reckoned as territory belonging to the city. All the inhabitants of this territory are citizens and jointly organize the life, political, economic, social, and religious, of the whole community. Foreigners, serfs, and slaves are the only persons excluded from the ranks of the citizens. In these city-states political power passes by stages from the hands of the clan king to the body of citizens, first to a group of leading families closely associated with the king in his duties, next to all landowners, and finally to the citizens generally; the first of these stages is called 'aristocracy', and the last 'democracy'.

The whole body of citizens draws up rules for the behaviour of each citizen individually and of the associated body. These compulsory rules receive the name of laws. They represent the conscience of the community, and express the will of the citizens in each city. As in the East, law is the means by which notions of right and justice are conveyed to the populace; but there is a difference. In the East, law is a part of the divine order, unalterable and binding on every man. But in Greece, though the law enjoys divine protection, it is not a divine revelation nor an unalterable rule of behaviour laid down once for all. In Greece laws are made by men. If a law offends the conscience of the majority, it can and must be changed; but while it is in force, all are obliged to obey it, because there is something divine in it and in the very idea of law. To break its injunctions entails punishment not only from men, the guardians of law, but also from gods. This rule of law in the city—of law created by the whole body of citizens—is one of the most characteristic features in the public life of Greece.

In any given territory the city has no rivals of a similar character. There may be other places where the population is concentrated; but these have no independent political life, and their inhabitants are citizens only of the central community. In private life the old clan divisions are kept up: each citizen is member of a brotherhood (*phratria*), family, and tribe (*phyle*); the last is a large subdivision of a clan. There is also a geographical division into districts (demes), each of which has some town or village as a centre. Within the limits of one clan there are often several city-states forming an alliance; one example is Boeotia. Such alliances are often due to certain cults common to a number of city-states, and then the alliances are called 'amphictyonies'.

Such is the general outline, identical in all city-states. But within the limits of this outline each city-state develops in its own way, so that endless varieties of the same system present themselves. We know most about the constitution of two city-states, which gradually step to the front of political life, and in whose history, as in a mirror, the whole history of Greece is reflected. I refer to Sparta in the Peloponnese, and Athens in central Greece. Next after these are ranked other states: Argos and Olympia in the east and west of Peloponnese; Messene beside Sparta; Sicyon on the northern shore of Peloponnese, not far from the Isthmus; Corinth on the Isthmus; Boeotia, including a number of cities, of which Thebes was the strongest and richest; Phocis, also including many cities which formed a religious alliance round the great shrine of Delphi; and Megara, close to Corinth and the nearest neighbour of Athens. A number of large cities, of which something was said in the preceding chapter, grew up in the islands nearest Greece, especially Euboea and Aegina. The chief cities of Euboea were Chalcis and Eretria.

Among these city-states a peculiar position is occupied by Sparta. In general, her constitution is not markedly different from the type just described. She is a community of citizens, such as we find elsewhere throughout Greece. But in this constitution there are a number of peculiar features, some of which, in a slightly different form, recur in Crete with its scores of cities and in the fertile plains of Thessaly; and these peculiar features gave Sparta her individuality and forced even Greek historians and thinkers to regard her system as exceptional.

Sparta forms the natural centre of Laconia, the fertile valley of the Eurotas. Of her early history we know little. In the Graeco-Aegean age Laconia was among the most powerful kingdoms of the Peloponnese. At the time of the Trojan war it was ruled by 'fair-haired' Menelaus and 'fair' Helen his wife, who, according to Homer, was the cause of the war. Homer represents Menelaus as one of the richest and most enlightened of Graeco-Aegean kings; and this is natural, because the Eurotas valley grows excellent crops, and the Laconian Gulf, into which the

Eurotas flows, has several convenient harbours which offer the shortest passage from Crete to Greece.

According to tradition, Laconia was conquered by Dorians at the end of the Dorian invasion and became the chief stronghold of the Dorian stock in the Peloponnese. In the eighth century B.C., and again in the seventh, Sparta, having become the capital of Dorian Lacedaemon, carried on stubborn warfare against her neighbour Messene, to acquire the fertile lands owned by this richest district of the whole peninsula. About the second of these wars we get information in the verses of Tyrtaeus, a poet born at Athens, who played a prominent part in the victory obtained by Sparta over a federation of Peloponnesian states, which had helped Messene to assert her freedom. Excavations carried out by Englishmen at Sparta have shown that she was at this time a rich country and in the van of Greek civilization. Her culture is of that semi-oriental type, together with a considerable number of Aegean survivals, which is noticeable in all the progressive districts of Greece in that age.

Whether the peculiar features of the Spartan system had taken shape as early as this time we do not know. By Spartan tradition they were assigned to a single reformer, Lycurgus, probably a mythical personality. Still it is very likely that tradition is right in considering the later system, as it is known to us from the sixth century to the fourth, as the result of one reform or of several carried out successively. We may suppose that these reforms were started amid the dangers and difficulties of the Messenian wars, when the inhabitants were forced to put forth all their strength in order to save the kingdom.

The chief peculiarity of the system is this. A group living in Sparta and called Spartiates, dominated a population many times as numerous. Of this subordinate population one part were called Helots. The Helots lived on separate farms in the domain of the city and in some parts of conquered Messenia; their position was that of state slaves, and the families of Spartiates made use of their labour. Another part were called *perioeci* or provincials. They lived in Laconia and Messenia, in the cities and the domains belonging to the cities; they enjoyed personal freedom and a certain measure of self-government; but in military and political affairs they were entirely subordinate to the dominating group. We do not know how this system came into existence. It is very likely that there were serfs in Laconia during the rule of the Graeco-Aegeans, and that the Dorians took over the institution. Some of the Messenians were reduced to slavery after the Spartan conquest already mentioned. It is probable, also, that the status of the Perioeci was due to the conquest, at some date, of independent cities, which were then united to Sparta as allies but inferiors.

The reform, already mentioned, of the Spartan constitution did not create these two inferior classes. Its object was rather to change the organization of the ruling class, and to define precisely the relations between it and the two others. It was, from first to last, emphatically a military reform, aiming at a military organization for the ruling class, who were probably identical with the group of Dorian conquerors. Within this group the reforms were democratic and socialist; it is the first attempt in history to introduce a thoroughgoing system of state socialism. The system retained some relics of the time when Sparta also was ruled by a group of aristocratic families. Thus the kings—two kings, one from each of the noble families of Europontidae and Agiadae—were still at the head of the government. There was also a body called *gerusia* or Council of Elders, consisting of thirty members including the two kings; these were drawn from a definite group of noble families and formed the chief instrument of government. But both these institutions were survivals. The real power belonged to the *apella* or popular assembly, consisting of all adult Spartiates who possessed full rights of citizenship and served as cavalry and infantry in the army. They elected the Council; they also elected the Ephors (overseers), who were the real rulers of the country and guardians of the constitution. It is true that the Assembly voted only on business submitted to

Fig. 10. Laconian black-figured cup. Two young soldiers are carrying on their shoulders a slain warrior. 6th cent. B.C. Berlin Museum.

them by the Ephors and previously discussed by the Council—individual citizens had no power to initiate legislation; but nevertheless no important decision and no law was valid unless it was confirmed by the popular assembly.

The peculiarity of Sparta was not the constitution: it was the creation of an absolute unique social organization, intended to increase the military strength of the country. All social and economic relations were based on absolute subordination of the individual to the state, and on the conversion of all the dominating class into a standing army, ready at any moment to take the field. Every adult Spartiate was, first of all, a soldier. Though he had a house and family of his own, he did not live there; and his days were not spent in providing for them or in productive labour, but entirely devoted to constant military training. Every adult Spartiate enlisted in one of the military divisions of the citizen army, and spent all his time in special clubs (*phiditia* or *syssitia*), where he was compelled to take part in the common meals. As all his time was taken up by his club life and training, the state relieved him of material cares by supporting him and his family. This was effected by giving to each man a considerable allotment of land together with one or more families of Helots. The Helots were bound to provide their owner and his family with a fixed annual quantity of foodstuffs, and to act as his servants in peace and on campaign. Part of the Helots' tribute went to pay the Spartiate's subscription to his club, and part to maintain his family.

From early childhood the Spartiate was trained to live for the State. A boy born in such a family, if he was pronounced healthy by a special board of elders, came at once under public supervision. Deformed or sickly infants, boys and girls, were exposed by the government, when they either died or were picked up by some charitable Helot. To the age of seven the children were cared for by their mothers and special government nurses. At seven the boys were removed from their families and entered a military group commanded by a young Spartiate; here they learned marching, gymnastics, music, and reading. They ate plain food cooked by themselves, and their bedding was of reeds gathered by themselves on the banks of the Eurotas. Gymnastic and military competitions were constantly held for their benefit. In order to develop independence, ingenuity, and dexterity, they were encouraged to steal and especially to steal food. But the unsuccessful thief was mercilessly beaten, not for stealing but for being found out. The girls went through much the same course of physical exercise as the boys, in order that the future mothers of Spartiates might be healthy. After marriage they led a comparatively idle life in the houses of their husbands.

Morally and socially the position of the Helots was deplorable. They were in absolute slavery to the State. They were kept under constant supervision; and from time to time the most vigorous among them were murdered. The most wary and intelligent of the young Spartiates were sent as secret agents of the government, turning up where they were least expected and dispatching undesirable Helots without trial. The economic position of the Helots was not so bad: their tribute of produce to their masters was strictly defined and not burdensome; and they had full liberty to improve their land and accumulate savings. But the Perioeci were much better off. The Spartiates were forbidden to engage in trade and industry, and not encouraged to sell their landed property, even when it was not divided into allotments; and therefore the Perioeci monopolized all the business of the country. They worked the rich iron-mines of Laconia; they manufactured weapons for the army, implements for agriculture, and articles for domestic use. Trade also was in their hands exclusively. The Spartiates, however, disapproved of foreign trade, and tried to make home products satisfy their needs. They feared that foreign goods would bring with them new demands and new ideas. For the same reason they retained iron coinage as the only recognized medium of exchange, though of course it was not current outside Sparta. The Spartiates kept a watchful eye on foreign visitors and resorted freely to the deportation of undesirable persons from other countries. This spirit tended to isolate Sparta from the rest of the world: she became self-centred—almost exclusively an inland power with a strong army but without ships either for war or commerce.

Such was the organization, political, social, and economic, which made Sparta a powerful factor in the life of Hellas. She alone possessed a standing army, large enough, considering the conditions of that age, strictly disciplined, and excellently trained. The other city-states, living under different conditions, had at their disposal a mere militia of citizens who were mustered only at the beginning of military operations. This military superiority made a strong impression upon contemporary observers, and they were therefore inclined to idealize the Spartan system. And it did enable Sparta to develop an extensive activity for conquest in the seventh and sixth centuries B.C. After the subjection of Messenia this policy was first directed against the neighbouring states of Elis, Arcadia, and Argolis. Arcadia, after long warfare, concluded an alliance with Sparta, recognizing her headship in their joint political and military proceedings. The attempts of Argos to make herself the leading power in central Peloponnese brought her into collision with Sparta, and also armed Elis against her, together with Corinth and Sicyon, the cities on and near the Isthmus. In the sixth century Sparta was able to disarm Argos and deprive her of Cynuria, a district bordering on Lacedaemon, and to make Elis, Sicyon, and Corinth members of a Lacedaemonian military league directed by herself. This was the first considerable league of the kind in the history of the Greek nation; and it made Sparta the controlling power in Greek politics, especially in times of difficulty and danger.

VI

ATHENS AND ATTICA FROM 800 TO 600 B.C.

Side by side with Sparta there grew up by degrees in Greece between 800 and 600 B.C. another considerable political power, which was destined to take the lead for several centuries in the politics and civilization of all Greeks. This was the city-state of Athens, the economic and political centre of Attica. We have seen how Sparta deliberately chose to confine her activity to operations by land and recognized no industry but agriculture. Athens, on the contrary, at all times made full use of her favourable geographical position and the resources of her territory.

The peninsula of Attica runs out eastward to the sea. Her harbours are connected with the East by a chain of large and small islands, which stretch to the coast of Ionia and Caria in Asia Minor. She is divided from central Greece and, in particular, from Boeotia by mountains which are fairly high but easily crossed. The island of Aegina in the Saronic Gulf forms a bridge between the Dorian world of the Peloponnese and the Ionian world of Attica and the islands. The Isthmus of Corinth cuts off Attica from the west, so that she had no direct and natural access to the Gulf of Corinth. The natural wealth of the country, though not great, was sufficient to support a considerable population. The valleys of the Cephissus and Ilissus, if tilled with care, produced fair harvests; the valley of Eleusis was more fertile. The soil was everywhere excellent for growing olive-trees. The mountains grew fairly good timber, which made ship-building possible. With regard to metals, there were mines of silver and lead, but no iron and no copper. Good clay provided fine material for the potter. The quarries of the adjacent mountains, especially Pentelicus, afforded excellent sorts of stone, marble, and lime, so that building on a large scale could be carried on.

It was more important to Attica that here the conditions were favourable for uniting a considerable territory round one political centre. She forms a single geographical unit, whose most convenient exit to the sea is formed by the two harbours of Athens, Phalerum and the Piraeus. Thus it was possible in Attica, as in Sparta, to form a single kingdom with a rather large territory. A divided Attica would have remained what she was in the Graeco-Aegean age—one among many centres of civilization and political progress; united, she became the single powerful political centre of the richly gifted Ionian stock, possessing sufficient population and sufficient natural wealth to make her the mistress of all Ionians, just as Sparta endeavoured to become the mistress of all Dorians. We must remember that the rest of Ionia was broken up into small political units in the islands, and that its development and expansion in Asia Minor were cramped first by Lydia and then by Persia. Political rivalry with Attica was impossible for any of the other city-states in central Greece; Boeotia was divided into a number of cities and had no satisfactory outlet to the sea; Corinth was a purely commercial power, her territory was always negligible, and she had also powerful rivals at her very doors—Megara on the Isthmus, and Sicyon on the north cost of the Peloponnese.

In Attica the process of unification was unlike the corresponding process of Sparta. One reason for this may be that there was no class of serfs as a basis of economic life in Attica of the Mycenaean age, and that the new order was established, not as a result of conquest, but by evolution and agreement. At all events, instead of foreign invasion and the reforms, military and social, of Lycurgus, we find a transaction of uncertain date, connected with the name of a mythical king, Theseus, and called by the Greeks *synoecismos* or *sympoliteia*. It is quite possible, in Attica as in Sparta, that the mythical name conceals the real name of some great statesman belonging to the eighth century B.C. But the transaction itself was this—that the separate communities of Attica, each of which had possessed its own individuality and its own centre for politics and finance, now agreed to form a single kingdom, with Athens for the single centre of political, economic, and religious life. It is not known whether this measure was preceded by a gradual rise of Athens which proved her superiority in war and peace to the other communities of Attica. But it is highly probable that this concentration, which was resorted to later in several parts of the Greek world, was due to several causes—the gradual destruction of the kingly power and the formation of a strong aristocracy in each of the separate communities, and the certainty that these aristocrats must join forces if they were to cope with domestic and foreign dangers. At any rate, tradition is unanimous that the change in Attica was gradual and peaceful, and free from the revolutionary convulsions familiar to the Ionian world of that age.

We know little about the constitution of Attica after this concentration was carried through. But it is probable that the class of large landowners, who at that time were also traders and pirates, took the lead in political and economic life. The rulers of the community, chosen from among the members of the ruling aristocracy, were three in number: first, the king who was also the chief priest; secondly, the polemarch who commanded the armed forces of the kingdom; and, thirdly, the archon, the representative of civil authority. With these were later associated six junior archons, called *thesmothetae*, as judges and guardians of the law. The nine chosen rulers of the state, or magistrates, to use the Roman term, did not form a single corporate body. The king, who had once been the head of the administration, gradually began to lose all political importance, retaining only his religious functions. Power was concentrated almost entirely in

FIG. 11. The palace of Thetis, the mother of Achilles, as represented on the so-called François vase (Attic black-figured). The palace shows the typical forms of a 'megaron'. 6th cent. B.C. Archaeological Museum, Florence. After Furtwängler-Reichhold.

the hands of the polemarch and archon. At the same time the tenure of all those archons or magistrates, which had been permanent, became limited. Eventually it became the custom at Athens for all the representatives of authority to hold office for one year.

The magistrates were elected, laws were passed, and perhaps decisions on war and peace were taken, by the *ecclesia* or popular assembly, which probably consisted of all citizens with full rights, that is, all those who formed part of the citizen army and fought in defence of the country. Together with the magistrates there acted a council of elders, the chief body of the state for political, religious, and judicial business; it was called the Areopagus after the hill on which its meetings were generally held, and was filled by representatives of the noblest families and, probably, by ex-magistrates.

Together with these gradual changes in the system of government there grew up a new division of the population into three social and economic groups. The first of these contained the large landowners, the second the traders and artisans who lived in the city, and the third the smallholders. At the same time the political rights and military duties of each citizen began to be reckoned not by his birth but by his property and income. The aristocracy became a timocracy. The necessity of creating a larger and stronger army was probably the cause of this innovation. The land-owning aristocracy, who had originally borne the whole burden of defending the country, was inclined to shift a part of this burden to the shoulders of other well-to-do citizens, and to concede to them in return a part of their own political rights. This new division for military and civil purposes was founded on the comparative wealth of various classes in the state—wealth connected with the possession of land. The highest class consisted of persons called *pentakosiomedimnoi*, those landowners who drew from their lands an annual income of not less than 500 *medimni* (700 bushels) of corn; the second class contained those whose income from land was not less than 300 *medimni*. These two classes served in the army as cavalry: when summoned, they had to appear on horseback and wearing the full equipment of the hoplite or heavy-armed foot-soldier; and as their horses were not used in battle but merely for mobility and to pursue a beaten enemy, they were, properly, mounted infantry. The third class consisted of those whose income was not less than 200 *medimni*; they were called *zeugitae*, and served in heavy armour but had no horses. Political rights were confined to these classes. Below them came the *thetes*, who lived by the labour of their hands and possessed no definite and regular income; some of them served as rowers in the fleet and as light-armed skirmishers.

The financial revolution described in Chapter IV affected

Fig. 12. Black-figured water-pot (hydria). The picture shows Athenian women filling their water-pots at a public fountain and chatting. 6th cent. B.C. Paris, Louvre. After Perrot and Chipiez.

Attica as well. There also, owners of vineyards and olive-groves made their appearance, the class of traders and artisans grew larger, and the population of the city increased steadily. In this new capitalistic society the position of the smallholder became more and more irksome. Money is needed for improvements, for additions to stock, and for the transition from corn to vines and olives; and when his sons set up for themselves, money is needed to stock their holdings. At the same time money is scarce and dear, while the law regarding debt is extremely harsh, and its application rests with the upper classes, the very people who own capital and lend money. Thus the smallholder is ruined and deprived not only of his property but of his freedom also by the law of debtor and creditor. Many escape this fate by becoming tenants of land which once belonged to them but has now been seized by moneylenders. The discontent of the lower classes grows steadily and takes an acute form. They seek and find men to lead them and organize them for the struggle against the dominant classes. Their war-cries are a fresh division of the land and the abolition of debt. In order to carry out this programme, an armed rising takes place, directed by the leader, who attempts, with the support of the masses, to concentrate in his own hands military and civil power. Disturbance of this kind was especially rife throughout most of the Greek world in the seventh and sixth centuries B.C. In many places the acuteness of class-warfare called forth 'tyrants' or 'judges' (called *aesymnetae* by the Greeks), whose business it was to smooth down extremes in either direction, to create a new and more democratic system, to devise and establish in writing the basis of a constitution and of civil and criminal law. They met with stout opposition from the aristocracy, especially the old aristocracy of birth and landed possessions; but they often found supporters, not only among the lower classes who possessed no political rights, but also among the middle class and the new aristocracy of commerce and industry. It is not without cause that this period in Greek history has been called the age of revolution and tyranny.

The history of Attica, during the course of these developments in the Hellenic world, is marked by one distinctive feature. For there the transition from one stage of civil government to another was accomplished more quickly and more peacefully, with none of those atrocious convulsions which make the life of many contemporary communities resemble an almost uninterrupted conflagration. In the course of a single century Attica made a clean sweep of her ancient institutions connected with the clans and families, and, for the first time, created a democratic state on the basis of a carefully considered legal system—a system no less logical, but more flexible, than the military system of Sparta. It is a remarkable fact that the constitutional changes of this period are everywhere associated with men of genius and brilliant personality—the first professional politicians, whose mythical prototype in Attica is the royal reformer, Theseus.

The dawn of political development in Attica reveals another

semi-mythical figure in the lawgiver Draco, to whom legend attributed the oldest written code of law. These laws are of interest, because they testify to the severity of the early criminal legislation which prevailed in an aristocratic Greek community; but it is hardly possible to believe, on the authority of late witnesses, that Draco was really the author of the first written constitution of Athens. Still we may well believe that party conflicts between the classes grew more and more acute in Attica, and that repeated attempts were made to set up a tyranny. There were many models to copy from: either at this time or earlier tyrants were ruling in Asia Minor, Italy, and the islands, and also nearer home—in Megara, the rival which contested with Athens the possession of the prosperous island of Salamis, and in the commercial cities of Corinth on the Isthmus and Sicyon on the north coast of Peloponnesus.

The great social and political reformer, Solon, is the first really historical name in Athenian history. Men of action, of this type, are common in Greece in the late seventh and early sixth centuries B.C. They are prominent and able representatives of noble families, men who have assimilated the results of Ionian culture, thinkers and rationalists, who believe in the omnipotence of government and statesmen to change social and economic relations, and who realize the effect of eloquence and literary propaganda. They are convinced that the causes of the never-ending class-conflict are clear to them, and consciously endeavour to reform out of existence that which they reckon as the root of the evil. With this object in view, many of them were forced to resort to armed force, and to make themselves tyrants, while others attempted to gain the same end by the peaceful method of legislation. Solon belonged to the latter class. Concerning his achievements even ancient writers knew little more than we do. Some writings by him, half-literary and half-political, have been preserved—short poems, which depict vividly the condition of Attica and speak of their author's reforms. Tradition associated with his name some essential features of democracy at Athens.

A number of laws written and placarded on wooden tablets were attributed to him with perfect justice; but a number of anecdotes, of doubtful historical authenticity, were piled by degrees upon the foundation of this fact. This composite tradition explains the different views taken even by ancient historians concerning the nature and extent of his reforms.

Nevertheless there is no difference of opinion on the main and essential points. Solon was elected archon in 594 B.C. The course of historical development had made the archon at this period the virtual master of political affairs. As archon Solon at once brought forward a series of reforms, upon which the future progress of Athens was built up. His main achievement was to mitigate the severity of the law which then decided the relation between debtor and creditor in Attica. Allotments of land which had been mortgaged to the rich were restored to the owners, and the debts cancelled. Freedom was restored to those who had lost it for nonpayment of debt. It was made illegal to advance money on the security of the landowner's person. Serfdom and slavery due to debt were abolished for all time coming. The amount of land that any individual might own was definitely fixed. The export of corn from Attica was forbidden; olive oil alone might be exported. The purpose of this last measure is obvious: it was to make speculative cultivation of arable land unprofitable and to simplify the transference of such land to smallholders. It is true that these reforms pleased neither of the contending parties: the poor hoped that all the land would be divided afresh and all debts cancelled, while the aristocracy lost heavily and had to seek new outlets for the investment of their capital. But, all the same, Solon had done a great work. The class of small landholders had been strengthened, and measures taken to maintain their strength. On the other hand, the capitalists' wealth was turned into a more profitable channel: the growth of olive-trees for the export of oil was stimulated, and trade and industry in general were encouraged. The beginning of Athenian coinage, toward the end of the seventh century, is related to this economic development. Athens also brought chaos into order by introducing a uniform system of weights and measures throughout Attica.

On the basis of these social and financial reforms Solon built his constitution. The chief innovation here was the admission of the lowest class, or *thetes*, to a place in the popular assembly. A new and important institution was the *Heliaea*, a law-court, in which any citizen could be a judge, membership being determined by lot-drawing in which every class of citizens, from the *pentakosiomedimni* to the *thetes*, could take part. Thus three most important functions of government—the election of magistrates, legislation, and the supreme control of conduct—were handed over to the whole body of citizens, irrespective of the class to which each belonged. On the other hand, the privileges of the highest classes were maintained: the magistrates, whose number and duties were unchanged, were still elected from the two highest classes exclusively. The Areopagus, or council of elders, retained its importance, but a new institution was added to it. This was the council of four hundred, with one hundred members chosen from each of the four tribes; it prepared the business which was afterwards discussed and disposed of by the popular assembly.

Though the reforms of Solon did not end the strife of classes, they paved the way to a victory for the popular party. The years that immediately followed his archonship were full of this strife. But it should be noted that Athens nevertheless was strong enough to begin a spirited foreign policy. She engaged in a struggle with Megara for the possession of Salamis; and there is no doubt that she also wished to claim a share in the commerce between the different parts of Greece. This foreign war, in which all the citizens, including the *thetes*, took part for the first time, had two important consequences. It was the first time that Attica interfered in the affairs of other Greek states, and imitated Sparta in trying to rule her neighbours and extend her territory at their expense. A collision with Sparta, who had been consolidating her leadership in the Peloponnese, was now inevitable; and the question was raised—who was to be the controlling power on the Isthmus, the bridge between central Greece and the Peloponnese? and who should take the lead in trade with the west? Secondly, this first considerable campaign revealed the importance of including every citizen in the army and of entrusting entire command to one capable general. Successful in the struggle against Megara, the Athenians owed the conquest of Salamis and Nisaea, the port of Megara, to the skilful leadership of Pisistratus, one of their own body.

Pisistratus was undoubtedly a prominent figure in Athenian history, not less important, and perhaps even more important, than Solon himself. Solon was a lawgiver and reconciler; Pisistratus was a military commander, the leader of a definite party, and a tyrant. After his success against Megara he came forward as the champion of the smallholders, and in 561-560 B.C. by their aid seized power at Athens. The aristocracy then united with the class of merchants and traders and twice forced him to go into exile for a time. But after some years' banishment he returned to Athens. He was cordially received by a considerable body of the citizens, who were weary of party strife. This time he remained at Athens as the supreme ruler of the state until his death in 528 B.C., when he bequeathed his power to his sons, Hippias and Hipparchus. They ruled for eighteen years.

The rule of Pisistratus may be considered as a turning-point, in many respects, in Athenian history. His tyranny did not destroy a single one of the democratic foundations which Solon had laid. His power was a mere superstructure on the top of Solon's constitution. The power of the aristocratic families was weakened, partly because most of them were banished and their land distributed among poor citizens, partly because the aristocratic bodies, the magistracy and the Areopagus, lost influence entirely and began to die away, thus clearing the ground for new democratic institutions in the future. When the tyranny fell and it was necessary to reconstruct public life, that life was not

FIG. 13. Red-figured vase. The picture shows Odysseus on his ship tied to the mast and the Sirens on the rocks singing him their alluring song. The ship gives a good idea of early Greek merchant ships. Early 5th cent. B.C. British Museum.

founded on a discredited and enfeebled aristocracy, but on a democracy strong and conscious of its strength.

The foreign policy also of Pisistratus had an important effect upon the future development of Athens. A powerful fleet and considerable improvements in the army assured to Athens a voice that must be heard in Greek politics. From this time onwards the strongest Greek powers of the day—Boeotia, Thessaly, and, above all, Sparta—had to reckon with Athens. Pisistratus, however, did not carry on a policy of conquest in southern and central Greece, satisfied with the safety from attack assured to him by his strong army and fleet. The sole object of his foreign policy was to make Athens powerful on the north-east coast of the Balkan peninsula, and on the shores of Macedonia, the Hellespont, and the Bosphorus. Thanks to him, the Athenians established themselves in Chalcidice, the Macedonian outlet to the sea, and also at Sigeum on the threshold of the Hellespont. This was a first step towards the extension of their influence over the Thracian Chersonnese, by which the fertile valleys of Thrace, closely connected at that time with the great Scythian kingdom on the north of the Euxine, communicated with the sea. It is interesting to note that Scythian mercenaries were first seen in the Athenian army during the reign of Pisistratus.

When Pisistratus died, he left Athens a considerable power, playing a conspicuous part in Greek politics, international and colonial. His sons continued his work; but their position was more difficult, as in all similar cases. For the power of every tyrant was in a high degree personal, and the transition to a hereditary monarchy was not easy. A conspiracy, due to the chance of a personal insult, carried off not only Hipparchus but also the conspirators, Harmodius and Aristogiton, and drove Hippias to adopt repressive measures and tighten the reins. Thus he lost the support of the majority, and it became possible for the exiles living at Delphi, with help from Sparta and in alliance with the discontented democrats at Athens, to undertake the enterprise of destroying the tyranny and restoring freedom. Thanks to the exertions of the Alcmaeonid family, the attempt succeeded: Hippias withdrew from Athens; and it became a question what shape this freedom, gained by an alliance between aristocrats and democrats, should assume.

Just as before the reforms of Solon, again a series of civil commotions preceded a radical reform carried out by Cleisthenes, one of the Alcmaeonidae. Cleisthenes supported an advance towards democracy. The aristocrats opposed his policy tooth and nail and called in assistance from Sparta; but this interference merely added to his strength and popularity. After a short occupation the Spartans were expelled from the capital, and Cleisthenes could begin his reforms and carry them through without interference from without or opposition from within.

The work of Cleisthenes differs from that of Solon and Pisistratus in this respect: he did not attempt to tinker at the existing system, but carried out a complete scheme which he had thought out in detail. His governing idea was to create a well-proportioned and completely co-ordinate state, based on the political equality of all the citizens, and on the participation of all in the working of the government machine. Existing institutions were neither destroyed nor abolished, but their life left them and entered into the new political bodies created by Cleisthenes.

The radical innovation due to the statesmanship of Cleisthenes was that he systematically introduced into the constitution the representative principle. At the same time the political centre of gravity was shifted to the representative bodies, and especially to the *Boule* or Council of Five Hundred, which became the main lever of the government machine. For this purpose Cleisthenes began by changing the whole system by which the citizens were classified, and created electoral districts of entirely new composition. The former division into tribes and phratries, though it continued to exist, lost all political importance. In place of these, the demes, or parishes grouped round the villages and small towns of Attica, became the chief electoral unit and the centre for the population in each place. All persons domiciled within the deme were registered as belonging to it, and the franchise was conferred upon every person so registered. The capital itself was divided into demes. It was no longer obligatory to belong to a *gens* or one of the old tribes. The demes were divided, according to their locality, into three groups: the city of Athens, the coast, and the plain of Attica with the hills. In each of these groups one of the main divisions of the population naturally outnumbered the rest: the commercial and trading element predominated in the city; sailors, dockyard hands, and fishermen on the coast; and landholders, large and small, in the interior of the country. Each of the above-mentioned groups was divided into ten *trittyes* with several demes in each; and three *trittyes*, one from each group, formed a tribe, so that ten new tribes were created out of thirty *trittyes*. In this way each of the three social classes was represented in each tribe.

These tribes became the foundation of all political and military activity. Each of them furnished a military unit, commanded by an officer called *strategus*. The magistrates, the members of the judicial assembly, and the Council of Five Hundred were chosen from each of the ten tribes. Within the tribe each deme had a local activity of its own, with an elective administration, a demarch, a local council, and a budget. The authorities attended to the local business, the local cults, and the local order. They were obliged to supply to the state lists of electors and tax-payers. The tribes also had representative bodies, with functions similarly limited. But the competence of the demes was strictly limited to local business of secondary importance. All important matters, even of local interest, were discussed and decided at Athens by the central assemblies. Attica was so small that no considerable municipal activity could find room beside the activity of Athens.

The demes and tribes were thus organized on purpose to secure an exact representation of the citizens in the Council of Five Hundred, the governing body of the whole country. This first endeavour to govern by means of a House of Representatives is highly instructive. Each deme, in proportion to the number of citizens on its roll, chose candidates for the council, and from these candidates the members of council were elected by lot, fifty in all being taken from each tribe. The existing House reviewed the moral qualifications of new members and rejected the unworthy. The council was not merely a deliberative body associated with the executive power, which was still retained by the board of the nine archons: it was a governing body, dealing with finance, war, and foreign policy. The magistrates, except in the case of some religious and judicial functions, were merely the executants of its decrees. Closely associated with the council were the *colacretae* and *strategi*, two boards now added to the magistracy; the former had to do with finance; the latter commanded ten companies of militia. The Council of Five Hundred was naturally too numerous a body to deal with ordinary business. Therefore such business was undertaken normally by a quorum, called a prytany, of fifty members, who held office for a tenth of the year under a chairman who sat for one day. Part of the prytany remained on duty day and night, eating and sleeping in the *Tholos*, a round building provided for the purpose.

Legislative powers did not belong to the council: laws were discussed and passed at meetings of the *ecclesia*, the popular assembly. Judicial authority remained with the *heliaea*, the court of popular representatives, elected by the tribes on the same principle and by the same method as the council. The magistrates—the nine archons, *colacretae* and *strategi*—were elected as before from the first two classes only, i.e. from the well-to-do citizens. This limitation of democratic ideas was dictated by necessity; for the state did not pay the citizens for the discharge of their public duties, nor even reimburse them for their incidental expenses. The army also definitely assumed the character of a national militia. Each tribe provided a regiment of infantry and a squadron of cavalry commanded by elective officers, called *taxiarchi* and *hipparchi*. The polemarch remained as a survival. Each of the ten *strategi* commanded the army in turn. The question of the navy, left untouched by Cleisthenes, was solved at a later date.

The reforms of Cleisthenes completed the creation of a strong and solidly organized Athenian state. While aiming at the same object as Sparta, Athens had attained it by different means. Her government was not based, as at Sparta, on the predominance of a single class over a subordinate population: she relied on attracting the whole body of citizens to the business of government; and she excluded none except the slaves and the foreigners resident at Athens, called *metoeci*. When the new system was created, these two groups formed a comparatively insignificant minority of the population, and it was not till much later that the question of their position became acute. This Athenian principle of government deserves to be called democracy, because the real master and ruler of the country was the people.

The constitution of Cleisthenes began working in 502 B.C. It did not, indeed, end the strife of parties or the uneven distribution of wealth. Both these evils remained, and there were conflicts, sharp and sometimes prolonged. But their acuteness was mitigated and almost abolished by the attitude of mind due to these reforms. Every citizen learned to regard the government not as an external and alien thing, but as something identical with the body of citizens, and each justly looked upon himself as a working part of the government machine. No Greek took such pride as the Athenian in his city and country; and nowhere in Greece was the consciousness of citizenship or the feeling of true patriotism so strongly developed.

VII

CIVILIZATION OF GREECE IN THE SEVENTH AND SIXTH CENTURIES B.C.

The seventh and sixth centuries B.C. were a great creative epoch in the history of human civilization. Those laws of thought, political organization, and art, which mark out European civilization generally and distinguish it in many important respects from the civilizations of the East, began to take shape at this time. The chief peculiarities of Greek culture, both then and later, were its individual, personal character and its boldness— the unbounded hardihood, one might say, with which it stopped at nothing, and its entire independence of religion, though the latter maintained a separate existence beside it.

But together with this bent towards individualism, we observe another trait which is easily reconcilable with it. Throughout Greek history we find among all Greeks an increasing consciousness that they belong to one nation and form one body; and this unity was indicated, not only by a common religion and a common language, but also by a common civilization, more or less identical among them all. This national feeling was powerfully promoted by colonization and the trade which kept pace with colonization. The tie that bound a colony to the Greek world was never broken: the colony always felt herself the true daughter of her mother city and resembled her almost exactly in all respects. On the other hand, the deep gulf that separated the Greek view of life from that of their new neighbours was realized with exceptional clearness by the colonists.

Fig. 14. Red-figured cup. The beautiful picture shows the god Apollo killing the Titan Tityos, who attacked Apollo's mother Leto. The mother of Tityos, Ge (the Earth), tries vainly to protect her son. The picture gives an excellent idea of Apollo as the god of right and civilization fighting against anarchy and barbarism represented by the elemental forces of nature. Attic work of about 460 B.C. Munich Museum. After Furtwängler-Reichhold.

Let us begin by dwelling for a little on the second of these traits, the feeling of nationality. In the dawn of Greek history it showed itself in religion. The primitive religious beliefs of the Greeks were the same as those of other peoples, the same as in the East—animism, or the belief that there exists in living beings an immortal part which is not identical with matter, the belief in a future life being derived from this; fetishism, or the belief in a mysterious power residing in certain inanimate objects, such as trees and stones; zoolatry, or the belief in the divinity of certain animals; and polytheism, which believes in an infinite number of gods and in the divinity of such natural phenomena as the sun and moon, thunder and lightning, rivers, springs, and forests. There was no national religion and could not be, because there was no nation. Each stock, each *gens*, each brotherhood (*phratria*), and each family had its own gods and its own rites.

It was the appearance of the so-called Homeric poems, during their first spontaneous expansion over the Aegean islands and Asia Minor, which first made the Greeks conscious that they were a nation. Through these poems and through their mighty culmination in the *Iliad* and *Odyssey*—a culmination which touched religion also and endeavoured to single out the common element in the religious ideas of all Hellas—the Greeks gained a clear conception of their national unity and realized the racial peculiarities of their life and religion. These poems set the figures of the chief gods before the eyes of the Greeks, gave to each of them a distinct form, forced men to believe in their nearness to humanity, and equipped them with attributes which every Greek recognized in himself.

Homer united the gods in one comprehensive family; the great monarch Zeus the Thunderer was the head of this family and governed it just as the Graeco-Aegean kings governed their households. At the same time Homer exalted the gods and Zeus in particular to a height beyond human attainment, placing them on the summit of Mount Olympus and illuminating them with the light of ineffable beauty. Homer became the Bible of the Greeks—the source from which they drew their conceptions of divinity, and which fixed for ever the divine images so familiar even to us. Supreme Zeus, ruler of gods and men; queenly Hera, his divine consort; Poseidon, lord of the sea; Ares, the terrible warrior; Hermes, the messenger of the gods; Aphrodite, born of the sea foam, ever young and lovely in her divine beauty; Hephaestus, the halting smith; the radiant Apollo—all these were clothed once for all in permanent forms of ineffable poetic loveliness.

Yet among these gods there was one in particular who became

especially near and dear to every Greek, and with whom they connected their new conceptions of divinity and its part in human life. This was Apollo. Originally the god of light in particular, but also the god of agriculture and stock-raising, he assumed by degrees new attributes. Like Heracles, a champion of humanity against the dark forces of nature, he comes forth as a defender and saviour. He overcame with his arrows the formidable Python, the serpent which personified the dark and dangerous forces of the underworld; and men, in gratitude for this exploit, built him his bright temple at Delphi, where all nature proclaimed the power of light to conquer darkness. Together with Heracles he was a builder of cities and their protector, and the patron of Greek civilization, especially of music. His first paean or song of victory he sang over the body of the slain Python. His oracles guided men along the path of truth and justice and advised them in their public and private affairs.

Still more important is the fact that, with the figure of Apollo, morality makes its first appearance as a part of religion. The god himself undergoes a humiliating penance for the slaughter of the Python, and feeds the flocks of Admetus. From his shrine at Delphi he holds forth a helping hand to others who have stained themselves with blood; by repentance and purification they are reconciled with their own consciences and with society; the god absolves them from their sins; for the matricide only there is no absolution. The religion of Apollo had a very great influence on Greece. The temple of Zeus at Olympia was not the only shrine where all Greeks worshipped: Apollo had two such temples— one at Delphi, the centre of an alliance, one of the most ancient in Greece, between several communities, and the other in Delos, where the religious life of all the Ionians was concentrated. In Asia Minor the place of Delphi was taken by the temple of Apollo at Didyma near Miletus, a shrine familiar to all Greeks. Pindar, one of the greatest Greek poets, claims to be a prophet who reveals the religion of Apollo and glorifies the god of light.

The worship of Demeter in her temple at Eleusis, originating

1. MARBLE STATUE OF
CLEOBIS OR BITON

2. MARBLE STATUE OF
A GODDESS OR PRIESTESS

Plate XII   EARLY GREEK SCULPTURE

1. The marble statue of Cleobis or Biton, carved by the sculptor
Polymedes of Argos; found at Delphi. Cleobis and Biton were the
two young men who drew the car carrying their mother, priestess of
Hera at Argos, to the temple. In reward for their piety the goddess
let them fall asleep after the sacrifice, never to awaken (cf. Herodotus I, 31). The statue is one of the earlier products of Greek
sculpture. The influence of Egypt is strong, but the statue is individual and shows a close study of the human body by the Greek
pupils of Egyptian sculptors. About 600 B.C. Museum, Delphi.

2. A beautiful and almost complete marble statue of a priestess or
goddess found in Attica. The statue shows all the peculiarities of
Greek archaic art when the Greeks were gradually becoming eman-
cipated from the rigidity of early art and beginning to take delight
both in the details of the feminine dress and in the rendering of the

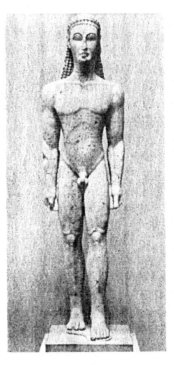

3. MARBLE STATUE OF
AN ATHENIAN YOUTH (KOUROS)

4. KORE

movement of the human body and in giving expression to the faces.
Early 6th century B.C. Berlin Museum.

3. Archaic marble statue of an Athenian youth. Such statues of
youths (*kouroi*) became fashionable as grave monuments in the late
7th and the 6th centuries B.C. The dead youth is represented naked
as he appeared in athletic competitions. Being semi-divine in his
after-life, he is represented larger than life. 615–600 B.C. Metropolitan Museum of Art, Fletcher Fund, 1932, New York.

4. Kore. From the last half of the seventh century, statues of women
were often dedicated to the gods at the Acropolis (and also in Eleusis and elsewhere) to secure divine blessing for the person represented by the statue. These statues were painted, and the women
wore Ionian dress. This particular kore is one of the 'Acropolis maidens'. 530–500 B.C.

in the second millennium, became universal among Greeks. Demeter, the Great Mother, had been a pre-Greek goddess, but the Greeks raised this cult to a high point of poetic symbolism and moralized it. Whereas Apollo was a god of all Greece, revered in every city and, as the 'god of our fathers', in every family, Demeter was more exclusive. She admitted to her mysteries only a chosen band of believers, only those who were pure in ritual and moral sense. Yet there was no distinction of sex or station: even slaves were included; but no foreigner was admitted. To the initiated she promised complete regeneration, or rather, a new birth during this life and bliss hereafter. At the solemn ceremony of initiation, her worshipper was cleansed from earthly taint.

A third cult, which spread by degrees over all the Greek world, was that of Dionysus. It reached Greece from Thrace probably, and was quickly diffused through Greece, Asia Minor, and Italy. By Thracians and Greeks, Dionysus was conceived as a suffering god: he personified the vegetation which dies in winter and is renewed in spring. In his youth he was torn to pieces by the Titans, the dark forces of earth, but is born again from himself, as young and beautiful as before. His worshippers, women especially, held nightly revels in his honour by torch-light on the mountain-tops. Dancing in ecstasy to the sound of cymbals and drums, they tore in pieces a sacrificed animal, whose blood they drank with wine, and so participated in the being and eternal life of their god. A group of religious reformers, who traced their descent to the Thracian minstrel, Orpheus, and called themselves 'Orphics', purified this worship of its rude primitive features and spiritualized it. The sacred writings of the Orphics taught that the soul, imprisoned in the body as a punishment for sin, is capable of purification. This purity is attained by a life of strict morality, even of asceticism, by participation in the great secret of Dionysus, the suffering god, and by initiation into his mysteries. To the initiated an endless life of happiness after death was promised. The Orphic cult of Dionysus was propagated outside Greece by a succession of missionaries who founded communities of believers, of which the most important and long-lived belonged to the Greek cities in south Italy. Among them were many thinkers of a religious turn, perhaps also Pythagoras, one of the founders of scientific mathematics and astronomy, and the head of a community which at one time governed the wealthy city of Croton.

These shrines, most of which were also oracular seats, were resorted to by all Greeks and served as a symbol of national unity. I have mentioned already the temple of Zeus at Olympia and those of Apollo at Delphi, Delos, and Didyma. Other oracular shrines were those of Poseidon near Corinth and of Zeus at Dodona in Epirus. The temples of the healing god, Asclepius, were national also. The sick and suffering flocked thither from all Greece, and schools of medicine were formed there by physicians, the pupils of the divine healer.

In connexion with some of these holy places competitions in honour of the god were instituted in athletic games, music, and poetry, and were open to all Greeks. From time immemorial the gods had been worshipped, not in Greece alone, with dance and song and competitions of various kinds. In these contests the youth of Greece sang hymns of praise in the god's honour; or reproduced scenes from his life in rhythmic choral dances, accompanied by music and singing; or vied with one another in running, jumping, wrestling, and the throwing of discus and the javelin; or appeared as drivers of chariots drawn by the swiftest horses.

In these games and in the very nature of the Panhellenic shrines the two characteristics of the Greek genius and of Greek life are conspicuous. The god was glorified by all Greeks: during the games thousands of Greeks from Greece proper and the colonies gathered at Olympia or Corinth met, conversed, discussed questions of interest to a section or to them all, and united in combined rites and offerings. But, on the other hand, almost every community in Greece or the colonies prided itself on its 'treasury', a beautiful chapel-like building within the temple precinct, where its great deeds were told in painting and sculpture; each community brought thither its best artists and best athletes, and coveted the honour of raising a statue of their victorious townsman on the open space in front of the temple. Not only did each city in this way assert its individuality, but the competitors did the same with equal emphasis. These youths were eager to excel, to thrust themselves forward, to display to all Greece their personal superiority. They strove with persistent toil to attain perfection of mind and body, and to wrest the prize from rivals like themselves, who had submitted to the same training for the same object. Their highest reward was gained when all Greece, in the person of the chosen judges, acknowledged them as national and public heroes, crowned them with a wreath of twigs from the sacred tree, and permitted their statues to be placed beside those of the gods.

The Greek, however strongly he felt himself a part of the Greek nation, was, first and foremost, a citizen of his own community and would sink his individuality for it, and for it alone. The interests of that community touched him nearly and often blinded him to the interests of Greece as a whole. Throughout Greek history the forces of disruption were stronger and more active than those of centralization; rivalry and separation, which found vent in wars between the states, were stronger than the tendency to agreement and coalition—a tendency which showed itself in treaties, alliances, and national arbitration, and laid the foundations of European international law. To the Athenian, the temple of his native goddess, Athena, on the Acropolis, the symbol of a united community and kingdom, was dearer than the temple of Poseidon in Calauria, the centre of a religious alliance between several communities akin to Athens, and dearer than the shrine of Apollo at Delos, the religious centre of all who used the Ionic dialect. Nevertheless, Attica, united round Athens, Boeotia, rallying round Thebes, Argolis, concentrating round Argos, and Sparta, ruling a number of Dorian communities and clans—each of these powers sought to become the centre of a still more extensive union; but each of them regarded such a union as a point scored in the competition between states, and treated the members of the union not as allies with equal rights but as inferiors.

The individual character of the national genius is seen with special clearness in the region of thought and of art, where local patriotism, far from hindering the development of personality, in many cases even encouraged it. The communities were just as proud of their great thinkers and artists as of their champions who won prizes at Olympia, and strove as eagerly for pre-eminence in culture as in politics. Discovery and invention, which in the East had been impersonal things, lose that character in Greece and are closely connected for all time with the personality of the discoverer. It is significant that all the earliest discoveries of the prehistoric past were attributed by the lively imagination of Greece to a definite inventor, who was, in many cases, not even a Greek. Thus the Greeks could tell at once that Prometheus had taught mankind the use of fire, and that Daedalus was the father of sculpture; they knew who invented the potter's wheel, and who was the first to forge weapons of copper and iron. Much more did they make mention of those who created their own civilization—that civilization which distinguished them from all 'barbarians' who spoke no Greek. Greece was proud of them, and with good reason: they laid the foundation of all our modern civilization, which is as individual as that of Greece.

In matters of science, technical skill, and art the Greeks were, in many respects, pupils of the East, and they never forgot this. It was in Asia Minor, where they were in constant connexion with the East, that they started on the path of progress themselves. But, while drawing freely from the stores of Eastern civilization, they refashioned all they received, and stamped a fresh character upon it. Their genius recognized no tradition, no unalterable rules. They approached each fresh problem as a matter for investigation. If the problem was solved, the next investigator treated the solution as merely a starting-point for further inquiry. Nature, the world, and man became at once for them matter for this kind of reflection and investigation. They were not content to register what they saw and accept its mythological explanation. They felt the rule of law in nature and tried to make it clear. Their first question was not 'How?' but 'Why?' When foreign travel made them acquainted with new countries and strange seas, they perpetuated their knowledge by drawing maps, and also at once began asking: 'What is the whole world? what is its shape, and what its relation to other worlds, the sun, moon, and stars?' And having raised such questions, they suggested answers—answers which were at first childishly simple, no doubt, but scientific and not mythological. Thus they became the creators of scientific geography, cosmology, and astronomy.

In their study of the world, the Ionian inquirers and thinkers —or philosophers, as they were called later—endeavoured to separate the chief and fundamental element in the creation. That a single substance underlies all matter was held first by Thales; and the question was discussed further by Anaximander and Anaximenes. All these three were Milesians. Thales found the primary substance of matter in water; Anaximenes found it in air; Anaximander, the creator of scientific prose and the first to publish his theory in a book, insisted on the infinity of the world, or rather worlds, and their perpetual interchanges. He also was the first to make a map of the world known to him. Still more profound were the views of Xenophanes, who migrated to Elea in south Italy and there founded the Eleatic school of philosophy. The unity of the world was his chief dogma. He believed one god to be the directing force of the world. 'He is all eye, mind, ear; he directs all things without effort by the power of his reason.' Polytheism and the legends told of the gods he treated as mere inventions of human imagination. God was perceived by reason, and reason led men to the knowledge of things. God is also moral force, and men should pray to God, in order to attain the ideal of justice. This is not the place to dwell on the

FIG. 15. Red-figured pot for wine and water (krater) found at Acragas in Sicily. One side of this krater is adorned with the figures of Sappho and Alcaeus, the two greatest lyric poets of archaic Greece. There was a legend based on some poems of the two singers that Alcaeus fell in love with Sappho and was rejected by her. This scene is represented on the krater. Attic work of about 480 B.C. Munich Museum. After Furtwängler-Reichhold.

beginnings of European science; but it is proper to repeat, that in Greece for the first time humanity treated nature and man as a problem that could be solved by reason.

In literature the same spirit of individuality is supreme. The Homeric poems may have owed their birth to a school of poets; but to the Greek they were the work of a blind old minstrel, whose native country was unknown but whose personality was nearer and dearer to every Greek. Homer is followed by a long succession of great writers in poetry and prose. A strong and brilliant personality belongs to each of them, and their work has such a definitely personal note that each of them has told us, in greater or less detail, his own biography in his writings. They all of them put their soul into their poetry. The first woman, the poetess Sappho, paints a most vivid picture of her own life, with the clubs or schools of Lesbian girls for a background—her passion for various members of the sisterhood, her jealousy of their future husbands, and the feelings with which she escorted them to a new life in households of their own.

The poets who were contemporary with Sappho reflect in their poetry all the life of Greece—a life full of movement, variety, and adventure. They are the true children of their time. They trade and travel and fight; they take an active part in revolutions; they flee from the battle-field or lead their comrades-in-arms to victory with their songs; they feast and love and are jealous; they lash the character and conduct of their fellow-citizens. Alcaeus of Lesbos is a warrior, an active politician. Archilochus of Paros is a needy adventurer, a stern warrior, an injured and resentful lover. Tyrtaeus, not himself a Spartan, sings his marching songs to the ordered ranks of Spartan hoplites. Anacreon of Teos, a poet in the courts of tyrants, sings of love and wine. Then there is Solon, the great Athenian reformer; Theognis of Megara, an injured and venomous aristocrat; Terpander of Lesbos, Simonides of Ceos, Stesichorus of Sicily—inspired writers of choric songs in honour of the gods. Last and greatest of the lyric poets is Pindar of Boeotia, that swan with strong snowy pinions, as he was called by later Greek and Roman bards, the inspired prophet of Apollo, who crowned with glory the conquerors at the Panhellenic contests. The poetry of them all has a personal note and conveys the individuality of the writer; the style, metre, and thought of each are his own. Most of the early philosophers already mentioned put forth their theories in poetic form.

But, together with poetry, prose also comes into existence. Of Anaximander I have already spoken. Travellers into far countries brought home with them many new impressions, and made acquaintance with foreign lands—their climate and flora and fauna, their religion, manners, customs, and history. Full of these new impressions, they told them to their countrymen at markets and on public squares, in temples and blacksmiths' shops; and from these narratives sprang the first tales of history, geography, and ethnography; they were called 'tales' (*logoi*) by the Greeks, and their authors 'talemakers' (*logopoioi*). The earliest tales were in verse; such is the story of Aristeas, how he travelled to the land of marvels, through the Black Sea regions and the land of the Scythians to Central Asia. Here legend and fact are bound up together; but, with Hecataeus of Miletus, prose takes the place of verse, and the narrative becomes a half-scientific treatise, in which mythology and history are fantastically blended with geography and ethnography. He is followed by Herodotus, the father of history and the first Greek historian; but still the distinction between science and literature is incomplete.

Political life was another source of prose literature. Disputes and discussions in the streets and at council-boards, attempts to write down and express exactly legal and constitutional principles in codes of law, decrees of law-courts and public assemblies —all these were written out in prose form and perpetuated on wood or stone or bronze. Hence proceeds the prose literature of law and politics, the speeches made before courts and assemblies, and the more austere and rigorous literature of official proceedings.

The singing and dancing of a chorus had long been used to express religious feeling. These differed at different festivals and in different cults; and in the worship of Dionysus they took a peculiar form which underwent a remarkable development in Attica. At the vintage festival it was customary for the chorus to dress up as birds or frogs or other animals, to come forward under the direction of the leader who presented them to the public, to sing songs of different kinds, and then to go off in a merry, noisy procession led by flute-players. This procession was called *comos*, and the performance itself comedy. At the spring festival of Dionysus the singers were disguised as goats and satyrs (imaginary half-animal creatures, spirits of the fields and forests, and the constant companions of Dionysus). These took turns with the 'answerer' (the Greek name for actor), who replied to the chorus in metre. From the goat-masks (*tragos* is the Greek for goat) the acting was called tragedy. The new form of ritual had a great success and became an established part of these festivals. From this humble beginning, Aeschylus, of whom more is said below, created Greek tragedy, one of the noblest triumphs of the Attic genius.

But religion was not content with expressing itself in the form of poetry, music, and dancing: the Greeks wished to see and touch their gods and give them dwellings worthy of their majesty. Zeus, Apollo and Demeter, Aphrodite, Dionysus and Poseidon, first came really home to their hearts when painters and sculptors, after long experiment, began to find fitting artistic forms for the divine inhabitants of Olympus. In sculpture we are able to follow their experiments, because a fairly large number of the statues which served to adorn the shrines and temples have been preserved, some of them the actual divine images which were worshipped by the faithful, while others were votive offerings—statues and statuettes dedicated to the god by his worshippers. Not a few of these have been found in different parts of the Greek world and are preserved in our museums. The painting with which the temples were adorned has perished; but the types of divinity created by the painters are repeated in the decoration of Greek vases, a subject we shall deal with later.

It is probable that painting preceded sculpture in representing not merely separate forms of the gods but scenes taken from mythology and perhaps also groups of worshippers. Sculpture followed the example, when it became the custom to adorn certain parts of a temple—pediment, frieze, and metopes—with reliefs and sculptures in the round or in bas-relief. Though their chief attention was given to religious subjects, the artists did not confine themselves to figures of the gods.

Greek art, and especially Ionian art, made immense progress in the course of the seventh and sixth centuries B.C. The delicate and beautiful floral ornament, which became one of the main features of Greek art, was perfected at this time. In the representation of men and animals advance was slower, especially in sculpture, which had to meet many purely technical difficulties; but by degrees these difficulties were surmounted. Beginning with a wooden post or board hewn into human shape, or with a stiff and lifeless idol of stone, the artist advances further and further in the truthful representation of the human body, conveys more and more accurately the anatomical structure and muscular surface, and reproduces the individual features with ever-increasing skill. The appearance of motion is added: one foot is advanced, the arms are raised, attempts are made to convey rapid movement and even flight, especially in the sculpture of imaginary winged figures. Treading in the footsteps of the painter, the sculptor learns to carve groups and to subordinate them to their architectural purpose.

Typical figures of the gods are evolved by degrees—Zeus in his majesty, Apollo, the graceful stripling, the ripe charms of Aphrodite, Athena, the stately maiden and formidable fighter. Art makes the attempt to embody ideas in colour and stone, and to create typical figures of humanity; and this power of creating types remains one of the leading features of Greek art. At the end of the sixth century, however, we notice in Ionian art the formation of some conventional tradition, some mannerism, some tendency to exaggerate details at the expense of the whole. Statues found on the Acropolis and dating from before the Persian wars prove this clearly. These defects of ancient Ionian art are shared to some extent by the sculpture of Greece proper.

The temples, the abodes of the gods, were worthy of their inhabitants. The modest house with its four walls, front room,

1. WRESTLING

Plate XIII EARLY GREEK SCULPTURE. RELIEFS.

1. A side of a base found with three others in the wall of Athens, which was built either in 337-322 B.C. or in 307, and for which the material of the wall built by Themistocles was used. The reliefs of this base are most beautiful examples of Athenian sculpture in the period of Pisistratus. The side shown depicts two wrestlers in the centre. The wrestler on the right is seizing the left arm of his opponent and is about 'to swing round to the front and by getting underneath him to throw him by leverage'. The wrestler on the left is trying 'to stop this swinging movement by placing his right hand on his opponent's left shoulder'. The athlete on the left of the group seems to be a jumper; the figure on the right is a javelin-thrower. The relief thus represents three of the five games of the pentathlon, the runner and the discus-thrower being omitted. About 520–510 B.C. National Museum, Athens.

2. Greek warrior found at Cyrene. Although of little artistic merit, the relief is historically important. It shows one of the Greek youths who colonized the Mediterranean shores and kept watch in the hostile world of the natives. The youth carries a spear, a typical weapon of a Greek warrior of the colonization period. Late 6th century B.C. Museum at Cyrene (Libya).

2. GREEK WARRIOR

3. ATTIC GRAVE-STELE

3. Attic grave stele of marble. (Detail.) The relief on the front of the stele shows the figures of the deceased, a young man and a young girl, probably his sister. The boy is naked and holds the funerary fruit, the pomegranate, in his left hand; an athlete's oil flask hangs on his right wrist. Semi-divine in death, he is represented larger than life. The girl holds a flower. The preserved fragments of the inscription seem to say that the monument was erected by a father and loving mother to the dead Phila (?) and Me(gakles?), who probably belonged to the powerful Alcmaeonid family. The stele was painted as well as carved. The heads are the finest part of this beautiful work of art. They are still conventional, but show a feeling for beauty of line and a strong decorative sense. About 540 B.C. Courtesy Metropolitan Museum of Art, New York.

4. MARBLE GRAVE-STELE FROM CHRYSAFA, NEAR SPARTA

4. Marble grave stele found at Chrysafa, near Sparta. The figures of
the deceased are represented seated on an arm-chair. Behind the
throne is the snake, symbol of the nether world. The deceased are
represented as hero and heroine enjoying a drink of wine. A youth
and a woman bring them offerings: a cock, a pomegranate, and a
flower. The relief, though not of very early date (late 6th century)
is very conventional and recalls wood-carving. Berlin Museum.

and two posts at the entrance, is converted by degrees into a majestic hall flanked by pillars, which, together with the walls, support the roof. These pillars, with their bases and capitals, become the main feature of the temple and define the order to which it belongs. The pillars themselves, the stone entablatures which crown them, the raised foundation, the walls and roof of the building, combine to form one artistic whole, where there is nothing arbitrary, but every detail is calculated and planned, where painting and sculpture are in strict keeping with the main lines of the structure, and where, nevertheless, nothing is stereotyped. There are no two temples in Greece which are exactly alike. The column, the main feature of the temple, is not confined to a single form. The massive Doric column has a flat cushion for a capital; the Ionic column, invented in Asia Minor, is more graceful and more elaborate, with its sculptured base, shapely fluted shaft, and the double volute of its capital; and then, still more graceful and more elaborate, comes the Corinthian column, whose capital reproduces the highly decorative foliage of the prickly acanthus. Noble columnar temples rise in all the great centres of Greek life. The temples of Artemis at Ephesus, of Zeus at Olympia, of Apollo at Delphi, of Hera at Samos—how clearly they convey the peculiarities of the Greek genius in all parts of Greece! In Italy and Sicily there still stand majestic productions of that genius, wonderful in the boldness of their plan and the harmony of their outlines.

But Greek art does not confine itself to the temples: from the earliest times it permeates the whole life. There is no clearer proof of this than the common pottery used for domestic purposes. Like the Aegean ware, and perhaps under its influence, it dislikes monochrome. And in no department is the variety and creative power of Greek genius equally conspicuous. Two simultaneous influences can be distinguished. The first is of Eastern origin. It prefers motley groups of animals, partly real and partly due to Eastern fancy; in the latter case the bright colours do not reproduce nature but confer on her a richness that does not be-

1. IVORY RELIEF FROM SPARTA. SPARTAN SHIP

Plate XIV GREEK ART OF THE 6th CENTURY B.C.

1. Semicircular ivory relief found in Sparta in the sanctuary of the great Spartan goddess Artemis Orthia. The raised border was probably inlaid with amber. The relief represents a warship about to sail. In the water are three large fish. Three warriors are seated on the deck facing the stern. Five round shields decorated with geometric patterns hang over the edge of the deck. Of the crew, one is fishing, another is crouching on the long beak below. Three sailors are working the rigging. A bearded man (the captain) is saying farewell to a woman who is meant to be on land. Behind the woman is a large bird. About 600 B.C. Museum, Sparta.

2. Picture on the inside of a Spartan kylix (cup). Black figures on a white background. King Arcesilas of Cyrene in Africa (Cyrene was a Spartan colony) is shown watching the lading and weighing of goods, possibly 'silphion' (a plant peculiar to Cyrene and extensively used in Greek diet). Note the realism with which the scene is painted, the intense movement in the picture, and the humour. The masterly rendering of the animals (the pet animals of the king, the monkey, and the birds) is quite remarkable. The scene illustrates well the growing commerce of Greece in the 6th century, and the part the Greek colonies played in this commerce. 6th century B.C. Cabinet des Médailles, Paris.

2. SPARTAN KYLIX. KING ARCESILAS OF CYRENE

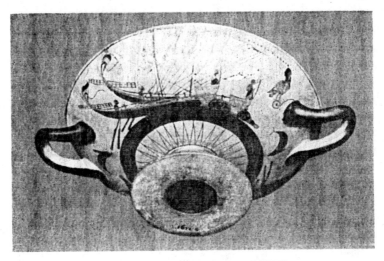

3. ATHENIAN KYLIX. ATHENIAN SHIPS

3. An Athenian kylix (cup). Black figures on red ground. From the workshop of the potter Nicosthenes. It is a beautiful scene full of life and elegance, showing two ships racing. About 530 B.C. Paris, Louvre.

119

long to her. Though the type of this pottery is the same everywhere, there is much local variety: if an Eastern vase from Rhodes be compared with another from Corinth, the comparison will show at once how much each presents that is local and peculiar. The other style is not Oriental but European. Poor in its choice of colour, and stiff in its simplified geometrical ornament, it develops quickly: ornament gives place to the human figure, though the figure is at first angular and stiff, and next the figures are combined to form groups. From this modest beginning the Attic vase is developed by degrees—the vase with black figures on a red background, in which the human figures are the main thing and the animals and floral ornament the accessories. These Attic vases, whose makers sign their names with pride on their work, reproduce before long each new artistic tendency and idea. While decorating these articles of everyday use, the artist feels freer than when working for temples and shrines. In painting vases he reflects all the full and various life of Greece—first of all, its religion, but not that alone. Love and feasting, the merriment of a holiday, weddings and funerals, men at the market or in the workshops, women in the seclusion of their apartments, children at their games, youths and girls in the palaestra and gymnasium—all these are revealed to us by the observant eye and ready hand of the Athenian vase-painter. And their mastery of design and drawing rivals even the majestic lines of the Greek temples themselves.

Such was Greece in the seventh and sixth centuries B.C. Without effort, in an impetuous outburst of genius, she overcame all the obstacles in her path. She knew what the East had accomplished, valued it, and made use of it; but she struck out for herself and created her own peculiar culture—a culture far more natural and intelligible to us than the civilizations worked out earlier by the East.

VIII

THE PERSIAN WARS

There is no doubt that in Hellas of the sixth century B.C. the leading part in economic and civilized life belonged, not to Greece proper, but to the Greek colonies in Asia Minor and, in some degree, to those in Italy and Sicily. The Greek cities of Aegina, Chalcis, Eretria, Corinth, Sicyon, Sparta, and Athens were far poorer and less civilized than Miletus, Ephesus, Samos, and Lesbos in the east, or than Sybaris, Croton, Gela, Acragas, and Syracuse in the west. The colonies had richer and more fertile territories, more extensive markets, and easier communication with the East. On the other hand, the position of these outposts of Hellenism was, from the political point of view, very precarious. In Asia Minor and also in Italy the cities were exposed to attack from their neighbours by land. The Sicilian Greeks were constantly menaced by the great maritime power of Carthage, backed by a powerful federation of Etruscan cities, to say nothing of their nearest neighbours—the tribes who inhabited the interior of the country. But even so they were safer than the Greeks in Asia Minor. For Etruria, though rich and civilized, was cut off from the colonies by the mountains of central Italy; their other neighbours were still in a primitive stage of development; and Carthage was only beginning to realize her strength and the necessity of a fight to a finish with the Greeks.

In Asia Minor the situation was different. The coast was occupied by Greeks. But even here a considerable part of the population which continued to live on the soil seized by the Greeks was neither Greek nor uncivilized. Before the Greeks came and conquered them, these tribes had enjoyed their own civilization and political institutions; and they kept this fact steadily in mind. They felt themselves closer to their Asiatic kinsmen than to their new masters. The record of central Asia Minor was distinguished, and traditions of the Hittite Empire survived in the new kingdoms of Phrygia, Lydia, and Lycia. Of these kingdoms Lydia lay nearest to the Greeks. During the seventh and sixth centuries B.C. she had survived the invading Cimmerians and Scythians, had rapidly grown strong and rich, and had become a powerful empire with distinct political and economic aims. As mediator between the East and the new world of Greece, and belonging to both of them by her position, nationality, and culture, Lydia was always pressing towards the sea. But the coasts were occupied by Phoenicians and Greeks. To oust the former was impossible: first Assyria, and then Persia, stood in the way. It was far easier and more natural for Lydia to expand towards the west, in the region of the Greeks.

The Greeks in Asia, just like the Greeks at home and in the West, all shared the same blood, religion, and culture, but were divided into a number of independent states, each with its own policy and traditions, which ran counter to the policy and traditions of its neighbours. Hatred and jealousy of these neighbours moved them more than hostility towards powerful but distant Eastern empires, about which they knew and cared little. Moreover, social and political strife was constantly going on inside each state, and led the contending parties to seek for support, irrespective of the source from which it came. And, finally, the strategic position of these cities was excessively weak. The territory of each was, in most cases, a river-valley, divided by a mountain ridge from the territory of its next neighbour along the coast. Thus communication was difficult by land; by sea it was not difficult but, owing to the much indented line of the coast, took much time. Meanwhile, the territory was freely exposed to the attack of any army from the interior of the country.

Of all these facts the Lydian Empire took full advantage and soon became preponderant in the political life of these cities. While giving much to the Greeks in the way of a civilization and commerce, Lydia took from Greece all that Greece could give, and the difference between the Lydians and Anatolian Greeks became fainter and fainter. By degrees Lydia was admitted to the band of Greek states as one of themselves, just as Macedonia was admitted at a later date. Lydian ambassadors, bearing rich gifts to Delphi and other Greek shrines, were as welcome guests as the ambassadors of Greek powers. It is not surprising that the Anatolian cities were speedily absorbed by Lydia in the seventh, and still more in the sixth century, and that such resistance as there was did not take the form of a combined national effort against an Eastern foe. The resistance was unmethodical and entirely ineffective. All the Lydian kings—Ardys, Sadyattes, Alyattes, and Croesus—worked deliberately at the task of subduing the Greek cities, and their activity prevented the Greeks from observing the growing power of the Medes and Persians. Hence the catastrophe of 548 B.C., when Cyrus defeated the armies of Croesus and took Sardis, was a complete surprise to the Greeks, who were now confronted by the Persians, a quite unknown enemy. Their sympathies were all on the side of Lydia, and Sparta even prepared to send part of her army to help Croesus.

Persia had little difficulty in conquering the Anatolian Greeks. Greece was far away and comparatively weak, while they themselves were crippled by disunion and the mild but corrosive policy of Lydia. All the coast soon became a part of the great Persian monarchy. But the new masters made little change in the internal life of the cities. Each of them retained its autonomy, kept up regular communications with the rest of the Greek world, and continued to be important as a centre of trade and industry. They were only bound in future to pay part of their revenue to their conquerors, and to provide soldiers and ships for the unending wars waged by Persia against Babylon and

Egypt. To all this the Anatolian Greeks were accustomed. They resented only the frequent interference of Persia in their party squabbles, and the support which they gave to tyrants. Tyranny became in time the prevailing form of government in the cities.

The absorption of these Anatolian Greeks was an important political factor in the history of the Persian Empire. These new subjects brought with them ideas and habits entirely unlike the ideas and habits which characterized all the rest of the kingdom. On the other hand, it was a political absurdity to rule Asia Minor and not to rule the coast also. But the ruler of the coast was bound to come in contact with the islands and with the complicated politics of all the Balkan peninsula and the Black Sea coast—a coast which was densely populated by colonists, mostly Anatolian Greeks. Thus, by the conquest of Asia Minor, Persia was drawn into European politics and forced to define, in one way or another, her policy in relation to Europe. The simplest solution of the problem, at least from the point of view traditional with Eastern conquerors, was this—that Persia should conquer and absorb Greece, thus including not merely a part but the whole nation in her Empire.

Conditions seemed to favour the execution of this project. Public affairs in Greece proper differed little from public affairs in Anatolian Greece. Both countries were divided into small states constantly at war with one another; in both there was the same jealousy between cities, the same internal divisions of each city into social and political parties, and the same readiness to make use of any allies in order to gain the immediate realization of political and party objects. Such political conditions made it seem an easy matter to conquer Greece. What Persia could throw into the scales in this contest seemed enormous and decisive—a great army, well organized and well disciplined—an excellent fleet, manned by Phoenicians and Anatolian Greeks, the most skilful sailors of the age; and the inexhaustible material resources of a wealthy kingdom. Distant campaigns must, no doubt, be undertaken; but did not the Persian armies march to the recesses of Central Asia and the boundaries of India? and had they not recently conquered mighty Egypt herself?

In extending their power the Persian monarchs never acted at random. They were excellent strategists: each campaign was rigorously thought out and carefully prepared. To them it was clear that the absorption of the Greeks in Europe was impracticable, unless the Persian frontier was advanced so as to meet the frontiers of the Greek states by land and sea. This meant that, before annexing Greece to their dominions, they must conquer the Greek islands and, above all, the north of the Balkan peninsula, the seat of the Thracian tribes, who were well known to the Persians in Asia Minor. There was this complication, however, that there Persia was confronted by the aspirations of another Iranian power—the Scythian Empire, which had by this time established itself firmly on the north of the Black Sea, and had also come into contact with the Greeks. This Scythian pressure towards the west and south Persia was bound to check before she turned elsewhere. At the time she did not contemplate the conquest of the Scythian kingdom in south Russia. That might be a problem in the remote future; but the pressing business was to drive the Scythians back from the Danube and prevent them from extending their sway to the Balkan peninsula. Darius undertook the task in a great campaign against Scythia about 512 B.C. He probably went no farther than the steppes between the Danube and the Dniester, and it seems that he succeeded on the whole; for the conversion of Thrace into a Persian province went on quickly and steadily after this date, with no hindrance from without.

Darius was prevented from carrying out his plans further by the revolt of the Ionian Greeks. The causes of this revolt we can only surmise; but it was certainly not connected with any Panhellenic movement intended to check the further advance of Darius; it did not even extend to the whole of Asia Minor. The southern and northern Anatolian Greeks took part in it, and a timid attempt to help them was made by Athens and by Eretria in Euboea, but no other power in Greece proper joined in. In fact it was hardly more than a revolt of Miletus and a few other Ionian cities. We must suppose that it was due to local causes and was undertaken because the Greeks overrated their own power and underrated that of Persia. Though they were well aware of Persia's weak points, it is obvious that they were blind to her real strength. The struggle was stubborn and prolonged (from 499 to 494 B.C.) but ended in the destruction of Ionia. Miletus was burnt to the ground and took long to recover from the heavy blows inflicted upon her.

This revolt played an important part in the history of relations between Persia and Greece: it confirmed the belief of Persia that it was imperative to proceed at once with the conquest of the Balkan peninsula. It is therefore not surprising that the first business of Darius, after crushing the revolt, was to send a force to the shores of the Hellespont and to northern Greece, in order to strengthen the authority of Persia, which had been weakened in these districts by the revolt. This was the immediate object of the campaign of 492 B.C.; but the large number of land and sea forces employed shows that, if all went well, a continuation of the campaign was contemplated, and an advance of the fleet and army into central Greece. But a large part of the fleet was wrecked off Mount Athos, and without the support of all their ships it was difficult to supply a large army through a long and troublesome campaign. Thus the Persians were forced to confine themselves to their main purpose, which was to strengthen Persian authority by the annexation of Thrace and Macedonia.

The campaign of 492 B.C. was only a first attempt. It was followed in 490 by a second, whose object, publicly announced by the Persian king, was to punish Athens and Eretria for their part in the Ionian revolt. This object was formally communicated to the Greek states by ambassadors who demanded of them 'earth and water' as a symbol of submission; what they really required was their neutrality in the coming contest. The proximity of the Persian dominions induced many of the Greek states not to reject these demands. But the real object of Persia was, undoubtedly, different. Making use of her naval superiority, she hoped by her second campaign to accomplish the task which Mardonius had begun, and not only to create a common frontier with Greece by land but also to connect Persia with Greece by a sea route, starting from the cities of Ionia and proceeding through the islands to the natural goal in Europe, that is, Attica and its harbours and the harbours of Euboea. Attica once seized, Persia had no other rival to fear at sea and might count on the conquest of Greece as certain. Considering the internal discord of Greece, it was easy to pit one state against another, and before long to knock out Sparta, the hope of Greece by land, with one decisive blow.

To seize Attica seemed a very simple matter. There was no quarter from which Athens could look for help. Close beside her was Aegina, a dangerous foe and rival; Sparta was far away, slow to act, and hardly conscious of her danger; Boeotia was openly hostile. There was no strong fleet at Athens; and the army of Attica had not much experience and no glorious traditions behind it. The new-born democracy found itself vigorously opposed by the aristocracy, which still retained some strength. Hippias, the last tyrant, was still living and hoped to return in the train of the Persian army. For these reasons Darius believed that Athens could be disposed of by a force landed from his ships.

His calculations proved partly true and partly false. Athens did, indeed, stand alone. But Aegina's intention of assisting the Persians was thwarted by Sparta. At Athens the friends of Persia were ready to act; but they would take no risks: the democratic army of Athens must be beaten first. Sparta did not refuse to support Athens, but her support was long in coming. The danger that threatened Athens and all Greece was enormous; and Athens recognized this, but Greece did not. When the Persian troops were landed on the plain of Marathon, Athens had either to surrender or to accept a decisive battle without any great

1. DARIUS AND A LION   2. THE BODYGUARD OF KING DARIUS

Plate XV   THE PERSIAN KINGS

1. Part of the sculptural decoration of the Great Hall with a hundred columns in the palace of King Darius (522–485 B.C.) at Persepolis. The king is shown fighting a horned lion, a personification of the brute forces of nature. End of the 6th or beginning of the 5th century B.C.

2. One of the bodyguard of King Darius. A long row of such figures adorned the walls of the staircase which led to the terrace on which his palace of Sus was built. Enamelled bricks. End of the 6th or beginning of the 5th century B.C. Paris, Louvre.

128

3. HEAD OF KING DARIUS

4. DARIUS FIGHTING HIS ENEMIES

3. Head of King Darius from the rock bas-reliefs of Behistun. Note the diadem, the skilful trimming of the beard and of the hair. The head is not a real portrait: it represents not the personal features of Darius but an idealized head of the Great King of Kings of the Persian Empire. End of the 6th century B.C.

4. King Darius fighting his enemies and trampling over their slain bodies. Between the king and his enemies is the holy symbol of Ahuramazda (the winged Sun-disk and the medallion with the bust of the god). Cast of a cylinder-signet. End of the 6th or beginning of the 5th century B.C. British Museum.

hope of victory. The chances on her side were not many, but there were some. The small compact army of Athenian and Plataean citizens—an army of infantry equipped with heavy weapons and covered with iron mail—inspired by their deadly peril, and fighting on their native soil and under familiar conditions, proved more than a match for their enemy. The Persians were much more numerous; they were picked troops and well provided; but they were light-armed and fought under strange conditions and had just completed a long voyage. It was a great piece of fortune for the Athenians that they were led by Miltiades, a skilful commander, who was familiar with the Persian army, having served with it during the Scythian campaign as the tyrant of some Greek settlements and local tribes in Thrace. His remarkable talents for war and his knowledge of the enemy played a great and almost decisive part in the brilliant and famous victory of Marathon.

The two armies which fought at Marathon were neither of them large, but the battle is of capital importance in the world's history. In the chain of Persian policy one link, and an essential link, was broken. Yet the battle might have remained merely a splendid exploit in the history of Athens, had it not been followed by a succession of crises in Persia which gave Greece a respite and a breathing-space for the next ten years. Darius, though he made serious preparations for it, was never able to fit out another expedition against Greece. After the failure at Marathon great caution was necessary. But he was old; the bureaucratic machinery of Persia worked slowly; in 486 B.C. Egypt revolted, and in 485 Darius died. Xerxes, his successor, needed time to take his bearings and strengthen his position at home. This delay was highly advantageous to Greece: it increased her resources and raised her spirit. The fame of Athens stood high in Greece. When her treasury was filled by thorough exploitation of the silver mines of Laureium, and when Themistocles came to the front and, with equal boldness and wisdom, insisted on the necessity that Athens should build a great fleet in order to resist future invasions, there was not a power in Greece that would have wished to hinder this addition to her military strength. Sparta and Aegina felt that opposition on their part was impossible. Still more important, the attitude of Greece towards the Persian peril changed during these ten years: all Greeks now realized that they might be enslaved by Persia, and realized also that the conflict was inevitable. Not that all Greece was preparing for the conflict throughout the ten years. Individual states did something in this way—but the important thing was this—that a public opinion, a feeling of common nationality, was formed to meet the struggle. But again, this does not imply that some of the states were not ready to yield and even to fight for Persia; but this had come to be looked upon as treason to the nation, and not as a legitimate course of policy.

Thus the next campaign, begun by Xerxes in 480 B.C., was carried on under different conditions. The preparations made by him were extraordinarily careful, and the plan of campaign excellent. The supply department was ably organized. The plan of 492 B.C. was adopted again: the army was to march along the coast, escorted by a vast fleet; the business of the fleet was to secure the provisioning of the forces and to guard it from being attacked in the rear. Great anxiety prevailed in Greece. Originally it was intended to bar the invader from Greek soil, by meeting him where the vale of Tempe gives admission to Thessaly. But this plan could not be executed, because it was easy to go round the pass. It was therefore necessary to abandon Thessaly to the invader. A second plan, pressed by the Athenians and all central Greece, involved co-operation of the fleet and army at Thermopylae, the key to central Greece: the army was to defend Thermopylae, and the fleet was to resist any attack by sea upon the rear of the army. But Sparta put forward a rival plan of her own: she insisted that the Isthmus should be defended and all central Greece abandoned without a blow. The plan of defending Thermopylae was practicable, if the army on the spot was large and the fleet did its duty. But, though the fleet did not fail,

Sparta and some of the allies sent forces which were insufficient for the defence, and the Persians were able to march round the comparatively small body of defenders. The Greek fleet thereupon sailed away to the coast of Attica. Some of the defenders of Thermopylae retreated; others, including Leonidas, the Spartan commander, were slain in unequal fight. The Persians had entered Greece.

Attica was their first victim. Boeotia, like most of central Greece, submitted to the invaders and rendered them zealous service. There were fresh disputes about the plan of campaign. To defend Athens was impossible, and the population of the city and of Attica was removed to Salamis and Aegina. Attica was soon overrun, and Athens was sacked and burnt. That it was now the turn of the fleet to act was beyond question; but where was the battle to be fought: off Attica or off the Peloponnese? The Spartans insisted that the Isthmus should be fortified and the Peloponnesian coast protected from invasion—a hopeless plan, considering the superiority of the Persian fleet. The Athenians demanded that the Greek ships should be concentrated between Salamis and the coast of Attica, where there was a chance of success because the gulf was too narrow for the Persian fleet to deploy in. Themistocles had great difficulty in securing that the battle should be fought at Salamis. Xerxes also wished this: he hoped to crush the united Greeks and to catch all their fleet in a trap by closing both ends of the gulf.

Battle was given and accepted; and the Greeks were completely victorious. It became necessary for the Persians to change their whole plan of campaign. Their fleet was not, indeed, utterly destroyed at Salamis; but it was so much crippled that the superiority at sea passed over definitely to the other side. And while the Greeks were masters of the sea, it was impossible to maintain a large invading army. They had fears also for their communications with their own country. Therefore Xerxes, with a considerable part of his army, started on the difficult march homewards. Part of the army was left in Thessaly with the object of renewing the strife in the following year, 479 B.C.

The situation in Greece, even after the victory of Salamis, was still precarious. To have beside her, perhaps for ever, a Persian province in northern Greece, with a strong army, was a terrible menace. But to this result the policy of Sparta tended. She continued to insist that central Greece must be abandoned and the Isthmus fortified. Meanwhile, the Persians re-fitted their fleet and sent it to defend the coast of Asia Minor; and they reinforced the army of Mardonius, a skilful general, who passed the winter in Thessaly. The spring brought them back to Greece. The plan of Mardonius was to cause a definite rupture between Sparta and Athens and then to conclude a separate peace with the latter. Once he had the Athenian fleet on his side, he could disregard the fortification of the Isthmus, and the conquest of the Peloponnese was assured. The Athenians were in a difficult position. They had to face a second invasion and a second devastation of their country; for Sparta obstinately refused to send her own forces and those of her allies to central Greece. Nevertheless, the Athenians found strength in themselves to return a decided refusal to the proposals brought by Alexander, King of Macedonia, the envoy of Mardonius. Attica was again occupied, her population was again removed to Salamis, and the destruction of Athens was this time completed.

When Sparta realized that the patience of Athens was nearly exhausted, and that, if Sparta continued to insist on defending the Peloponnese, a separate peace between Mardonius and Athens and the utter collapse of the Spartan plan of campaign were inevitable, then, and not till then, she decided to give up this plan and dispatch her army to Boeotia. A strong Spartan army took the field at once, and was joined by the militia of other Greek states; the whole number amounted to 100,000 infantry, heavy-armed and light-armed. Mardonius at once evacuated Attica. The two armies met not far from Plataea. At first the Persians had the upper hand. Mardonius had excellent cavalry as well as a strong force of infantry. Hence Pausanias, the Spartan king, who commanded the allied Greek army, was hampered in his movements and obliged to keep to the hilly ground between Boeotia and Attica. The difficulty of the Greek position increased with the duration of the campaign. The Persians had the fertile lands of Boeotia and Thessaly for a base, whereas the Greeks had to draw all their supplies from as far off as the Peloponnese. Again, the Persians were united under one command; but the Greek generals were apt to quarrel even on the field of battle. The Greeks were saved by an error on the part of Mardonius. When Pausanias shifted the front of his army towards the hills, for protection against the Persian cavalry, Mardonius took this manœuvre for a retreat, and gave battle under circumstances which made his cavalry useless. As at Marathon the Persian infantry were beaten by the hoplites; but this time the hoplites were Spartans.

At the same time, in order that the Persian fleet might be kept aloof from the struggle in Greece, the Greek ships sailed eastwards to the island of Samos, where a Persian army and fleet were stationed at Mycale. The Greeks disembarked and offered battle. Betrayed by the Ionian Greeks, who predominated in that division of the Persian army, the Persians were cut to pieces.

As the result of Plataea and Mycale, the Persians were forced to abstain from any further interference in Greek affairs and to abandon the conquest of Greece.

While these events were taking place in Greece an equally stern struggle was going on in the West between the Sicilian Greeks and Carthage. I have spoken already of this important Phoenician colony on the north coast of Africa, of her commercial relations and growing prosperity. By degrees Carthage reduced to subjection the other Phoenician colonies on that coast and also a number of tribes in the interior. In the sixth and fifth centuries B.C. she was a strong imperial power, governed by a small group of her noblest and richest citizens, and possessing a powerful army and fleet, manned partly by citizens and partly by mercenaries. Her trade was directed chiefly to the north and north-west. I have said already that she had to face the competition of Greek cities in Sicily, Italy, and Gaul, and that this led to constant bloody collisions. At the beginning of the fifth century, simultaneously with the third Persian invasion of Greece, and possibly in collusion with Persia, she equipped a powerful fleet and collected a large army, and hurled them upon Sicily, hoping to seize the whole island and expel the Greeks at one blow. Fortunately for the Greeks, Sicily was in such a position that she was prepared to meet the foe. Gelon, tyrant of the city of Gela, an able and ambitious statesman, had created a powerful empire in Sicily; and Syracuse, the richest and strongest city in the island, had come under his sway shortly before the Carthaginian invasion. Making use of the resources thus obtained and of the general apprehension, he collected a great army and met the invaders near Himera. The skill of the general and the favourable conditions—the Carthaginian cavalry had been wrecked while crossing from Africa—gave victory to the Greeks. It was long before Carthage was in a position to renew her attack.

Greece had defended her freedom. Persia and Carthage, it is true, were still great powers, but Persia advanced no farther: she had to think of defence instead. Greece had escaped the fate of Asia Minor: she never became, even for a time, the province of an Eastern monarchy.

IX

THE ATHENIAN EMPIRE

After Plataea and Mycale the struggle with the Persians in Greece proper was at an end. Persia recognized that, as things were, she was unable to conquer Greece and cut it up into Persian satrapies. But this does not mean that war between the two nations was ended: it still dragged on, inevitably; and the only question was, what form the struggle would take, and which side would play the active or the passive part. It was possible for Persia to abandon all hope of immediate conquest, and yet to maintain her common frontier with Greece and her possessions in the Balkan peninsula, Asia Minor, and the islands.

The period of fifty years which divides the battle of Plataea from the beginning of the Peloponnesian war is a period about which little is known. Herodotus ends his history with the taking of Sestos in 478 B.C.; Thucydides made it his business to describe and explain the great struggle between Sparta and Athens for primacy in Greece; and the later historians—Ephorus, Theopompus, and others—who recorded not episodes merely but the whole of Greek history, have come down to us, if they have come down at all, in mere fragments. Those fifty years were not marked out by any central incident of arresting interest, and therefore found no historian fit to rank with Herodotus or Thucydides.

It was impossible that Persia should give up the struggle. But she had suffered such shrewd blows in Greece that the ponderous framework of the Persian Empire, with its immense territory and motley armies, obviously needed some respite in order to concentrate these armies and prepare for a fresh attack. But this respite Greece refused to give. She never stopped fighting, even temporarily; instead of defending herself, she became aggressive. She made it her object to push the Persians back to Asia and deprive them of immediate contact with the Aegean. This military object was at the same time a national object: what mattered most was to restore their independence to the Greek cities on the Aegean coast. We are ill informed of the way in which this policy was carried out. I have said above that we have but meagre records of the period following the Persian wars; and such information as we have refers mainly to the internal affairs of Greece and not to the struggle against Persia. These internal affairs became more complicated as Athens rose in political importance. There was increasing friction between her and her neighbours; and behind those neighbours was Sparta, ever turning a suspicious eye on the increasing wealth and importance of Athens.

The main incidents, however, of this struggle are known. It was directed originally by Sparta. Before the war Sparta had been the chief political and military power in Greece; to her, with Athens coming next, had belonged the first place in the actual conduct of the war; her army had won the battle of Plataea. But Sparta was ill suited to take the lead in a contest which was waged chiefly by sea and on the outskirts of the Greek world. Such a war demanded a more flexible and active machine than the constitution of Sparta. Her military strength was limited and could not be squandered here and there in large numbers. Her domestic affairs, her relations to the Helots and Periocci made it necessary to retain at home a large military force, the majority, indeed, of those Spartiates who formed the nucleus of the army. This concentration of Spartan force in Greece, instead of Asia Minor and Thrace, was required also by the complicated political situation of the Peloponnese, where Sparta's

1. RED-FIGURED ATTIC CUP.
THESEUS AND AMPHITRITE

2. RED-FIGURED ATTIC CUP.
ATHENIAN WARRIOR AND HIS FATHER

Plate XVI   GREEK POTTERY OF THE 5TH CENTURY B.C.

1. Attic cup (red figures on black ground) from the workshop of
Euphronios, the great Athenian potter and painter of the late 6th
and early 5th centuries. Found at Caere in Italy. The picture, which
is splendidly illustrated by the beautiful victory-song (*paean*) of
Bacchylides, recently found, represents the Athenian national hero
Theseus. He had been challenged by the Cretan King Minos to
prove that he was really the son of Poseidon. Fearless, he jumped
from his ship into the sea, and supported by a sea-monster Triton
met the sea-queen Amphitrite in her palace. His protectress and the
patron of his city, Athena, assisted him; and he received from the
queen both recognition and rich gifts. The picture is one of the most
beautiful of archaic vase paintings. It is important from the historical point of view as well. It shows that, from the time of Pisistratus,
Athens regarded herself as the mistress of the sea. About 500 B.C.
Paris, Louvre.

2. Attic cup (red-figured) showing an aged citizen helping a young
man to put on the arms of a hoplite. The expression of deep sorrow
is masterly. Such were the fathers of those who fought for their
country at Marathon, Salamis and Plataea. About 480 B.C. Vatican,
Rome.

3. RED-FIGURED ATTIC CUP.
OEDIPUS AND THE SPHINX

4. RED-FIGURED ATTIC CUP.
JASON AND THE DRAGON

3. Attic cup (red-figured) in the style of Duris. Oedipus is seated on a rock meditating the riddle of human life which the Sphinx, a beautiful winged woman with a lion's body, has asked him. A beautiful symbol of the time of the great Greek thinkers, especially the Sophists, who tried over and over again to find a logical solution of the riddle of life. About 480 B.C. Vatican, Rome.

4. Attic cup (red-figured) in the style of the painter Duris. The picture shows Jason, the first Greek sailor, who went on the ship Argo to Colchis in the Caucasus to bring back the golden fleece. He met here the dragon which guarded the fleece, entered its huge body or was swallowed by it, was rescued, and finally killed the monster. The picture shows Jason coming out of the dragon's mouth under the protection of Athena. The fleece hangs near by on a tree. The picture demonstrates how early Athens became interested in the Greek colonies on the Black Sea and wished to be recognized as their protectress. About 480 B.C. Vatican, Rome.

leadership depended upon military superiority alone. Finally, as we have seen, Sparta was an agricultural and inland kingdom: her wealth was limited, and no war could be carried on with success at sea and on the outskirts of the Greek world without large expenditure.

All this taken together inevitably drove Sparta to resign the leading part in the further struggle against Persia. But a leader there must be, and the only possible leader was Athens. Her fleet was the best in Greece; her army was considerable, including as it did all the citizens of the state, i.e. the immense majority of all the population inhabiting Athens, the Peiraeus, and all Attica; and the fleet could easily convey detachments of the force to wherever they were needed. Besides, after the democratic reforms of Cleisthenes, her domestic affairs were in order; and indeed the citizens, busy with military enterprises, had no time to think of anything else. And lastly, the spirit of patriotism had risen high in Athens, in consequence of Marathon, Salamis, and Plataea; and the fame of the Athenians, as excellent soldiers and sailors and sagacious politicians was very great. It is no wonder that Athens coveted the direction of the struggle against Persia, and obtained it.

Though Greece proper, i.e. the cities dotted about the Balkan peninsula, was not much concerned in this contest, to the islands and the cities in Asia Minor it was a matter of life and death. These parts of Greece took therefore an active part in it, combining, under the presidency of Athens, in a marine confederacy with a centre at Delos—a confederacy which gave birth to the Athenian Empire. The principles of this irrevocable alliance were—that each of the allies should take part in the war and be represented at the council of the league, and each might contribute money instead of men and ships. Under these conditions it was natural that the presidency should belong to Athens. Possessing larger forces and greater wealth than the other allies, she commanded a majority of votes in the council; she alone had men enough and energy enough to convert the money of the allies, in case they were unwilling or unable to take an active part in the war, into ships and soldiers. On the Athenians, as directors, the chief responsibility fell; and their importance on the council was naturally in proportion to their responsibility.

By the action of this confederation the Aegean was gradually cleared of the Persians. The Hellespont and the Sea of Marmora joined the alliance, or, in other words, became Athenian waters; the most important points were garrisoned by colonies of Athenian citizens; and by degrees the Persians were squeezed out of the southern Aegean also. The chief actors in this systematic warfare against Persia were new. Aristides, a general at the battle of Plataea and founder of the Confederacy of Delos, had left the scene. So had Themistocles, the hero of Salamis and the creator of the Athenian fleet. His last achievement was to fortify Athens and the harbour of Piraeus with walls. With her land and sea bases thus fortified Athens could carry on freely her activity at sea, and could be indifferent to the possibility of attacks by land against her capital and harbour. Later, like most statesmen of the Athenian democracy, Themistocles was prosecuted and exiled. His remaining days he spent in Persia.

The chief figure at Athens now was Cimon. He led the aristocratic party and supported the 'balance of power' in Greece, that is, a policy of peace and agreement with Sparta and the other Greek states. Thus he was peculiarly well fitted to direct the foreign policy of Athens, as things then were. Like his father, Miltiades, and like Themistocles, he had great ability. His chief exploit was his victory over the Persians at the river Eurymedon c. 468 B.C., which decided the mastery of the southern waters. After this defeat the Persians had no marine base except the coasts of Palestine, Syria, Phoenicia, and Egypt.

This battle completed a series of operations against Persia, which were closely connected with the invasion of Greece. The Greeks realized clearly that the danger of a fresh invasion was not to be feared in the immediate future. But this did not imply that the struggle was over. Persia was still a strong marine power

1. RED-FIGURED KRATER. KING DARIUS

Plate XVII GREEK POTTERY OF THE 5TH
AND 4TH CENTURIES B.C.

1. Red-figured wine-vessel (*krater*) found at Canusium in Italy.
The leading idea is the triumph of Europe over Asia. The most important part (our figure) represents the preparations of Darius for
his eventful expedition into Greece. Darius is consulting his council,
one of the Persian nobles is speaking. Below, the treasurer collects
the war-tax from the tax-payers. In the upper row to the left the
divine protectors of Greece (Athena, Hera, Zeus, Nike, Apollo,
Artemis), to the right the personification of Asia led into war by the
goddess 'Apate'—Deceit, Illusion. It is the first act of the great historical drama treated by Aeschylus in his 'Persians' and by Herodotus
in his 'Histories'. Italiote Greek work of the 4th century B.C. Naples
Museum. After Furtwängler-Reichhold.

2. Red-figured amphora (vessel with two handles). The picture shows the Lydian King Croesus on the pyre after his army was defeated by the Persian King Cyrus. The story was famous in Greece and was used by Herodotus to show how unstable fortune is and how quietly a 'wise' man takes the inevitable. Attic work of about 500 B.C. Paris, Louvre. After Furtwängler-Reichhold.

3. Red-figured cup. Achilles is represented slaying the Amazon Queen Penthesilea, with whom, according to the epic poets, he was in love. To the right, one of the Greeks; to the left, one of the Amazons in Oriental costume. Attic work of about 460 B.C. Munich Museum. After Furtwängler-Reichhold.

143

with outlets to the Mediterranean, and sooner or later she might return to a policy of attack with increased experience and increased knowledge. But no Greeks except the Athenians realized this danger. The rest felt themselves free from immediate menace, and thought it unnecessary to preserve, with an eye to the future, the naval organization which they had created for the contest with Persia. Thus a process of decomposition began in the confederation. The allies resented the supremacy of Athens and aimed at complete political independence.

There were now two alternatives before Athens—either to renounce the mastery of the Aegean and revert to the state of things before the Persian wars, or to convert the confederation into an Athenian Empire; in other words, to rule the allies instead of presiding over them, a result which could only be secured by force. She was induced to take the second of these courses, partly by her conviction that the struggle with Persia was not yet over, and partly by other considerations. Athens had become a great city: a large part of the Aegean trade was concentrated there; and she had become an important centre of industry. The population had greatly increased: to the citizens were added a multitude of aliens (*metoeci*) who did not possess the franchise but settled in the city in order to carry on trade and industry; the number of slaves also had risen greatly. The loss of mastery over the sea would certainly have arrested this development; and also it might have forced on Athens a return to the conditions that existed before the Persian wars; and such a return would inevitably have brought with it serious internal convulsions. Hence she chose the second course and proceeded to convert the confederation into an empire, in which the citizens of Athens ruled over the citizens of other states, and the contributions of the allies became tribute instead.

This decision affected the whole policy of Athens, both at home and abroad. The leaders of the democratic party—first Ephialtes and then Pericles—became assertors of the imperialistic ideas and aspirations cherished by the citizens. The activity

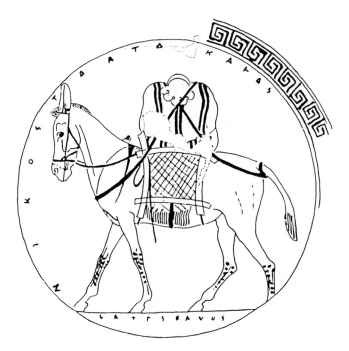

FIG. 16. Red-figured cup. The picture shows a beautiful pack donkey, a familiar figure in the bazaars of the East. Attic work of about 480 B.C. Boston Museum. After Hartwig.

of Ephialtes was short-lived: soon after his first public appearance he was mysteriously murdered. But Pericles guided Athenian policy for many years, and always found support in the popular assembly. He was a strict and consistent champion of the view that Athens should be at once a democracy and a great imperial power; he was an excellent orator, and a wary and sagacious statesman. It is with good reason that the time between the banishment of Cimon in 461 B.C. and the beginning of the Peloponnesian war is generally called the Age of Pericles.

The decision was taken, and Athens became the centre of a great empire, a democracy herself, but with a number of states dependent on her and ruled by her in all matters except those of purely local interest, and thereby deprived of their political independence. This decision altered the policy of Athens towards her nearest neighbours and towards Sparta, and also affected her relation to the Persian monarchy; and in both cases the new policy was due to economic causes and mainly to commercial considerations.

Between the seventh and fifth centuries B.C. Greece created her own flourishing manufactures, developed and improved her production of wine and oil, and found for her wares a number of markets, where they were appreciated more and more and found increasing sales. The chief markets were Italy, Gaul, and Spain in the west, Macedonia, Thrace, and the Black Sea coast in the north and north-east. In the east also, Athenian vases and the large quantities of Greek, especially Athenian, silver coins found all over the Persian Empire from Afghanistan to Egypt attest almost uninterrupted commercial relations with the Greek world in the fifth century. The Phoenicians, driven out of the Aegean, were still masters of the lucrative trade with Egypt (though the Greeks tried to compete with them there as early as the seventh century B.C.), and tried hard to oust the Greeks from all the western trade. It is therefore no wonder that the imperial fleet of Athens aimed its first blows at the Phoenicians, attacking them in Cyprus and Egypt, the main centres of their trade in the eastern Mediterranean. Success in the struggle for these markets would have enabled Greece to attack Phoenicia itself. But both these Athenian expeditions ended in failure. When endeavouring to support the Egyptian revolt against Persia (460–454 B.C.), they lost a considerable detachment of soldiers and a powerful squadron of ships; in Cyprus, having recalled Cimon from banishment to lead their army, they won a battle (450 B.C.) but reaped no considerable advantage from it. Cimon died of disease during the campaign. They were forced to make peace with Persia and leave the question of Phoenicia to be settled by future generations.

Athens was unsuccessful against Persia, because she was at the same time drawn into strife with her nearest neighbours and with Sparta. Her empire was by no means consolidated at this time, and she was forced, as we shall see later, to fight against her own allies or subjects. In this case the war with Aegina, Corinth, and Boeotia was due to the same economic and commercial motives which had embroiled her with Persia. Aegina was an old enemy and a rival. Corinth with her western colonies excluded Athens from the Etruscan sea, the West, and the great grain-markets of Italy and Sicily. The economic expansion of Athens had to be directed at the undeveloped countries on the Adriatic Sea. But for Athens, with the growth of her manufactures and the conversion of her fields into vineyards and olive groves, the import of raw materials and foodstuffs was a question of life and death. Italy and Sicily could supply both her needs more fully than any country except Egypt. The northern markets, still only in process of development, could not produce enough to satisfy the needs of the great Athenian Empire, increased as it was by the accession of the Ionian cities.

Repeating the policy which they had employed against Phoenicia, the Athenians did not attack Corinth directly, but tried to weaken her by seizing Aegina and forcing her into the alliance, by depriving Megara, the neighbour of Corinth and Athens, of all commercial importance, and by establishing her own ascendancy in Boeotia. This attempt to extend her influence in Greece proper naturally involved collision with Sparta, to whom (and to all Peloponnesians) the neutrality of the Isthmus was of vital importance, because they depended largely on the import of corn and raw material from Italy and Sicily. The struggle dragged on from 459 to 447 B.C., and Athens in the end was unsuccessful. Aegina, indeed, became part of the Athenian Empire; but she was unable either to cut off Megara from the sea or to strengthen her own position in Boeotia. Again she was obliged to end the war by an unprofitable peace which was concluded, first for five years, and then, in 446, extended to thirty. Sparta consented to make peace, though the question of Athenian ascendancy in central Greece was by no means settled. But she could not help herself: she was weakened by a long struggle against the Helots, from 464 to 459 B.C., and by repeated complications with Elis and Arcadia, members of the Spartan military league, and with Argos, her stubborn enemy.

Unsuccessful in her grand imperialistic schemes, Athens was now obliged to deal with the affairs of her confederacy, in other words, of her new dominions, and to consolidate her position in those parts of the world where her supremacy was as yet undisputed—in Thrace and on the Black Sea coast. The wish to impress the dependent cities and extend the bounds of the empire explains the cruise undertaken by Pericles. In command of a great fleet he visited the coast of the Black Sea and the Crimea, where a number of military colonies were planted, probably by Pericles himself, and many Greek cities were annexed to the empire. While Athens was fighting Persia and her Greek neighbours, the process was going on which converted the maritime confederation into the Athenian Empire. In 454 B.C. the treasury of the league was transferred from Delos to Athens; most of the allies, except Samos, Lesbos, and Chios, became dependent and paid tribute; and they were all obliged at this time to refer most of their suits at law to the decision of the Athenian courts. All this was exceedingly displeasing to the 'allies', as the subjects of the Athenian Empire were still officially called; and they resented the constant interference of Athens in the internal affairs of cities which still considered themselves independent. Thus Athens had constantly to deal with 'revolts' among the allies. Some of these, e.g. the revolt of free Samos, which refused to remain a member of the league, and the revolt of Byzantium, were very formidable and were quelled with great severity.

The internal life of Athens was influenced by her ambitious foreign policy. The consistent development of that policy was guided mainly by the lower classes—by the citizens engaged in navigation, trade, and manufacture. They were the masters, and all public institutions were re-fashioned, to suit them, in the spirit of extreme democracy. The political centre of gravity was now transferred from the Council of Five Hundred to the popular assembly, in which the law required that all important business should be decided, such as questions of foreign policy, of war, and of food-supplies. Once in each prytany (a period of thirty-six days) the public assembly reviewed the proceedings of the magistrates, with power to suspend and bring them to trial, in case of any irregularity. Under these conditions the magistrates confined themselves to executing the decisions of the assembly; and the council merely discussed beforehand the business which the assembly had subsequently to decide. Every member of the assembly had the right to speak and even to initiate legislation. But the latter right was hedged about with certain safeguards. Agenda of the assembly was prepared by the Council, and the motions had to be approved by it, although the people could amend the proposed text. However, any citizen could attack a decree in the courts for constitutional reasons.

The board of ten generals (*strategi*) acquired great importance at the same time and formed a kind of cabinet. This was a survival from the troubled times of the Persian wars. All foreign and domestic policy was concentrated in their hands. If their policy was successful, they might be re-elected an indefinite number of times; in case of failure, they were sometimes tried and sentenced to exile or death. Their high position was quite natural in a state where the centre of gravity lay in foreign and military affairs, and in the ruling of an empire. There was also an army of executive officials, all appointed annually by lot, and serving partly in Athens and partly abroad. Their chief business was the finance of the empire.

There was a third body which played an important part in public life. This was the Heliaea or judicial assembly in which citizens were paid for their duties. This body monopolized by degrees all the forensic business of Athens. It consisted of 6,000 members, 600 taken by lot from each tribe. They were divided into committees of 500, but the number was sometimes greater than this, sometimes less. The jurors swore to give their verdict in accordance with the laws, and, in cases where the law could be interpreted in more than one way, according to their conscience. The number of suits, especially when swollen by business of the empire, was very large and took long to decide. The magistrates merely prepared the case and took no part in the decision. Advocates and defenders were not admitted to the court: each party had to appear in person. The verdict was determined by a simple majority.

Such was the final form of democracy. Neither in foreign nor in domestic affairs did it lead to any specially brilliant consequences. To it, in considerable measure, Athens owed her failure in the struggle with Sparta, and her fall.

X

THE PELOPONNESIAN WAR

The continued existence of the Athenian Empire started a problem in Greek politics. Which was the stronger, the centralizing forces personified in that empire, or the opposite tendency towards independence in each separate community? It is remarkable that the Athenian democracy, while taking the path of imperialism, at the same time supported the democratic cause in all the states dependent on Athens. She reckoned that the democrats, most of whom belonged to the industrial and trading class, would support the commercial imperialism of Athens, even if injury were done to the political independence of the separate communities. However selfish the policy of Athens might be, yet she made the seas safe for traders and admitted her allies to some share in the advantages of her commercial ascendancy. About 450 B.C. Athens made the use of her silver coins, measures, and weights obligatory in her empire. In this way her dominion became a common trade market.

'Self-determination' and 'a balance of power'—these had once been the watchwords of most Greek cities. Now they were proclaimed chiefly by the adherents of aristocracy—the wealthy landowners and smallholders. Sparta sympathized to a certain extent with this programme: she was prepared to concede to her allies a larger measure of self-government, even in political affairs, than Athens was willing to grant. She supported, therefore, in all ways the aristocratic and oligarchic factions which existed in every Greek community and even at Athens. She left no stone unturned, that the conservative policy, which was bitterly opposed to Athenian imperialism and sympathized with the constitution of Sparta, if not with her military league, might become the policy of as many Greek states as possible.

But the difference between the Spartan attitude and the Athenian attitude towards these fundamental questions of Greek politics does not explain why these two powers were infallibly bound to meet in armed conflict—a contest which was destined to continue till the strength of the combatants was utterly exhausted, and to end in the complete triumph of the separatist tendency. The turn of events in the first half of the fifth century B.C. was such that the coexistence of a maritime Athenian Empire and a Spartan league of inland states enjoying some measure of political independence was perfectly possible; and this might seem the most reasonable solution of the difficulty for an indefinite time to come.

The explanation of the conflict is therefore to be found not merely in the fundamentally different view of politics taken by two almost equally matched powers in Greece, but also in a succession of accompanying incidents, which ripened and hastened on the clash of arms. The growing trade and industry of Athens and the states in alliance with her, including the islands and Anatolian cities, made the question of the Western markets, which had not been settled by the wars of 500–450 B.C., still more acute. Corinth and Megara would not and could not put up with the increasing competition of Athens in Italy and Sicily. The success of Athens in her trade with the West is proved by this one fact—that from 500 B.C. her pottery drove out, all over Italy, the product of all other Greek centres of the manufacture. If imports from Athens grew thus, the exports from Italy and Sicily—corn, cattle, and metals—would soon pour exclusively into the Piraeus; and then Athens would have an ascendancy, not merely commercial but political also, in all the north and west of the Peloponnese. For those districts could not support their own population and depended absolutely upon food exported from the West; but this trade would be monopolized by Athens. Sparta also, though not interested in export trade to the West, was menaced by this danger and therefore inclined to listen to the complaints of Megara, Corinth, and Sicyon.

It was a turning-point in the long rivalry, political and economic, between Athens and the Peloponnese, when Athens made up her mind that certain questions concerning Megara and Corcyra were ripe for settlement. Pericles was induced by continual friction with Megara to take the decisive step of declaring a blockade of the city. And at the same time Athens was compelled to take a definite line in the Western question. In 433 B.C. Corcyra, a rich colony of Corinth and the natural bridge between Greece and the West, finding that her commercial interests were constantly at variance with those of her mother city, expressed her readiness to enter into alliance with Athens. To do this was to cut off from Corinth her last chance of stemming the rush of Athenian trade to the West, and to put the control over the western trade-route, which was commanded by the harbours of Corcyra, in the hands of Athens. For the presence of an Athenian fleet in those harbours would hand over to Athens all the Italian and Sicilian trade. She had at this time allies and friends in both countries, few but faithful. Sparta had to decide whether the western waters should be given up to Athens or not. It was almost impossible for Athens to withdraw: to check the expansion of her trade was to endanger the very existence of her empire. And lastly, Athens was aiming at complete control over the Chalcidian peninsula, which involved her in a prolonged contest with Potidaea. Potidaea, an ally of Athens but a colony of Corinth, was unwilling to part with her last scrap of independence and to become a member not of the Athenian confederation but of the Athenian Empire.

Sparta decided for war, though her prospect of victory was not very bright. It was a contest for mastery of the sea and de-

1. RED-FIGURED WINE-CUP. HERACLES AND THE AMAZONS

Plate XVIII   WAR IN THE ART OF
THE 5TH CENTURY B.C.

1. Red-figured wine-cup (*kantharos*) painted by Duris. The picture
shows the fight between Greeks, led by Heracles, and Amazons. The
idea is to represent the victorious fight of Greece against the East.
Attic work of about 490–480 B.C. Brussels Museum.

2. Red-figured cup painted by Brygos. The pictures represent the
capture of Troy by the Greeks with all its horrors. On one side we
see Priam taking refuge at the altar of Apollo, and Neoptolemos, the
son of Achilles, using the boy Astyanax to brain him with. On the
other side a wild fight is going on. The heroic woman who defends
her boy is Andromache. Attic work of about 480 B.C. Paris, Louvre.
After Furtwängler-Reichhold.

2. RED-FIGURED CUP. CAPTURE OF TROY

manded, above all, a fleet and money; and she, as an inland and agricultural power, possessed neither. Nor was the Corinthian fleet a match even for the fleet of Corcyra. Athens, on the other hand, had a fleet, a large reserve of money, control of the trade-routes, a great number of men for service in the fleet and army, and considerable wealth amassed by individual citizens. It is no wonder that Pericles insisted upon war. Still, Sparta did not act without definite grounds for her action. Her chief superiority lay in her army. If Athens decided to fight a pitched battle in defence of her territory, which the Greek cities generally did in their wars with one another, Sparta could easily defeat her on land; and such a defeat might naturally lead to disruption of the Athenian confederation and defection of the allies, in other words, to civil war within the empire. It is probable, too, that Sparta disbelieved in the strength of the Athenian democracy: on the eve of the Persian wars she had managed to interefere in the domestic affairs of Athens and had met with support in the city itself.

Beginning in 431 B.C., the war dragged on for twenty-eight years of almost continuous operations. Thucydides, a contemporary and himself an actor in the war—he was at one time in command of an Athenian force—has left us a description of it, which is one of the noblest monuments of the Greek genius in literature and art—a masterpiece both in detail and in its general survey of a period of primary importance. The course of the war is therefore known to us in all its particulars. The general outline is as follows. The first ten years are somewhat monotonous. The Spartan plan was to invade Attica year after year in harvest time, in order to reduce the population to despair and force the Athenians to fight a decisive battle. Sparta also endeavoured, without much success, to sow division among the subjects of the Athenian Empire. The policy of Athens was to abstain from an engagement on Attic soil, and on this account the population was withdrawn into the city. At the same time the Athenians took every means to seize the western sea-routes, i.e. the route through the Corinthian Gulf and round the Peloponnese. This was not easy, because most Greek cities in Italy and Sicily were hostile; many of them were Dorian colonies, and Syracuse, a purely Dorian colony, was more hostile than others. Further, it was imperatively necessary for Athens to keep full control over the northern and eastern waters; but this again was a difficult and complicated business. To secure the former of these objects it was not enough to hold the entrance of the Corinthian Gulf: it was necessary to have a maritime base and, if possible, more than one, on the coast of the Peloponnese itself.

Athens suffered a heavy blow when, in 430 B.C., at the very beginning of the war, a destructive plague broke out in the city and crippled her just at the very moment when the exercise of her full strength might have decided the war in her favour. The plague also carried off Pericles, whose genius had sketched out the main lines for conducting the war, and who held all the threads of it in his own hands. Yet, in spite of this incalculable calamity, the strength of Athens was so great that the course of events was, in general, favourable to her. But neither side was able to inflict a decisive blow upon the other. The western trade-route remained open, even after Athens had seized two points in or near the Peloponnese—Pylus and Cythera—and actually captured at Pylus a considerable Spartan force. It became clear that to control one end of this route was not enough, and that a powerful base at both ends was indispensable. As it was, the Peloponnese kept up connexion with Italy and Sicily and could not be forced to surrender. It must have surrendered, had it been possible for Athens to stop the importation of food, especially of grain, from Italy and Sicily.

But Sparta's plan of forcing the Athenian army to fight a decisive battle was a failure also. The devastation of Attica was ineffective, for the Athenian fleets retaliated by ravaging the Peloponnesian coast, and her control of the Black Sea route secured to Athens a supply of grain and fish for food and of raw materials for manufacture. Revolts among the allies were ruthlessly suppressed. The single success of Sparta was the seizure of Amphipolis in Macedonia and of Chalcidice; but these places were not of vital importance to Athens. Meanwhile the strength of both antagonists was beginning to fail, and the peace party in both countries became prominent and importunate. After ten years of war, when Cleon, the chief of the war-like and imperialistic party, was killed in Thrace and predominating influence passed to Nicias, a man of small ability and a lover of peace, Sparta and Athens concluded a peace and even an alliance. This peace, which dates from 421 B.C., is called in history the Peace of Nicias.

Lasting this peace could not be. The Athenians were conscious of their strength and aware that the chance of victory was still, on the whole, on their side. Still the foundations of the Athenian Empire were shaking, and their confederation was threatened with gradual dissolution from within. The Persian spectre again raised its head in the East, and Persian gold found easy access to the pockets of orators who attacked Athens in the allied cities. Nothing but complete success could save Athens: a partial victory was little better than defeat. This point of view was expressed in set terms by Alcibiades, the nephew of Pericles, an able general and dexterous politician, and an incarnation of the virtues and vices which marked Athenian character in her time of empire. The military problem and the political problem were both clear to him. In Greece Sparta was invulnerable. Decisive success was attainable only by complete control at sea; and, for this purpose, it was necessary that the Greeks in Italy and Sicily should be included in the Athenian confederation. Syracuse was the Athens of the West; and it could not be expected that this Dorian rival should enter the alliance of her own free will. One course remained—to compel her to come in. This was the design of Alcibiades. If successful, it would bring speedy and certain victory; and failure was improbable, because no one expected such a step on the part of Athens.

The enterprise was planned and carried out on a great scale. In 415 B.C. a formidable expedition was suddenly sent westwards. The plan of campaign was carefully worked out, and all the threads of it were in the hands of Alcibiades, its author and the leader of the expedition. But at the very start a decisive blow was dealt to their design by the Athenians themselves. His political opponents first prosecuted Alcibiades on a frivolous charge, and then prevented an investigation while he was still on the spot; when he had started, they stirred up the people against him and condemned him in absence. This was a fatal blow to the whole enterprise. He fled to Sparta and revealed to the Spartans all the details of his plan. Nicias, his successor, had no plan of his own and was incompetent to devise one. For all this, the Athenian armament was so powerful that at first the capture of Syracuse seemed possible. But Nicias was slow and made mistake after mistake. Sparta had time to throw reinforcements into Syracuse under a competent general, who had got accurate information from Alcibiades concerning the resources of Athens and the weak points of the expedition. The affair ended with the complete destruction, in 413 B.C., of the Athenian army and navy.

So the stake was lost and the fate of the Athenian Empire settled. The chief assets of Athens, her fleet and her reserve, had perished at Syracuse; for nearly all the reserve had been spent in fitting out the expedition; and it was impossible to replace them. And yet the weakness and poverty of Sparta prolonged the agony for nearly ten years more. For victory Sparta needed a fleet, and for a fleet she needed money; but she and her partisans in Greece, already ruined by the war, could supply neither of these requisites. The Italian and Sicilian Greeks were never inclined to give her active and steady support, and now they were threatened with a fresh attack from Carthage. Persia was the one possible source from which funds might be got for continuing the war. Sparta did not hesitate: she even agreed to hand back the Greeks in Asia Minor to Persian rule. But Persia was slow to act.

Each satrap in Asia Minor had a policy of his own to carry on, so that the affair took time. Also Sparta prolonged the negotiations, because she could not all at once make up her mind to betray the interests of Greece. The proposal was that Persia should send a Phoenician squadron to assist Sparta, and should provide pay for the crews of the Spartan ships.

Of this delay Athens took advantage. The general despair after the Sicilian disaster had enabled the oligarchs to seize control for a few months and to set up the Council of Four Hundred. But the democratic party soon turned them out and adopted as their watchword 'a fight to a finish', whereas the oligarchs were anxious to stop the war as soon as possible. In the restoration of democracy a leading part was played by the fleet; and the fleet also insisted that Alcibiades should be pardoned. The exile had quarrelled with Sparta and fled to Asia Minor, where he was now trying to hinder the negotiations between Sparta and the Persian magnates. Restoration from exile, a fresh outburst of patriotism at Athens, and the hesitations of Sparta, enabled Alcibiades to gain considerable successes during the next four years. In 410 B.C. he won a great naval victory off Cyzicus and began by degrees to bring pressure on the Spartans and Persians. But a trifling failure incurred by one of his subordinates at Notium in 407 B.C. gave a handle to his enemies at Athens, and they contrived to secure his condemnation in absence. He fled to the coast of Asia Minor and watched from there the course of the war. At the same time an energetic satrap made his appearance in Asia Minor, in the person of Cyrus, younger son of Darius II; and Sparta found in Lysander a skilful, brave, and ambitious general, not inferior in his aptitude for war to Alcibiades himself.

After the expulsion of Alcibiades the Athenians made one more great effort. The chief object of the Spartans and Persians was to seize the north-eastern waters and so to deprive Athens of food-supplies from the Black Sea; they had already driven her from the Anatolian coast and some of the chief Aegean islands. An Athenian fleet was now sent to defend the Hellespont and began with success: the Spartans were defeated at Arginusae in 406 B.C. But the battle was fought during a storm, and many Athenian sailors were drowned. The failure of the generals to rescue their drowning men caused an explosion of anger in the popular assembly at Athens. The generals were deprived of their command, and those of them who had come home were put to death. Such summary justice did not encourage their successors. To this cause among others the Athenians owed their final and decisive defeat, which took place at Aegospotami near the entrance of the Hellespont.

With the fleet the last hope of Athens perished. She was forced to accept the terms of peace dictated by Sparta in 404 B.C. The walls of the Piraeus were levelled, and also the walls connecting the fortifications of the Piraeus with those of Athens; the fleet, with the exception of twelve ships, was destroyed; and Athens was forced to join the Lacedaemonian league, in complete dependence upon Sparta. She continued, however, to exist as an independent state, in spite of the persistence with which Megara and Corinth demanded her complete destruction. Sparta even carried her magnanimous policy so far that she did not require Athens to retain the oligarchical government set up by Lysander, which was carried on by Critias and the rest of the Thirty Tyrants. When Thrasybulus overthrew the Thirty and restored the democracy, this revolution was quietly accepted by the Spartans.

The fundamental question of Greek politics was thus settled, and settled once for all. Local freedom and self-determination for each state had been bought; and the price paid was the collapse of the one attempt to consolidate Greece into a single political unit. It is true that this attempt was based on the ascendancy of one state over all the rest. We shall see later that Greece endeavoured to settle the question of national unity by resorting to federation. But by that time the existence of an independent Greek power, based upon an association of free city-states, was altogether out of the question.

XI

GREEK CIVILIZATION AND SOCIAL
DEVELOPMENT FROM 500 TO 400 B.C.

After the defeat of Persia by Athens and Sparta, Athens became
the chief political power in the Greek world, especially in central Greece, the islands, and Asia Minor; and to her also fell the
leadership in economic development and in culture. In these
departments, Sparta had neither the power nor the wish to rival
her, and Asia Minor was entirely dependent upon her. The
Greeks in Italy and Sicily still kept their economic and cultural
importance but such outposts of Hellas had little influence on
the life of those Greeks who lived round the Aegean. Athens, on
the other hand, had acquired not only great political influence
but a still greater moral authority. Greece recognized that
Athenian persistence and patriotism had saved her, when the
whole nation was threatened with the fate of the Ionian Greeks.
For this reason Athens and all her doings were now watched
with intense interest by the whole nation.

Life at Athens itself underwent radical changes. The city had
become the capital of Hellas, and the citizens were conscious of
this. Perhaps the growth of the city itself is the most obvious
proof of this change in the position of Athens. In the sixth century B.C. the city, though large, had grown up irregularly; its religious centre was on the Acropolis, which had once been occupied by the fortified palace of the kings and was now consecrated
to Athena, the guardian goddess of Athens, and the site of her

modest temple of local stone. Pisistratus did much for Athens. He built a large and convenient central market, improved the water-supply, erected a stately entrance to the Acropolis and a new central temple to Athena on the same hill. All this was swept away by the Persian invasion. When the city was recovered by its inhabitants, they found it in ruins. From 479 B.C. the work of making good the destruction went busily on. Cimon was conspicuous in this task. He rebuilt the city, particularly the market-place, which served also as an exchange and a social club, and was the place where some political business was transacted. Beside the marketplace, one of his relatives built the famous *Stoa Poecile*, or Painted Colonnade, decorated with paintings, some of them by a celebrated artist, Polygnotus. Of these paintings some represented heroic actions belonging to the legendary past; but others depicted such recent achievements as the battle of Marathon.

The Acropolis, however, still lay in ruins. Pericles, the director and organizer of the Athenian Empire, undertook the task of restoring it. Millions were spent by Athens to turn the Acropolis into one of the most perfect of architectural productions, adorned with a whole museum of masterpieces in stone and in colour. The work was still going on during the Peloponnesian war, at the very time when the shipwreck of Athenian power was drawing near. In realizing his artistic design Pericles was assisted by the architect Ictinus, and by Phidias, the greatest of Greek sculptors. Their intention was to make the Acropolis a splendid dwelling-place for Athena, reigning above the city and symbolizing the power and might of Athens, both as an empire and as the heart of Greek civilization. It was still a fortress at the time of the Persian invasion, but it ceased now to be a fortress; the centre of Athens had no further need of fortifications. On its slopes there were no private houses and no shops; only a few shrines, including that of Asclepius, enlivened the steep sides of the hill. A stately staircase, ending in an elaborate entrance supported on pillars (Propylaea), led up from the plain below. In

1. STATUE FOUND IN THE SEA NEAR CAPE ARTEMISIUM

Plate XIX   ZEUS. SCULPTURE OF THE 5TH CENTURY B.C.

1. The statue found in the sea near Cape Artemisium. The statue, larger than life-size, is an exceptionally well-preserved masterpiece of Greek bronze-casting. It represents a god, Zeus or Poseidon, hurling his (lost) weapon against the enemy. First half of the 5th century B.C. National Museum, Athens.

2. Zeus and Ganymede. This terracotta statue of Zeus and Ganymede originally ornamented a building in Olympia. Zeus, who has descended to earth, carries away Ganymede. The boy clutches at a cock, love-gift of the god. About 470 B.C. Museum, Olympia.

2. ZEUS AND GANYMEDE

one wing of this entrance was a picture-gallery. Over the staircase, on the right-hand side as you went in, there rose on a high bastion the beautiful temple of Athena Nike, the guardian and defender of the Acropolis. The whole surface of the hill was converted into a level terrace, divided by the Sacred Way. Both sides of the Way were lined by a forest of votive offerings dedicated by Athenian citizens to their great goddess, and by the archives of the Athenian democracy—the most important decrees of the popular assembly, engraved on stone. To the right and left of this Way rose the two dwelling-places of Athena.

To the right is the mighty Parthenon, the home of Athena Parthenos, a great Doric temple, with a gabled roof and columns all round it. The east of the building was occupied by the *cella*, the real temple, the dwelling of the goddess; here by the inner wall stood the ivory and gold statue of Athena; two rows of columns divided the *cella* into three aisles. Behind this was a chamber in which the treasures of Athena were kept. The rich sculpture which adorned the temple told the spectator the history of the relations between the goddess and the city. Over the columns, on their outer side, in the metopes (or spaces between the triglyphs) the struggle of civilization against the forces of primeval chaos was unrolled—the Lapithae, the oldest Greek inhabitants of Thessaly, conquering the Centaurs, half-men and half-horses; the Greeks conquering the East personified in the Amazons; and the gods conquering the giants. Of the pediments (or triangular gables at the ends of the temple) one represented the birth of Athena from the head of Zeus, the other the strife between Athena and Poseidon for possession of Athens. Lastly, the famous frieze which ran round the outer wall of the *cella* represents the Pan-Athenaic festival—the annual procession of Athenian citizens to the shrine of the goddess. In life-like groups they move towards the temple—priests and victims for sacrifice, magistrates, maidens carrying the garment newly woven for Athena by Athenian women, reverend elders leaning on their staves, and noble youths riding on thoroughbred horses. A group of gods looks on.

On the other side of the Sacred Way was the Erechtheum, one of the most refined and beautiful examples of the Ionic order of architecture. This second dwelling for Athena was built in the dark days of the Peloponnesian war; it was dedicated to Athena Polias, the protector of the city. This one building united the worship of Poseidon, god of the sea and sea-borne trade and formerly the protector of Athens, with that of Athena, the new mistress of the Athenian Empire, who brought with her the olive-tree to her city. Between the Propylaea and the Erechtheum stood a colossal bronze statue of Athena Promachos (the Champion), the golden gleam of whose spear-point could be seen by sailors approaching Athens from the sea.

Such was the centre of Athens as a great state, unrivalled in Greece. The rest of the city was mean and insignificant by comparison, with its narrow crooked streets, modest houses, shops and workshops, noise, dust, and mud. All the inhabitants lived in more or less identical conditions. Many of the citizens were rich, but they built themselves no luxurious palaces. It was a public scandal when Alcibiades broke the custom and adorned the walls of his house with painting. Athens was a democracy, and the rich were afraid to make themselves conspicuous by display and extravagance. Besides this, the men at Athens did not spend much of their time at home. The market-place; the Pnyx, where the popular assembly met; the law-courts and the council-chamber—these were the places where the higher classes passed their time. The lower classes worked in the docks and warehouses of the Piraeus, or in their shops and workshops. All classes alike devoted their spare time to bodily exercise and games, for the sake of health. For this purpose a number of gymnasiums, wrestling-schools, and paddocks surrounded by colonnades were constructed in the suburbs; and here all the population of Athens, young and old alike, practised running and wrestling,

1. THE ACROPOLIS

Plate XX GREEK ARCHITECTURE

1. The Acropolis. The large temple in the centre is the Parthenon.
To the right is the temple of Nike (the goddess of victory). To the
left of the Parthenon is the Erechtheum.

2. View of the ruins of the Parthenon, the grand creation of Pericles, Ictinus, and Phidias.

3. Two of the famous temples of the Greek city Poseidonia (now
Paestum) in South Italy. Poseidonia was one of the flourishing
Greek cities of Italy in the 6th and 5th centuries B.C. The site was
abandoned in the 9th century A.D. This explains the splendid state
of preservation of the ruins as shown on our illustration, which shows
two of the temples: in the foreground, the so-called temple of Poseidon (in fact, of Hera), with six Doric columns on the fronts and
twelve on the sides, a regular Doric temple; farther off, the oldest
and the largest, the so-called 'Basilica' with nine columns on the
fronts and eighteen on the sides, an excellent example of an early
Doric temple. The 'Basilica' belongs to the early part of the 6th
century B.C.; the temple of Poseidon to the 5th.

2. THE RUINS OF THE PARTHENON

3. TWO OF THE TEMPLES OF THE GREEK CITY POSEIDONIA

1. PART OF THE MARBLE FRIEZE OF THE PARTHENON

Plate XXI GREEK SCULPTURE OF THE
5TH CENTURY B.C. THE GODS

1. Part of the marble frieze of the Parthenon. The whole frieze is
about one metre high and 160 metres long. It shows the procession
of the Panathenaea, the chief festival of the Athenian calendar, in
honour of Athena. The procession consists of young men on horseback and in chariots, of old men, of musicians, of offering-bearers.
The priest assisted by the priestess is folding the beautiful 'peplos'
(garment) of the goddess which has been woven by noble Athenian
women. And finally the gods are watching the majestic procession.
Our section of the frieze represents three of the group of the gods:
Poseidon, Apollo, and Artemis. Whether the frieze was designed by
Phidias and carved under his direction or not is a matter of contro-
versy: certainly it breathes the spirit of Phidian art. About 440 B.C.
Acropolis Museum, Athens.

2. MARBLE RELIEF FOUND AT ATHENS. ATHENA

2. Marble relief found at Athens, representing Athena looking at a
pillar (*meta*) which marked the starting point (and finish) of a
course in sports contests. The goddess seems to ponder over the
choice of the winner in the contest. National Museum, Athens.

Plate XXII GREEK SCULPTURE OF THE
5TH CENTURY B.C. RELIEFS

1.–3. Three marble slabs adorned with reliefs found in the Villa
Ludovisi at Rome. It is still a question to what kind of structure the
slabs belonged. Probably an altar. Equally controversial is the explanation of the figures. A young and beautiful woman is represented
either in a crouching position or emerging from the soil or from the
sea. Two other women are helping her. On the short sides we see a
seated woman placing incense on a thurible, and a naked girl playing
a double flute. Some scholars suggest that the central figure represents Aphrodite emerging from the sea, others think that it is Leto
giving birth to the twins Apollo and Artemis as described in the
Homeric hymn. Another related set of similar reliefs is in the Boston
Museum of Fine Arts. The reliefs of the Villa Ludovisi are a fine
product of Ionian sculpture of the early 5th century, soft and gracious. About 470 B.C. Museo delle Terme, Rome.

1. RELIEF FROM ELEUSIS. DEMETER, TRIPTOLEMUS, KORE

Plate XXIII MYSTIC ELEMENTS IN GREEK RELIGION

1. Relief found at Eleusis, the great centre of the cult of Demeter and of the famous Eleusinian mysteries. The bas-relief shows the gods of the place: Demeter (to the left) gives Triptolemus the corn-ears that he may go out and teach; Kore, the daughter of Demeter, with the Eleusinian torch, puts a crown on the head of Triptolemus. The relief shows the typical features of the great art of Phidias. It is a little earlier than the frieze of the Parthenon (Pl. XXI). Middle of the 5th century B.C. National Museum, Athens.

2. RELIEF FOUND IN ITALY. ORPHEUS AND EURYDICE

2. Relief found in Italy. Orpheus, the mythical hero of the Orphic mysteries, came down to Hades to rescue his bride Eurydice. Having charmed the rulers of Hades by his music, he received permission to take her back to life, on condition that he lead her back without looking at her. He did not fulfil his promise, and Hermes is gently taking the poor young bride back to the nether world. The great mystery of life and death was the main point in the teaching of the Orphics. A copy, made in Roman times, of an Attic work of the late 5th century B.C. Naples Museum.

played ball, and threw the quoit and the javelin, and then plunged into the cold water of the pools which formed part of these establishments. Here, too, the education compulsory for every young Athenian was carried on. The boys were trained for war and for competition in the local and Pan-hellenic games; they also learned reading and writing, and elementary mathematics, but their chief study was music, singing, and the reading of literary masterpieces, especially the poems of Homer.

Women did not play that part in the life of Athens in the fifth century which they had played when Greece and Ionia were ruled by aristocracies, and which they still played in Sparta. The time of their political influence, of their importance in public life, and of their literary activity had gone by. As late as the beginning of the fifth century, Elpinice, the sister of Cimon, exercised considerable influence on Athenian politics; but in the age of Pericles, Aspasia, with her personal ascendancy over that great Athenian, was an exception. Democracy banished women from the street to the house: the kitchen and the nursery, and the *gynaeceum*, a special part of the house reserved for women and children, now became their sphere.

During this century the two unenfranchised classes, the *metoeci* or resident aliens and the slaves, steadily increased in numbers and became more prominent in social life. The former class was deliberately attracted to the city by the political leaders. The citizens themselves were too busy with agriculture and public affairs to give much time to trade and manufacture. Therefore the aliens, who had no other occupation or interest except commercial affairs, became the instrument which, more than anything else, created the extraordinary economic development of Athens in this century. They controlled the merchant-ships of Athens, the banks, now an important feature in financial life, and the large factories. They suffered under one disability: they might not own land within the bounds of Attica. Although liable for military service, they had no political rights. They did not constitute a class by themselves: in society no distinction was made between an alien and a citizen.

Another notable feature of fifth-century Athens is the rise of slaves, if not in legal status, at least in social and economic importance. The industrial activity of an Athenian citizen was based upon slave labour. If he owned a factory, the power that ran it was his confidential slave who directed the workmen; and some of the workmen also were slaves. If he was a trader, a slave was his right hand. If he owned a bank, all the business was managed by slaves and freedmen. There were, no doubt, other slaves of lower rank, mere outcasts and beasts of burden, like those who perished by hundreds in the silver-mines of Laureion, spending whole years in hard labour. But such slaves were not visible at Athens. Those employed in trade and manufacture lived in the same way as the rest of the population. Many of these forced themselves to the front as dexterous men of business and eventually received their freedom. An Athenian conservative of this century, in the course of a malignant pamphlet directed against Athenian democracy, notes with good reason that it is impossible to distinguish slaves and aliens from citizens in the streets and squares of Athens, because all classes dress alike and live in the same way.

Such was the city of Athens, the pulse of Athenian life. But the city must not make us lose sight of the country; for there the majority of Athenian citizens were to be found. After the time of Solon and Pisistratus the country came into favour again. In the demes of Attica, in farms scattered over hill and valley, in the forests that clothed the mountains, thousands of citizens spent their lives—small landowners, husbandmen, vine-dressers, olive-growers, shepherds, and charcoal-burners. They had no liking for the city and were a little afraid of it. But they were devoted with all their heart to their country, and came in their thousands, when they were needed, to the popular assembly. The existence of this class explains the fact that the Athenian state, in spite of its democratic constitution and boldness in speculation, never ceased to be, on the whole, conservative and devoted to the past.

But the most remarkable change at Athens in this century was in the region of the intellect. Among the poets and thinkers of the previous century Solon is the one Athenian citizen who finds a place. Now things are entirely different: the majority of prominent thinkers and writers are either Athenians or, if citizens of other states, live at Athens. In Asia Minor a few representatives of the fountain-head of Greek philosophy are still at work—Heraclitus, for instance, the first to understand and appreciate the importance of motion in the universe, as well as Leucippus of Miletus and Democritus of Abdera, who founded the Atomistic School. But Anaxagoras, a native of Clazomenae in Asia Minor, lived and worked at Athens. In the West also a group of philosophers was busy; but Empedocles of Acragas, who carried on the Eleatic philosophy, invented the theory of four elements and taught evolution and the survival of the fittest, found no successors in his native country: it was at Athens that Anaxagoras supplemented the theory of elements by introducing Mind (Nous) as the cause of evolution of an infinite variety of 'seeds'.

These examples show how quickly the intellectual centre of gravity was shifted to Athens. The conditions were favourable. Athens opened up opportunities, unequalled elsewhere, for original genius. Nowhere else was there such perfect freedom of thought and speech; nowhere else did men take such a keen interest in every novelty. The democracy, indeed, insisted on its right to dispose of the persons and lives of the citizens, when this was demanded by the interests of the state. A law passed in the popular assembly was all-powerful. Democracy feared too influential leaders of the strong minority as a possible source of revolutions; therefore it removed them by the device known as ostracism, and sentenced them to exile without disgrace. But with the private life and pursuits of the citizen, with his thoughts and words, democracy did not interfere but suffered each man to live as he chose.

In religious matters the Athenians were more conservative. While leaving men free to speak and think as they pleased, they were jealous in maintaining the ancient traditions in religion. Socrates, as we shall see later, fell a victim to this conservative feeling. Religion consisted chiefly in certain rites, and these rites were a special object of veneration to the Athenian citizen. Hence the people resented outspoken attacks on the gods and their worship; and Anaxagoras, charged with impiety, had to leave his adopted country and depart into exile. But when attempts were made to spiritualize and purify religion, and when a tendency towards monotheism, such as we see in the plays of Aeschylus, began to develop, the popular reception of these changes was attentive and respectful. There is no doubt indeed that the drama raised the religious conceptions of the people to a much higher level. The Eleusinian Mysteries, also, rise higher and higher in reputation and just at this period become closely connected with Orphic rites.

Such were the surroundings of those marvellous achievements in intellect and art which permeated Athenian life of the fifth century B.C. and at once became standards of perfection for all Greeks. Tragedy ranks among the highest creations of Greek genius in this age. Aeschylus, as I have said already, was its creator. In the dialogue between the chorus and the narrator he introduced a second narrator, and this apparently trifling change in the mechanism of the drama, this introduction of a second actor, made it possible to convert the ritual acting at the festival of Dionysus into real drama and real tragedy, the same, in its essential features, as the tragedy of our own stage. The dialogue between the actors, divided up by songs from the chorus, enabled Aeschylus to thrill the spectator with pictures of the intense passions that fill the heart of man, while he supplemented these in the choric songs with his own feelings and reflections. The plots of his plays were almost all taken from

1. SOPHOCLES   2. EURIPIDES

Plate XXIV   GREAT MEN OF 5TH-CENTURY ATHENS

1. and 2. Sophocles and Euripides. Bronze statues of three great tragedians were erected in the theatre of Athens, built about 330 B.C. Roman marble copies of statues or busts of Sophocles and Euripides (but not of Aeschylus as yet) have been identified. Made three generations after the death of both poets (in 406 B.C.), the statues in the theatre were not portraits in our sense, but ideal images of the authors of two different kinds of tragedy. The statue of Sophocles, now in the Lateran Museum, Rome, was unfortunately modified by a modern restoration. The bust of Euripides (nose restored) is in the Naples Museum.

3. THUCYDIDES

4. SOCRATES

3. Bust of Thucydides, the first scholar-historian, who wrote the history of the Peloponnesian war. The bust may be a copy of a contemporary portrait of Thucydides. The face is individual, not typical. Holkham Hall, England.

4. A charming statuette of the great philosopher Socrates. The long beard, the nose and the square head are typical of the portraits of Socrates. The statuette is probably a work of the early Hellenistic period, inspired, of course, by earlier portraits. British Museum.

mythology and not from actual life. But mythology offered such an endless variety of vivid stories in the lives of gods and heroes, that it was not difficult to get from these stories material for human drama. His plays, and those of his successors, were arranged in trilogies: that is, he produced three plays together on one subject, and also a satyr-play, a parody of tragedy, to end up with; but each of the three had to be complete in itself, while the connexion between them was maintained by the identity of the dramatis personae. Aeschylus wrote a great number of tragedies, perhaps as many as ninety. Seven have been preserved, and they include one trilogy, the *Oresteia*—the tremendous story of a son's vengeance on his mother for the murder of his father, and of the son's tortured conscience and final purification. The *Persians* is an exception to the rule: the subject was taken from recent history—from the Persian war, in which Aeschylus himself had taken an active part and fought in the ranks at Marathon. In the general opinion of antiquity, with which modern criticism entirely agrees, Aeschylus, from the artistic point of view, not merely created the tragic drama but also wrote tragedies whose perfection has never been surpassed either in ancient or in modern times.

Sophocles was a younger contemporary. The number of his plays was even greater—the titles of 111 are known to us—but only seven, with half of one satyr-drama, have been preserved. Three are connected by a common subject, being taken from the story of the royal house at Thebes—*Oedipus the King, Oedipus at Colonus,* and *Antigone;* but each of these is complete in itself and describes a separate series of events. Last comes Euripides, a younger contemporary and rival of Sophocles, and the author of 75 tragedies, of which 19 have survived. Though not enjoying much success in his lifetime, he became the idol of later generations and of Roman readers.

Athenian drama is astonishing for its literary perfection: the language is copious and richly coloured; the imagery is infinitely various, sublime, and beautiful; the metrical skill and the power of construction are altogether exceptional. But its chief importance is distinct from these excellences, and lies in this—that in it for the first time men saw their own hearts held up before them by the poet, and saw the process of conflict in that heart—conflict with itself, with circumstance, with society and government, with the laws of God and man. For all that, Athenian tragedy is practical and draws its inspiration from contemporary life and circumstances; it does not eschew politics, it takes a side in the settlement of many social problems. It is hard to convey in a few words all the wealth contained in Greek tragedy of the fifth century B.C, and no less hard to indicate the difference between the three equally great tragedians. For the historian of Athenian culture it is sufficient to point out that the appearance of this form of art gave rise to an entire revolution in the minds of those who first witnessed it: they carried with them from the theatre a whole world of new conceptions and ideas; they learned to look deeper into their own hearts and to bear themselves differently towards the inner life of their neighbours.

Comedy also exercised a strong influence upon the Athenians. Later in development than tragedy, and owing much to tragedy, it was the work mainly of Eupolis, Cratinus, and Aristophanes. The last alone is known to us; he lived during the Peloponnesian war and wrote forty-four comedies, of which eleven are preserved. Comedy did not touch mythological subjects, but drew its matter from the medley of passing events. It pays no attention to the experiences of the human heart. It passes judgement on topics of the day, or even of the hour, in a fanciful and highly comic spirit. The emancipation of women and their position, the teaching of Socrates and the Sophists, the question of war or peace, the personality of this or that statesman, theatrical innovations—such are the topics brought upon the stage for discussion and for mockery of the most merciless and outspoken nature. Comedy was a kind of chair for political and social deliverances, from which the author chats with the citizens and holds up to ridicule whatever seems to him to deserve laughter—laughter which is sometimes gay, sometimes sharp and even cruel, but always outspoken.

These same questions of morals, politics, and social life, which were raised by tragedy and comedy in a poetical and artistic form, were also forced upon the Athenians in their daily life. They passed laws in the popular assembly, they prepared bills in the council, they judged suits in the law-courts. On the vote of any individual might hang the life or death of the foremost and best of his fellow-citizens. Each individual had to vote on complicated political issues—issues that often affected the very existence of the state. Each decision evoked criticism and ridicule, and often hatred and ill-feeling; and no citizen could escape his share of responsibility. It is clear that the majority, in the assembly and the law-court, wished to vote according to their conscience. Often they were required to justify their opinion before an audience. But there was no preparatory training for these responsible duties. The professional politician was still unknown. Hence the average citizen sought guidance and felt the necessity of political education; he was often conscious of his own helplessness. He began to demand teachers who should instruct him how to reason, to think, and to speak. And such teachers were forthcoming.

Some of these were themselves seekers after truth and gave light to others merely by the way, while others made a profession of their teaching. The name of 'sophists' was given to both classes by the Athenians. The sophists were willing to teach all comers how to think and reason, how to speak and write. The most original thinkers, the most powerful reasoners, the most lucid and eloquent speakers, got the greatest reputation and attracted the largest classes. In natural sciences they took little interest: they concentrated their study on man, society, and the state; and they approached these topics with an open mind and with no ready-made solution of difficulties. 'Man', they said, 'is the measure of all things', meaning by 'man', human reason. That which seems to us to be truth and which convinces others is discovered by a process of logical reasoning; hence the most important thing is, to be able to think and argue logically, or, in a word, to convince others. Such was the general tendency of thought among the sophists; but it is hard to indicate any detailed instruction in which they all agreed. They were not a school of philosophers, though a succession of philosophic schools took rise later from their activities. One thing they had in common: they all sought plausible answers to troublesome questions. They sought these answers in different directions and by different paths; but these paths were always the paths of logic and dialectics, and the answers were never laid down as dogmas. And, lastly, their chief interest was in political and social questions; they deserve to be called the fathers of sociology and political science. We know that Protagoras, one of the most famous sophists, first discussed the origin of society and the state, and tried to settle the problem by logic. Another, Hippodamus of Miletus, was the first thinker who constructed a purely ideal state and society. He was a mathematician and engineer who invented a method of laying out a city in squares somewhat like the squares of a chessboard—a method which he put in practice when the Piraeus, the harbour of Athens, was rebuilt. Other sophists worked on similar lines: thus Thrasymachus preached that the strongest and best have a right to power, and there were also defenders of communism and anarchism. One fundamental notion pervaded all their teaching—that the part of human life determined by nature is natural and therefore indispensable, but the part created by man himself is conventional and transitory. This notion is very clearly expressed in the fragments of a treatise *On Truth,* by the sophist Antiphon, a contemporary of Aristophanes, and the butt for many of his bitterest sarcasms; his philosophy, founded on the atheism of Democritus, was purely materialistic.

In the second half of the fifth century a figure of extraordinary originality and power towers over the sophists. This is Socrates.

Socrates was not a professional teacher: he was a seeker after truth. Wherever Athenians gathered together, there he was to be found day after day, and there he started endless discussions on the main problems of life and conduct. He began by refuting with the edge of his logic the answers given to his questions by those present; and he prepared the ground for a reasonable and accurate solution by the way in which he raised each problem and by his preliminary objections. Thus he reached by degrees a position from which he could define the chief conceptions of the human mind: he asked, what is virtue? what is beauty? what is justice?—and so on. We do not know what his positive teaching really was: our sources are meagre and inconsistent. These sources are the *Memorabilia* of Xenophon and the series of *Dialogues* by Plato; both were pupils of Socrates. Xenophon was a man of moderate ability and slight philosophic training, Plato one of the greatest thinkers in the world's history; and it is difficult to reconcile their statements. There was much in the teaching of Socrates which Xenophon did not understand; and Plato may have attributed his own doctrines to his teacher. Still we must suppose that the immense influence of Socrates upon all later speculation, and the fact that all subsequent philosophic schools traced their descent from him, prove one thing—that he imported some new element into philosophy which caught the attention of all contemporary thinkers. It appears that this novelty was partly the predominant importance which Socrates attached to man, and the soul and conscious self of man, and partly the enthusiasm with which he called on men to 'know themselves' and so to lead better lives both as individuals and members of associations, including the chief association, i.e. the state. Socrates had no definite political views and was not an opponent of democracy; but he saw its weaknesses clearly, especially its entire failure to train the citizens for the business of government; and he urged them to increase their knowledge and develop their reasoning faculties. Nor was he an atheist: he believed in the gods and habitually made offerings to them; and he felt the presence of a divine being, his *daimon*, within his own breast. His religious belief was, like that of Aeschylus, the belief in a superior being and ruler of the world. But there was something irritating and provoking in the mission of Socrates. There were few citizens to whom he had not proved how little they knew, how badly they reasoned, and how ill-founded were their most cherished opinions. It is therefore not surprising that the conservative Aristophanes attacked him fiercely in one of his comedies, and that an accuser named Anytus was found to prosecute him for 'disbelief in the gods recognized by the State, and for corrupting the young'. And we can understand how the Athenians were glad to rid themselves of this 'gadfly' and coolly condemned him to death, though he had honestly performed all the duties of a citizen.

Thirst for knowledge and pursuit of truth created also in men's minds a lively interest in the past. Every Athenian wished to know the events of the recent past and the Persian invasion, and to understand how Greece had been able to cope with that danger. We have seen that the Ionian thinkers took some interest in past history, and that some writers had already appeared in Asia Minor who collected facts about the history of the Anatolian Greeks and the Eastern nations who lived near them. No wonder then that Herodotus, one of those Asiatic Greeks and a native of Halicarnassus, a partly Carian and partly Dorian city, undertook to relate to the Athenians the history of the Persian wars. He had migrated to Athens and, as an Athenian citizen, took part with other Athenians in founding the colony of Thurii in Italy. Well read in the historical literature of the Ionians, he was himself a great traveller. He visited Egypt and Babylonia; he knew Asia Minor well; he may have paid a short visit to Olbia, at the mouths of the Dnieper and the Bug. In every country his unbounded curiosity led him to visit historic places with their monuments of hoary antiquity; he collected the tales told by the natives in explanation of these monuments; he had an eye for the manners and customs of the inhabitants and the characteristics of the country. With even greater enthusiasm he questioned at Athens those who had themselves taken an active share in the Persian wars, and those whose fathers and grandfathers had been concerned in the events which led up to the Persian invasion. He studied the monuments connected with that invasion, and collected the tales and legends that had grown up around them. He had especial pleasure in conversing with priests and drew much material from the lips of the priests at Delphi. And in this way his great work, his history of the Persian wars, was composed.

He was not content with a dry narrative of events. He wished, above all, to understand the past, and therefore prefixed to his history a sketch of those countries with which the history was in some way connected. His descriptions of Asia Minor, Persia, Babylonia, Egypt, and Scythia are of fascinating interest, although many of his notions concerning the history of those countries have turned out to be incomplete and inaccurate. When he proceeds to the story itself—to the gradual development of strife between Persians and Greeks, the general course of events is accurately stated throughout, though it is stated from the Athenian point of view, because Herodotus had become at Athens an eager partisan of the Athenians. Without Herodotus, the 'father of history', we should know as little of the Persian war as we do of the political history of Greece before that war and in the interval that divides it from the Peloponnesian war. His history was published in 430 B.C. He was the only writer who collected information about the war when those who fought in it were still living; and all later narratives by Greek historians make use of him as their main source.

In details, however, Herodotus is often inaccurate. He paid little attention to the exact chronology of events; he had little understanding of military matters; he describes many places which he had not himself seen. While we are aware of this, we are often unable to correct his errors owing to the lack of other authorities. Often he gives us a purely personal impression of incidents; and here, too, it is difficult to correct him. At times he lends too ready an ear to marvels and legends. But he generally recognizes how shaky the foundations of historical knowledge sometimes are. When he meets with different versions of the same incident, he is helpless; for the methods of historical criticism were unkown to him. But we are grateful to him for this, that in such cases he hands down all the versions known to him, leaving the reader to choose among them. A place of honour belongs to Herodotus in the history of mankind and of Greek civilization. He is truly the 'father of history'. He was the first to treat history, not as a collection of interesting stories about gods and men, but as the object of scientific investigation.

That the next Greek historian, Thucydides, should approach his task from a different standpoint is natural enough. An Athenian, born and brought up in the atmosphere of the fifth century at Athens, he had seen the tragedies of the three great dramatists on the stage, had listened to the sophists and may have met Socrates himself, had taken an active part in public life, and served as one of the generals in the Peloponnesian war. He witnessed that war from beginning to end, and survived it all with its successes and failures. On him, as on all the best Athenians, the defeat of Athens left a profound impression; and he laid upon himself the task of telling to present and future times the whole truth about the war, as he saw it and as he understood it. He possessed abundant and excellent material, which his knowledge of affairs and war enabled him to turn to account. When Amphipolis was seized by the Spartans in 424 B.C., he was in command in the north of Greece, and suffered banishment in consequence of his failure. But exile enabled him to become better acquainted with the antagonists of Athens, to understand their mental attitude, and to appreciate their points of superiority. Such was the material and such the experience he possessed, when he undertook the work of an historian, and determined, not merely to describe, but also to explain the Peloponnesian war.

For this purpose he had, first of all, to collect the ascertained facts in their exact chronological sequence. That was no easy task: passion burned too fiercely on each side, and the historical facts, framed in their proper environment, came home too closely to the hearts of both peoples. But Thucydides faced the problem of representing the facts in their reality, and of stripping off the wrappings in which they were disguised. And he did this with extraordinary precision, following scientific rule and applying all those methods which we call historical criticism. If he was not the father of history in general, he was at least the father of critical history and the first of all who have written the history of their own times. But even more must be said. In his eyes the facts were only a means; the end was to throw light on them and explain them, and the explanation was not to be theological, like many of the explanations in Herodotus, but based upon rationalism and logic. To establish the causal connexion between events was the supreme object of Thucydides. His whole exposition aims at discovering causes —causes as distinct from motives—and proceeds by a strictly logical method, with no concessions to feeling or belief. While engaged in this work Thucydides realized the part played in history by personality, and also its occasional helplessness in the face of economic and social movements. He understood the 'psychology of the herd' and the mighty part it has played in history; and he understood much else, reaching a height to which many modern historians aspire in vain. Thucydides was in history what Aeschylus was in tragedy. Once again Athens had produced a man who was not merely a pioneer in a new and important branch of human creation, but actually approached perfection in that sphere. The ancient world never produced a second historian of equal genius and scientific insight; and he has few rivals among historians of our own day and of the recent past.

What we observe in the development of the drama, of historical inquiry and historical narrative, and in the sphere of

Fig. 17. Red-figured cup found at Vulci (Italy). The picture represents an Athenian foundry. To the left the stove, to the right smiths working on a bronze statue, on the walls various instruments and the products of the shop. Attic work of about 480 B.C. Berlin Museum. After Furtwängler-Reichhold.

philosophy and rhetoric, is equally noticeable in the history of the plastic arts, and especially of sculpture. The history of painting is more obscure, because we possess no direct copies of the great decorative and easel paintings, and can only judge of them by the imitations on purely decorative vases, where the artist has to take account of the nature and proportions of the object decorated, and, in general, to restrict himself to two colours, red and black; and we can learn something from the influence exercised by painting upon sculpture. It follows that Polygnotus and the other great painters of the fifth century are still to us mysterious figures. About sculpture we have much fuller information: in the Parthenon sculptures we possess a number of original works by great masters; we have also a multitude of later copies, more or less exact, taken from the great statues of the fifth century, and contemporary reproductions of those statues in small bronzes, terra-cottas, and coins.

By the end of the sixth century B.C., side by side with the

1. BRONZE HEAD OF A CHARIOTEER   2. SEATED GODDESS

Plate XXV   SCULPTURE OF THE
5th AND 4th CENTURIES B.C.

1. Head of bronze statue found at Delphi. The statue belonged originally to a group which, according to the inscription, was dedicated at Delphi by Polyzalos, the ruler of Gela in Sicily, brother of the rulers of Syracuse, Gelon and Hieron. The dedication took place probably in 474 B.C. in memory of a victory in racing. The group represented a chariot drawn by four horses. The head is that of the charioteer. It is a magnificent piece of work, still a little archaic in its supreme simplicity. Probably a work of one of the sculptors of the Peloponnese or of Aegina. 474 B.C. Delphi Museum.

2. Marble statue of a seated goddess of West-Ionian workmanship. It is a beautiful work of mature archaic sculpture, elaborate in details and splendid in its general conception. Early 5th century B.C. (time of the Persian wars). Museum, Berlin.

3. APOLLO   4. HERMES OF PRAXITELES

3. Marble statue of Apollo from the west pediment of the temple of Zeus at Olympia. The sculptures of this pediment represent the fight between men (Lapiths) directed and helped by heroes (Pirithous and Theseus) and the Centaurs, representing the elemental forces of nature. Apollo stands in the centre and dominates the pediment sculptures by his beautiful, majestic figure. He is helping the Lapiths and represents the forces of civilization and order. About 460 B.C. Museum, Olympia.

4. Hermes, by Praxiteles, the greatest Athenian sculptor of the 4th century B.C. The statue was found at Olympia in the temple of Hera, where it was seen by the writer Pausanias, who, in the time of the emperor Marcus Aurelius, compiled a description of Greece. The statue represents Hermes playing with the infant Dionysus. It is one of the few original statues by great Greek masters which have remained to us. For the art of Praxiteles see the text. Museum, Olympia.

Ionian schools of sculpture, independent schools were growing up in Greece proper and in Italy. The rapid development, technical and artistic, of sculpture is proved by many remains—from Aegina, from the temple of Zeus at Olympia, from the ornament of various treasuries of Greek states at Delphi, and from the decoration of Italian and Sicilian temples, especially at Selinus; step by step it cast off the conventionality that marks Ionian sculpture of the sixth century, and the heavy solidity of the archaic period in general. Nowhere was this development so rapid as in Athens after the Persian wars. Till then Athenian sculpture had been merely a branch of Ionian art; but now it discarded Ionian influence altogether, and the work of Athenian sculptors became free and independent. The advance went on with dizzy speed, and at the head of it stood Myron, with his statues of gods and athletes. It reached its zenith in the person of Phidias, the greatest sculptor of this century, who worked under the direction of Pericles and adorned Olympia and other centres of Greek civilization as well as Athens. His most famous statues were the Athena in the Parthenon and the Zeus at Olympia, both chryselephantine—that is, the head, hands, and feet, with the dress, were made of gold and ivory, and the remainder of wood. Polycleitus was a younger contemporary of Phidias; his statues of athletes, like the statues of gods by Phidias, set the standard at once; and his Hera at Argos was ranked with the Zeus at Olympia.

The essential features of this new Greek art are these: complete victory of the artist over his material and the technical difficulties which hampered him earlier; the endeavour to idealize the human body, not by copying nature nor by correcting it, but by searching out in nature that which is most perfect and nearest to the ideal which has formed itself in the artist's mind; and, lastly, the skill to embody in statuary ideas cherished by the artist, especially the idea of divine majesty and divine power. These sculptors are familiar with nature: they have studied it thoroughly; they have mastered the anatomy of the human body;

Fig. 18. Red-figured water-pot (hydria) found at Ruvo in South Italy. The picture represents a potter's workshop with workmen (three boys and one girl) painting vases of various shapes. Athena is bringing a crown to the best painter. Victories are crowning the other two boys. The poor girl got no prize. Attic work of the middle of the 5th century B.C. Ruvo, Caputi Collection. After Perrot and Chipiez.

they understand the beauty of drapery flowing down in various folds; they can harmonize the lines of the body with the lines of the drapery. But they do not copy nature slavishly. Their athletes, for example, are unsurpassed in the representation of the nude male body. The Discobolus of Myron embodies all the strength and beauty and life of the youthful frame at the moment of its most intense physical exertion. In the bronze charioteer from Delphi we admire the severe stateliness of the youth who stands at his ease, wearing the long garment that falls down in straight folds. Still more perfect is the sculpture on the pediments and frieze of the Parthenon. It may not have been carved by Phidias himself, but it was certainly carved under his direction and by his pupils.

Phidias surpassed himself in his representation of the supreme deities. We possess only poor copies of these statues, and must trust the judgement of the Greeks and Romans who saw the originals. Their evidence testifies to the ineffaceable impression, both artistic and religious, produced by these masterpieces. The Zeus of Phidias was the same omnipotent father of gods and men, terrible and also gracious, the same ruler of human destiny,

Plate XXVI   GREEK ART OF THE 4TH CENTURY B.C.

1. The grave-stele of a noble Athenian lady, Hegeso. She is seated in all her Phidian beauty in a chair; before her is her maid with her jewel-box. Late 4th century B.C. Cemetery of the Ceramicus, Athens.

2. The bas-relief of Dexilaos. The burial ground before the double gate (*Dipylon*) which led to the potters' quarter (Ceramicus) in Athens was in use from the 8th century B.C. on. At the beginning of the 4th century, the rich obtained family plots here. High terraces were built upon which memorial monuments were placed. The tombstone of Dexilaos stood in the middle of such a terrace which belonged to the family of a certain Lysanias. As the inscription under the relief states, Dexilaos, at the age of twenty, fell in 394 B.C. at

3. FIGHT BETWEEN AMAZONS AND GREEKS

Corinth, one of the five Athenian 'knights' lost in this battle. However, he is represented as striking the vanquished enemy. The relief on the restored terrace still stands over his grave in the Ceramicus at Athens.

3. One of the slabs of the sculptured friezes on the monument of Mausolus of Caria. The two friezes, one representing the fight of the Amazons and the Greeks and the other the fight of the Centaurs and Lapiths, probably adorned the massive base of the monument, while a third frieze—a chariot race—ran above the columns. The sculptures were the work of the most famous Greek sculptors of the 4th century: Scopas and Leochares, Timotheus and Bryaxis. It is possible that the passionate fight of Greeks and Amazons on our slab is the work of Scopas. British Museum.

1. RED-FIGURED CUP BY DURIS. ATHENIAN SCHOOL

Plate XXVII POTTERY OF THE 5TH CENTURY B.C.

1. Red-figured cup by the painter Duris. It represents an Athenian school of the 5th century B.C. The boys are being taught music (lyre and flute), Greek literature, writing. Attic work of about 480 B.C. Berlin Museum. After Furtwängler-Reichhold.

2. RED-FIGURED CUP. HERACLES AND DIONYSUS

2. Red-figured cup. On one side Dionysus is represented seated on a couch watching a Satyr dancing. On the other Dionysus and Heracles, the god of ecstasy and the god of duty, are having a banquet together. Two Satyrs are acting as servants; one has just stolen a cake from the table. The picture illustrates the worship of the two great gods of the Greek religion who had originally been men. The painter has probably taken his inspiration from the so-called Satyr drama, a comic performance ridiculing divine beings. Attic work of about 470 B.C. British Museum.

1. A POLYCHROME ATTIC LEKYTHOS. GRAVE OF AN EPHEBUS

2. AN ATHENIAN LEKYTHOS. CHARON, HERMES, AND THE DEAD

Plate XXVIII GREEK PAINTING. POLYCHROME VASES OF THE 5TH AND 4TH CENTURIES

1. One of the most beautiful lekythoi (grave-vases) with polychrome painting on white ground. The picture represents the grave-stele and the grave-tumulus (behind the stele) of a young Athenian. On the

3. RED-FIGURED VASE (LEKANIS). DECKING OF A BRIDE

tumulus, green branches; on the stele, a 'taenia' (ribbon); on the steps of the base of the stele, offerings of wreaths and oil-flasks. Before the stele stands the deceased in the dress of an ephebus, while a girl brings grave-offerings in a basket. The style makes one think of Phidias. Attic work of about 440 B.C. National Museum, Athens. After Riezler.

2. An Athenian lekythos. The picture shows Charon, the ferryman of the nether world, receiving a dead woman from the hands of Hermes, 'the leader of the souls' (Psychopompus). The little winged beings in the air are souls. Attic work of about 450 B.C. National Museum, Athens. After Riezler.

3. A red-figured vase (lekanis). The subject of the picture is the decking of a bride. The bride is represented among her girl-friends. She is receiving various gifts and being dressed for the wedding ceremony. Various religious rites preliminary to the wedding are being performed by her friends. Little Loves flying and running among the girls give the significance of the scene. Attic work of the middle of the 4th century B.C. Gold and white are extensively used. Museum of the Hermitage, Petrograd. After Furtwängler-Reichhold.

whom we find in the poetry of Aeschylus. The head alone is poorly reproduced on coins of Elis; but even this conveys that impression of divinity which we feel also in reading the tragedies.

As in the sixth century, art was not confined to the temples and public resorts of the city: it permeated the whole life of a Greek. This fact is proved to us most distinctly for that period by Greek vases. In that century the supremacy of Athens in the manufacture of pottery was virtually undisputed: her vases are found everywhere—in Egypt, Italy, Sicily, the south of France and Spain, the Black Sea coast, and even in the capital of the Persian Empire. Black figures on a red background had now given way to red figures on a black background. These vases represent the highest point ever attained in this branch of decorative art: many of them are really great artistic productions, for the grace and variety of their shapes, and for the decoration, in which the drawing is severe, exact, and extraordinarily rich, and the grouping of figures in scenes taken from the life of gods and men quite masterly. Like contemporary drama and contemporary sculpture, the vases reflect every phase of Athenian life. Even politics are not excluded: there are many drawings by the great vase-painters of this age which can only be explained thus; for instance, the marriage of Theseus with the sea typifies the maritime imperialism of Athens, and scenes from the life of Jason refer to Athenian aspirations in the region of the Black Sea.

A special group of Attic vases was not satisfied with the combination of two colours only, black and red. These are the *lekythoi*, tall, slim funereal vessels, and also some vases in the shape of men, animals, and mythical creatures. In the former, the figures, in rich combinations, are painted in natural colours on a white ground; while the vases shaped like the deities and mythical beings of the next world are covered all over with soft and brilliant colouring. From these vessels we get some idea of the painter's art in the fifth century, both in easel-pictures and in decorative work.

XII

GREECE IN THE FOURTH CENTURY B.C.

The Peloponnesian war ended in a victory for the decentralizing forces in Greece; but that victory was not complete or decisive. When Athens was crippled and the Athenian Empire destroyed, competitors for the succession put in an appearance, one after another; and even the Athenians themselves considered that their defeat was not final and that their dreams of restoring the empire might yet be realized. Though Sparta had issued from the war victorious, properly speaking, there was no real conqueror. All the partakers in the strife were weakened; all were confronted by sore points and difficult problems in domestic and foreign policy; and Sparta, in her new part as queen of the seas, had to face more trouble and responsibility than other states. Greece expected ₁of her that she should restore order and tranquillity at sea as well as on land. But this needed men and money, because force alone could maintain order. She was obliged to adopt Athenian policy without possessing Athenian resources. During the war Persia had acted as paymaster; but her money was not given for nothing, and now she sent in the bill: she demanded the restoration of the cities in Asia Minor which had formerly belonged to her.

Persia was still a powerful, wealthy, and well organized empire. It is true that her reputation had suffered greatly from her failure in Greece. Further, a strong detachment of Greeks had fought for Cyrus in his struggle against his elder brother, Artaxerxes, for the succession in 401 B.C., and had succeeded in retreating from Babylonia after the defeat of Cyrus. This retreat was described by the Athenian, Xenophon; and the whole episode demonstrated afresh to the Greeks their superiority to the Persians in tactics and strategy. Yet the situation remained essentially unchanged. Greece was crippled and split up and torn by mutual hatred between the states; Persia was still a very rich country with a powerful army, and well acquainted with the state of affairs in Greece. In an armed conflict Greece would have no chance at all; but the Persians had changed their tactics since the time of Marathon and Salamis. They were convinced that a steady stream of their gold would break up Greece more and more, until any form of national union would be impossible, and Persia, without having recourse to a fresh campaign, would find it easy to reduce Greece to the position of dependent vassal.

So Persia made her first move at the end of the Peloponnesian war. Sparta, constrained by public opinion and conscious that further demands from the same quarter were inevitable, was not inclined to surrender the Greek cities in Asia Minor. This made war certain, and war in Asia, not in Greece, offensive war on the side of Sparta, and defensive on the side of Persia. At one time, Sparta and especially Agesilaus, her able king and general, dreamed of a national war waged by all Greece against her old enemy, and of decisive victory in the struggle. But that dream remained a dream. Not even the ruthless measures taken by Lysander, when he kept garrisons and military governors in all the chief cities, could weld Greece together. Persian gold did its work, and when Sparta in 395–394 B.C. made the first serious effort to attack Persia, she was soon forced to give up operations in Asia for the defence of her own military supremacy in Greece. For at this time, 394–391 B.C., the Athenians rebuilt their walls and refortified their harbour, while the vassals of Sparta, profiting by the absence of her forces in Asia, were planning and carrying out new and, in some cases, very surprising alliances, which involved a rearrangement of forces among the city-states.

Sparta was obliged to make concessions which amounted to capitulation. Her supremacy in Greece was secured; but the price paid for that security was the freedom of the Greek cities in Asia Minor. It must be said that these cities shed few tears at their restoration to Persia, since it promised them great commercial advantages at the loss of political independence: they had never enjoyed either under Athens or under Sparta. The conditions of the treaty concluded with Persia in 386 B.C. by the Spartan ephor Antalcidas, are notable: the Persian king, like Flamininus the Roman general and the emperor Nero in later times, bestowed freedom on all Greek communities, except the cities in Asia, which became subject to Persia, and except the islands of Lemnos, Imbros, and Scyros, which remained in the possession of Athens; rigorous war was declared against all who refused to submit to this settlement. The treaty did not touch the supremacy of Sparta; for it did not forbid pacts and alliances between individual states, such as formed the legal basis of that supremacy.

Meanwhile, Greece became more and more discontented with Spartan rule, and the difficulty of maintaining that rule became greater and greater. Persia and Syracuse, Sparta's allies, could not give her active assistance: the former was fighting hard against the process of disruption which had taken an acute form in her vast empire; and the latter was far away and entirely occupied with Sicilian and Italian affairs. Yet Sparta needed external support to control her empire, so large, so scattered, and so constantly disturbed. Constant wars had involved heavy loss of life, chiefly among the Spartiates, and the number of Spartan citizens with full rights was now dangerously reduced. On the other hand, the government of their foreign possessions was so profitable to the governors that the Spartiates took no steps to increase their numbers and treated every attempt in that direction as revolutionary. They preferred to ignore the transference of land, either allotted by the state or acquired, to the hands of women, rather than fill up their ranks by admitting Spartans without full rights, Perioeci, and Helots. Consequently, the Spartiates were too few to defend Sparta, to command the scattered garrisons of the empire, and to carry on foreign wars.

The rivals of Sparta meanwhile were gaining strength. A comparatively long peace had encouraged a renewal of Athenian trade. At the same time the former allies of Athens, oppressed by the Spartan garrisons and the *harmosts* who commanded them, sighed for the good old days of the Athenian confederation. The conditions seemed favourable for renewing that confederation on more equitable terms. Elsewhere, the power and influence of Boeotia and of her chief city, Thebes, were growing in central Greece; and hatred for the Spartan garrison which held the Cadmea, the acropolis of Thebes, was growing also.

For all this, the Greek world was surprised, first, by the news that a detachment of Spartan invincibles had been beaten by the Theban, Pelopidas, and later by the complete victory won by the Boeotian militia over a picked Spartan army at Leuctra in 371 B.C., when Sparta, backed by all Greece and confident of victory, was marching to suppress the obstinate Boeotians. The Thebans owed this victory entirely to the military genius of Epaminondas: he had reformed the tactics of Greek militia forces, won considerable victories, and inspired Boeotia to rise against the oppressors of Greece. The victory of Leuctra and the invasion of the Peloponnese led to the separation of Messenia from Sparta; and thus the military strength of Sparta was undermined; for many Spartiates had their allotments of land in Messenia, and could no longer maintain themselves and their families without them. The political state of Greece, bad enough already, was made worse by the collapse of Sparta. The last power which had tried, more or less successfully, to deal with the growing anarchy, now disappeared. Sparta ceased, and ceased for ever, to play the leading part in the life of Hellas.

There was no one to take her place. The second Athenian maritime alliance was formed on purpose to fight Sparta; but, when she lost political importance, the Athenians endeavoured to convert it into an empire by the same harsh measures which they had used before the Peloponnesian war. The result was resentment among the allies, war, and the dissolution of the alliance. The supremacy of Boeotia was bound to be short-lived and precarious: she had neither the historic past and the wealth and civilization which created the Athenian Empire, nor that excellent professional army of citizens which formed the strength of Sparta. The effect of her supremacy in Greece was purely destructive: she crushed the last attempt made in Greece to create the semblance of a national power with the resources of a single city-state.

When the Spartan league had fallen to pieces and Thebes was growing steadily weaker, the political condition of Greece can only be defined by the word 'anarchy'. The observers of that day, reflective and clear-sighted men of affairs, such as Xenophon and Isocrates, Plato and Aristotle, saw all the horror of this anarchy, but saw no way out of it. And indeed there was no way out for those whose political views could never rise above the limits of the Greek city-state, and its peculiar conception of freedom. For such men freedom meant simply the possession of certain political rights—rights strictly limited to the inhabitants of their native city and the limited territory belonging to it. The sovereignty of the city, its complete political independence, was an axiom in all Greek political science. Whatever interfered with that sovereignty seemed to a Greek intolerable slavery; and this is why Greece struggled so obstinately against Athens and against Sparta, choosing political anarchy rather than subjection to any one city-state.

Syracuse also, when she attempted to unite the western Greeks into one kingdom, was foiled by the same deeply rooted prejudice of the Greek mind. For a time the attempt was successful. Under the pressure of constant danger from Carthage and from the Italian peoples, the Greeks in Sicily and Italy endured the military dictatorship of Dionysius, tyrant of Syracuse and an able statesman. But when he died in 367 B.C., his empire in the island and on the mainland fell to pieces. Some decades later the same fate overtook the short-lived Syracusan Empire of Agathocles, another tyrant of Syracuse. Here also the failure was due to this—that the despotism of Dionysius and Agathocles was built up on the basis of a city-state, which, in its Greek form, was incapable of becoming the centre of a great national and political union.

Thus the Greek city-state, in the two centuries of its development, proved unable to create a national union of Greece, and reduced Greece to a condition of political anarchy, which must infallibly end in her subjection to stronger and more homogeneous governments. Apart from the tendency to separation innate in the Greek mind, the blame for this failure lies largely on the constitution of the city-states, and, most of all, on democracy, the most complete and progressive form of that constitution. Democracy in Greece proved unable to create a form of government which should reconcile the individualism characteristic of the nation with the conditions essential to the existence of a powerful state, namely, civic discipline and a preference of the general interest, even when it appeared to oppose the interest of particular persons or classes or even communities.

The fifth century B.C. was exceptionally favourable for the growth of individualism. The extension of trade, the great technical improvements in agriculture and industry, the supremacy of Greece in the world's markets, her production of oil, wine, manufactures, and luxuries for all those countries to which her colonists had penetrated—such conditions had enabled the Greeks to show their enterprise in the sphere of finance, and to abandon more primitive methods in favour of a capitalistic system and a production aimed at an unlimited market with a demand constantly increasing in amount. The rudiments of such a system are noticeable at Athens even earlier than this century. The transition to capitalism was made easier by the existence of slavery, as an institution everywhere recognized, whose necessity and normality no one questioned. The slave markets provided slave labour in abundance; and the growth of political anarchy only increased the supply of slaves and lowered the price of labour. But capitalistic enterprise was interfered with by the state: within the limits of small states it was difficult for the capitalist to go ahead: their territory was too small and the competition of neighbours too severe. And apart from this, within each state capital had to fight the socialist tendencies of the government and its inveterate jealousy of all who, either by wealth or intellectual and moral superiority, rose above the general level. Thus capitalism and individualism, growing irresistibly, came into constant conflict with democratic institutions; and the conflict led to utter instability, hindered the healthy development of capitalism, and turned it into speculative channels with which the state was powerless to interfere.

Among the characteristic peculiarities of Greek democracy is its view that the state is the property of the citizens—a view which includes the conviction that the state is bound, in case of necessity, to support its members, to pay them for performing their public duties, and to provide them with amusements. These expenses had to be defrayed by the state either out of the public funds, including its foreign possessions and the tribute paid by the allies, or, if these funds were insufficient, at the cost of the more wealthy citizens. In extreme cases the state resorted to confiscation and requisitioned, on various pretexts, the riches of the well-to-do. When the government sold corn and other food below the market price, or paid the citizens for attendance at the popular assembly and for serving as judges, members of the Council, and magistrates; when it gave them money to buy tickets for the theatre and fed them for nothing in times of dearth—in such cases the usual procedure was to squeeze the rich for the means; they were compelled either to lend money to the state, or to undertake, at their own cost, the management of certain public duties, for instance, the purchase and distribution or sale of corn. They were required also to fit out warships for service, and to pay and train choruses and actors for theatrical performances. Public burdens of this nature were called *liturgiae*.

The same levelling tendency is shown by the state in every department of life. The equality of all citizens was a principle of democracy; and where it did not exist forcible measures were taken for reducing all alike to the average standard, if not to the standard of the lowest citizens. In public life all citizens might and must serve their country as magistrates; hence most of the magistrates were appointed by lot and the method of choice was abandoned. In private life, sumptuary laws aimed at the same object; and equality in morals was secured by laws which prescribed definite rules of conduct. And lastly, in order to preserve equality in matters of the intellect, thinkers and scholars, whose opinions appeared subversive of religion and government, were again and again prosecuted. I have already spoken of the fate of Anaxagoras and Socrates.

Democracy had good reason for prosecuting thinkers and men of learning. For they submitted the city-state to merciless criticism based upon a profound study of its essence. Some peculiar social institutions, such as slavery and the isolation of women, were repeatedly dealt with, from different points of view, by Euripides and Aristophanes. There is a remarkable review of Athenian democracy, witty, profound, and, in places, malicious, in an anonymous pamphlet of the fifth century; the writer is unknown, but was evidently an important figure in the politics of the day. But the heaviest blows suffered by this form of constitution were dealt by the sophists and by Socrates, of whom we have already spoken. Plato, the disciple of Socrates, and Aristotle, the disciple of Plato, summed up the results of this criticism and investigation: in their political writings they gave an excellent and detailed account of such a constitution in its development and practical working, classified all the possible forms which it might assume, and planned the formation of a new and more perfect city-state out of the elements actually existing in Greece.

Democracy was not the only form of government in Greece in the fourth century B.C.; and democracy in one state differed from democracy in another. It appeared in a moderate form at Athens. For Athens still possessed a numerous class of small landowners, an important element in the population of Attica. This essentially conservative class voted, at times of crisis, with the higher class of the city population, and so prevented the proletariat, who were mostly sailors or dock labourers in the Piraeus, from keeping power in their own hands for long. Economic conditions worked in the same direction: men who could earn good wages at Athens were not inclined to give up their earnings for the small sum paid to judges, councillors, and magistrates; so that in practice the business of government was generally left to the richer and more educated classes. And lastly, the ordinary citizen, who had not received the necessary education, felt himself lost in complicated political affairs, and gladly made them over to professional politicians to manage.

A serious danger to the city-state lurked in this tendency of most citizens to hold aloof from politics. Men lost the taste for public life; they felt that public duties, especially the duty of military service, were a grievous burden, and retired more and more into private life; they were thankful to any one who could govern in such a way as to relieve the citizens, as far as possible, from the current business of the state and the necessity of serving in the army. I said above, that democracy was not triumphant everywhere in Greece. Many states were ruled by an oligarchy, that is, by a small group of the richest and most influential men, others by a tyranny, in which one man, supported by hired soldiers, was supreme. Both these forms of government rested on a practice new in Greek life, and partly due to the distaste for public life already mentioned—I mean the gradual substitution of hired professional soldiers for an army composed of citizens.

From the earliest period of Greek history it was the custom of Eastern monarchs to base their military strength largely upon detachments of Greek mercenaries. The stormy politics of Greece were constantly pouring a stream of young and healthy men into the market, where they could be bought. They served in the armies of the Persian kings and satraps; and the vassals of Persia, the Carian kings, for instance, relied upon them. In the fourth century B.C. even the Greek city-states began to use mercenaries for foreign wars. Oligarchies employed them; and so did tyrants, in order to keep the power they had seized.

The case of Panticapaeum, the richest of the Greek colonies on the Black Sea, may serve as a typical example of the way in which the power of a tyrant was maintained for a long time by means of mercenary forces. Panticapaeum, a colony of Miletus, had become a tributary vassal of the Scythians; acting as middleman between Scythians and Greeks, it had grown rich by the export of grain and fish. In the second half of the fifth century B.C. it fell into the hands of tyrants. The decisive factor in this revolution was the hostility between two sections of the population in Panticapaeum and the other Greek cities on the straits of Kertch, which controlled a large part of the Crimea and all the Taman peninsula. The natives formed one section, and the Greek settlers the other; and the tyranny of Panticapaeum was established in order to reconcile the interests of both. It maintained itself for a long time and was converted into a hereditary monarchy, thanks to the strong mercenary army employed by the tyrants.

But if the political life of fourth century Greece was unsatisfactory, her economic life was not. Agriculture everywhere became more intensive and therefore more productive: old-fashioned methods were generally abandoned. Economic progress was powerfully aided by Greek science, which turned its attention to technical improvements. Specialists collected the results of private experiments, studied them and published them, and so created a science of agriculture. Evidence for this will be found in a short treatise by Xenophon, an Athenian citizen, the same who saw service with the younger Cyrus in Persia as one of his mercenary soldiers. Similarly the culture of the vine and the olive was placed on a scientific basis.

Industrial activity was no less intense. The factory system, indeed, was never adopted—I have already pointed out how difficult it was for a sound capitalistic system to grow up in Greek cities; but workshops of moderate size with a score of workmen, partly free and partly slaves, abounded in every large city. The work done there was highly specialized, different shops turning out different parts of the same article. Thus, in the manufacture of candelabra, four sets of workmen might be employed in four different cities: the first would make the metal branches, the second the stem, the third the pedestal, and the fourth the lamps to be placed on the branches.

The development of trade and industry was facilitated by the abundance of monetary tokens, especially in silver, which were coined by each of the larger cities. Special repute was enjoyed by the Athenian 'owls', silver coins bearing the figure of an owl. Persian gold and the gold coins of Cyzicus and Lampsacus circulated everywhere. The increasing amount of money gave birth to the banking industry and set credit transactions of a firm footing. Banks at Athens in the fourth century B.C. did essentially the same business as our own do now: they received deposits and kept them, made payments on the order of the depositors, gave credit to merchants and traders, received real and personal property as security, and acted as brokers between capitalists and parties in need of credit. Improvements were made in commercial documents and civil law. International trade gradually created a civil law of nations, or rather, a law of cities.

The expansion of trade and, still more, of industry depended largely upon slave labour. The slaves at Athens were numerous, but they were distributed in groups of moderate size over the different departments of industry. Great plantations and large factories, equipped with servile labour, were both unknown in Greece. The mines were the only exception to this rule. In outdoor and indoor work the slave was a member of a great family. In the fields he often worked side by side with his master, ate the same food, and slept under the same roof. In the workshop he rubbed shoulders with the free artisan, did the same work, and received approximately the same wages, i.e. a sum sufficient to cover the necessaries indispensable for a single man. In building the practice was the same: slaves and free citizens of Athens worked together to raise the Parthenon and Erechtheum. We may suppose that the same conditions held good in other parts of Greece.

Greece was now passing through an economic and social crisis which gradually became more acute. The essential features of the crisis were the shortage of foodstuffs which is referred to frequently in literary and epigraphic sources, proletarianism, and the spread of unemployment, both illustrated by the growing number of Greeks who became mercenary soldiers in Greece and abroad. There were many causes for this economic unbalance. Greece was not rich in natural resources and had to depend on importing food as well as raw materials for her industry. The forests of Greece, once productive, had now vanished. In addition, Greece suffered from over-population. The remedies were colonization and the export of wine, oil, and manufactured products. When, in the fifth century, before the Peloponnesian War, the influence of Greek civilization had made these exports familiar commodities to the native inhabitants of Spain, Gaul, Italy, Sicily, Egypt, and the Black Sea coast, Greek export trade rose immensely. The graves of Scythian nobles contain great amphorae once filled with wine and oil and quantities of Greek ornaments; the graves in Etruria and southern Italy are as rich in the same objects; and both bear witness to the importance of Greek exports. In exchange Greece imported from the countries mentioned above the raw materials required for her industries, and foodstuffs to support the population of her cities—immense quantities of corn, salt fish, metals, hides, flax, hemp, and timber for shipbuilding. The importation of slaves was also important.

But Greek colonial expansion ended in the middle of the sixth century, and the market for Greek exports, which had been expanding rapidly in the sixth and fifth centuries b.c., shrank considerably in the fourth century and was no longer able to absorb the goods that Greece had to offer. The reason was that the other countries had gradually developed their own agriculture and industry and competed with Greece proper not only in their own markets but also in foreign trade. Such countries as Italy developed their own viticulture and production of olive oil. In the Persian Empire, during the Peloponnesian War, local silver coins, often imitating the Athenian 'owls' (silver pieces bearing the figure of an owl), had already begun to supplant Greek coins. Finds in northern Italy show that around 400–375 B.C. the importation of Attic vases to this region dropped to about one-fourth the amount bought before the Peloponnesian War. At the end of the fifth century, Attic vases were sold in southern France in increasing quantities, but the competition of imports from southern Italy soon became fierce, and this French market, too, was lost after 350 B.C. In this way Greece became less and less able to pay for the imported goods which she absorbed in ever-increasing quantities.

The crisis in the foreign commerce of Greece together with the anarchic political conditions brought about the difficult economic situation in which Greece found herself at the time of Alexander the Great. The decline was gradual. Greece was faced with the necessity of readjusting her economic and political life.

XIII

MACEDONIA AND HER STRUGGLE
WITH PERSIA

In the middle of the fourth century B.C. the position of affairs within the Graeco-Oriental world may be described as follows. Greece was torn by political and social anarchy. The principle of autonomy for the different city-states had been victorious over the principle of unification, either in empires, like that of Athens, or in federations, like that of Boeotia; and this victory led to painful consequences in the foreign and domestic affairs of Greece. Of the eighty-five years that divide the beginning of the Peloponnesian war from the conquest of Greece by Macedonia, fifty-five were filled with wars waged by one state against another. Every considerable Greek city experienced at least one war or one internal revolution every ten years. Some cities, such as Corcyra, were perpetually under the strain of revolution, past, present, or future. These convulsions were social rather than political. Abolition of debt and redivision of land had become the programme of the popular party. At Athens the strife of parties was carried on without those atrocities which attended it at Argos, for instance, or Corcyra; yet the democracy, when restored after the Peloponnesian war, included in the jurors' oath a clause that no person taking the oath should demand abolition of debt or a redivision of land.

Anarchy in politics being thus complicated by social anarchy, Greece was filled with exiles from different cities, homeless adventurers, prepared to follow any leader and serve any cause for pay. In the cities the number of citizens with full rights grows smaller, and the unenfranchised, both freemen and slaves, become more important in society and in finance. The militia of citizens is no longer competent to bear the burden of foreign and domestic wars; patriotic feeling is less keen; every one tries to shirk military service by some means or other or to buy exemption. The citizen army of heavy-armed hoplites vanishes from the scene, and the new fashion is a mercenary force of light-armed peltasts. The same conditions prevailed in the fleet also.

What Greece had lost politically, Persia seemed to have gained. It looked as if a Persian conquest was imminent, and as if the enslavement of Greece was inevitable. From this point of view only is it possible to understand the fanciful notion represented by Isocrates—that there was no salvation for Greece, unless all Greeks would combine to attack Persia; but who was to lead them remained uncertain. Nor were the fears of Greece exaggerated. It is true that the process of disruption was going on even in Persia. The more Asia Minor prospered in consequence of her active share in the international trade organized by Greece, the more stubbornly did the different parts of the country strive to cut themselves loose from the Persian monarchy. Asia Minor in the fourth century consisted virtually of a number of half-Greek monarchies which paid tribute to Persia. And the same tendency was shown by the satraps who represented Persian power in the country: each of them, if he had the chance, was ready enough to declare himself independent. Things were no better in Egypt. During this century she was constantly in revolt, and was brought back each time under the Great King's sceptre with difficulty and not for long. Phoenicia was less unruly: her competition with Greece in trade and finance strengthened her connexion with Persia. About the state of central Asia we are ill informed; but there, too, the same process of disruption into separate kingdoms was going on.

For all this, Persia was still a mighty empire. Under Artaxerxes

Ochus, a contemporary of Philip of Macedon, she showed her strength by dealing with the seceders and restoring the unity of the empire by harsh and cruel measures. But she was weakened partly by dynastic disputes, and partly by her stubborn conservatism in military matters. The war with Greece had proved the great superiority of the heavy-armed Greek infantry to the light-armed troops of Persia; but still the Persians did not even attempt to improve their standing army, and ignored the mechanical skill, especially in siege operations, which the Greeks had attained. While recognizing Greek superiority they refused to reform their own army, and preferred to add to it detachments of Greek mercenaries, who were, of course, swamped in the heterogeneous mob that fought for Persia. And it must be remembered that each contingent sent to swell the Great King's army carried its own national weapons and fought in its own national manner. Yet, as I have already said, Persia was the only power in the civilized world of that day which had immense material resources and endless reserves of fighting men at its disposal. Disunited Greece was, beyond doubt, far weaker than Persia.

The position was very similar in the West. Carthage became more and more the predominant power. Her trade grew, her territory increased, she went on annexing African tribes who furnished her with good soldiers. She did not, indeed, score any decisive successes over the Sicilian Greeks; but she succeeded at least in establishing herself in the west of the island when the empire of Dionysius came to pieces. It was also an ominous presage that the Greek population in Italy was growing steadily weaker, as one city after another fell into the hands of their semi-Hellenized neighbours—the native clans of south and central Italy. This weakness of the Greeks encouraged the growth of one of these clans—the Latins with their capital of Rome in the centre of the peninsula, who had inherited from Etruria the ambition to unite Italy under one government.

More or less similar was the position of the Greeks in relation to the peoples inhabiting the north of the Balkan peninsula. On the borders of central Greece and strongly influenced by her civilization, three considerable powers were growing up which Greece could not disregard; these were Epirus with an Illyrian population, Thrace, and Macedonia. All three kept up constant relations with Greece; and in each there was a marked tendency to concentrate in the hands of a single dynasty the control over all the inter-related clans which made up the population. Instead of hindering this process Greece was more inclined to help it on. This patronage of upstart and more or less Hellenized nations we can trace with special clearness in the policy of Athens. To Athens all these countries, and especially Thrace and Macedonia, were very important from the point of view of commerce. Thrace was steadily becoming an agricultural country and increasing her export of corn to Greece. She had abundance of cattle and was one of the sources which furnished a constant stream of slaves. In all these ways her services to Greece and especially to Athens were like those of the distant kingdom of the Bosphorus, on the Kertch strait, which forwarded to Greece an immense quantity of grain, hides, fish, and slaves, supplied by the dwellers on the steppes of south Russia, subjects of the Scythians. In addition, Thrace and south Russia exported metals, especially gold, which was dug up in Thrace or carried from the Ural mountains through Scythia into Greece.

Macedonia was no less important to Athens and to all Greece. She possessed excellent timber, especially the pine-wood required by Athens for shipbuilding. The only other sources for a supply of good timber were round Mount Ida in the north of Asia Minor and the mountains in south Asia Minor and Syria; but all these districts were included in the Persian Empire, and practically inaccessible to Athens and the rest of Greece. The pine forests of Macedonia also produced great quantities of the pitch and tar indispensable for building ships. Epirus, with its primitive and purely pastoral population, was of less importance to Greece.

In all these countries Athens found it more agreeable to deal with a single person in possession of executive power than with a number of petty tribes and rulers; and the productiveness of the land also was increased by political unity. For this reason Athens kept up friendly relations with the kingdom on the Bosphorus (see Chapter XII), even after the tyranny of the semi-Hellenic Spartocidae had been established there; and in Thrace, when the Odrysian kings were able for a time to unite a number of Thracian clans under their rule, Athens showed them favour. Thus also there were ties of friendship between Athens and the kings of the Macedonian coast. Two of these, Archelaus, who reigned during the Peloponnesian war, and his successor, Amyntas, were Athenian allies in the north and highly valued by her. In those days no one at Athens dreamed that a strong Macedonia would ever be a danger to Greece.

But vast possibilities in the way of civilization and political development were now opening up before Macedonia. The origin of this people is still an unsettled question. Perhaps they were Greeks, just as the Aetolians and Acarnanians were; perhaps they belonged to the family of Illyrian or Thracian clans; or perhaps there gradually settled in Macedonia detachments from each of the three Indo-European stocks above mentioned, overspreading a non-Aryan population and gradually blending with it to form a new nation in many respects unlike the Greeks. But no certain conclusion is possible. The Greeks found their language difficult to understand, and ranked them as 'barbarians'. It is clear that the language was a dialect of Greek, with a strong infusion of foreign words, phrases, and expressions. For the future fortunes of Macedonia it was of more importance that the valleys on her coast, together with her mountainous district, including Paeonia, form one geographic and economic whole, divided by lofty mountains from Epirus, Illyria, and Thrace. These parts of the country are bound into one by three great rivers, which are quite large enough for navigation—the Haliacmon (now the Bistritza), the Axius (now the Vardar), and the

Strymon (now the Strumnitza). The natural wealth of Macedonia was abundant and various—rich mines, excellent forests,
extensive pastures, and wonderful cornfields. On the pasture
lands horses were bred as well as sheep and oxen. The level land
on the coast runs along two deeply indented bays—the gulfs of
Therma and the Strymon; and these bays are divided by the
peninsula of Chalcidice (now Mount Athos). There are good
natural harbours in both bays, especially in the former, where
Therma (afterwards Thessalonica and now Salonica) is still
among the most important roadsteads of the Mediterranean.
Greeks had long before this time settled on the coast of Macedonia and both the bays; Amphipolis had been built on the
Strymonian gulf. Macedonia used the Greek cities for exporting
her produce; and they served her also by introducing Greek
civilization.

Under these conditions, Macedonia naturally grew rich in the
palmy days of Greece, especially after the Persian wars, and her
higher classes became more and more Hellenized. Nevertheless,
the process of political unification, complicated by the continual
intrigues of the chief Greek states and by the dynastic quarrels
inevitable in monarchies, went on slowly in Macedonia, till the
second half of the fourth century B.C., when the efforts of Archelaus and Amyntas pushed it forward with some success. In this
way it became possible for Philip, who succeeded Amyntas on
the throne in 360 B.C., to take as his task the complete unification
of Macedonia; by this means he could create a powerful kingdom
and begin extensive political activities in Greece, with the definite object of heading the Greek nation in a crusade against
Persia. By long and persistent labour he succeeded in reforming
the political and military system of the country. Out of a feudal
kingdom based upon clanship he made a powerful empire, ruled
by a single head and depending on a standing army, well trained
and well supplied. The nucleus of this force was supplied by
small landowners, who served as infantry and formed the pha-
lanx which later proved invincible. The large landowners, the

former feudal aristocracy, now became the king's 'Comrades', and furnished the army with a force of heavy-armed cavalry superior to any then existing.

Philip introduced into his army all the latest improvements in Greek tactics, which he had learnt during his long residence at Thebes with Epaminondas, and also adopted all the Greek mechanical appliances for war. By means of this army he was able to check the disruptive tendencies of the country, to protect his frontiers against attack from their northern neighbours, to cripple the Odrysian kingdom of the Thracians, his most serious rival, and even to penetrate farther north and inflict some blows on the Scythian kingdom, which at this time was expanding southwards and westwards and seizing one part of the Balkan peninsula after another. At the same time he never relaxed his efforts to annex Thessaly and that strip of Macedonian coast which was occupied by Greeks. Without access to the sea, a wider political influence over the whole Greek world was out of the question. By degrees, and after a succession of wars, the Greek cities in Macedonia, Paeonia, and Chalcidice, became part of his kingdom.

I said above that in his youth, and before he ascended the throne, Philip spent a long time at Thebes while the Boeotian league was at the height of its power. There he became thoroughly familiar with the features of contemporary Greek politics; and there, probably, he conceived the plan of using the political and social anarchy of Greece, in order to unite that country under his own leadership, for the purpose of a common attack on Persia. He learnt the details of Greek politics even more thoroughly during the struggle for mastery on the Macedonian coast, which first brought him into collision with Athens. The Athenians were beginning to understand the greatness of the danger which threatened their political and commercial interests, if Macedonia were converted into a strong maritime empire.

Philip interfered in the complicated politics of Greece herself, after he had finally annexed the Greek cities of Chalcidice and destroyed many of them, during 349 and 348 B.C. His pretext was a mournful business, typical of the time and place, which was transacted in northern Greece. A small alliance of Phocian cities had been at war with Boeotia from 356 B.C., when Boeotia declared a Sacred War against Phocis for laying hands on the property of the Delphian temple. The Phocians, taking advantage of their own proximity to Delphi and the weakness of Boeotia, had seized the temple with all the treasures amassed there, and used their spoils to create a strong army of mercenaries; they then proceeded to enlarge their territory at the expense of their neighbours, Boeotia and Thessaly. Thus they came into collision with Philip and were driven out of Thessaly by him. Just at this time Philip had overcome the Athenian defence of Chalcidice and had forced Athens to conclude a treaty of peace. He was now at liberty to interfere in the affairs of Greece. On the invitation of the Amphictyones, the official guardians of the Delphian temple, he undertook the command in the contest with the Phocians, defeated their army and destroyed their cities, and imposed on them an annual tribute to make good the losses suffered by the temple. The Phocians were expelled from the Amphictyonic assembly, and their place there was taken by Philip.

When Macedonia in this way became recognized as a member of the family of Greek states, Philip came forward with his plan of uniting Greece into one allied kingdom under the political and military direction of Macedonia. The statesman and soldier saw clearly that the question of his domination over Greece could not be settled in his favour without a decisive conflict against Persia. For, under the vigorous rule of Artaxerxes Ochus, Persia laid claim to Greece as her own property, and regarded her as the regular source of those mercenary troops which made it possible to maintain the unity of the monarchy. Hence the intention of Philip to unite all Greece was a serious threat to Persia; and her gold was actively employed in Greece to support hostility to Macedonia.

In the diplomatic strife between Macedonia and Persia, Greece had a hard part to play. She had early realized Philip's aspirations. There were a band of idealists in the country—the most important of them, Isocrates, has been mentioned already —who saw that the city-state was powerless to effect a union of the nation, and realized the Persian peril; they were therefore inclined to endure dependence on Macedonia, if only they could defy the Persian spectre and the yoke of the 'barbarian'. Macedonia they recognized as a Greek power; and in submission to Macedonia they saw the one possible solution, the only means of preserving for Greece her importance and her prominence in the political life and civilization of the world. One of the most active supporters of this policy at Athens was the eloquent orator, Aeschines.

But the majority in Greece took a different view; and they found a leader in Demosthenes, a forensic orator and statesman, a determined foe of Macedonia and a champion of old traditions. To Demosthenes and his followers the matter at issue was the freedom of Greece, which by them was identified with the city-state—its independence, its right to settle its own affairs, domestic and foreign, without interference from others. Opposed to this freedom was monarchy, in which they saw the mortal foe of the peculiar constitutional principles so dear to every Greek. It would not be just to describe Demosthenes and his party as opponents of national unity; but they were determined on one point: they would not buy national unity at the price of political freedom. Nor was there any reason to suppose that their dreams of a united but free Greece were merely fanciful. At the moment Greek freedom was menaced by two enemies, of whom Macedonia was the more immediate and Persia the more remote. Of two evils they chose what seemed to them the least. To be conquered by Macedonia meant immediate slavery; to conquer Macedonia, even with the help of Persian gold, did not necessarily mean slavery to Persia. A Persian conquest was a bugbear which few Greeks were frightened of. They had a lively remembrance of the previous wars, and were convinced that they could defend their country a second time from the invader, if he ever came. On the whole, the only immediate danger to freedom came from Macedonia; and from that danger Greece must, at all costs, be protected.

We may well wonder that the Greeks, in spite of their political anarchy, were able to struggle so long and so successfully in defense of their independence. Demosthenes contrived to bring together such irreconcilable rivals as Athens and Boeotia, to tear up the treaty concluded with Macedonia, and to bring matters to an open conflict between the two antagonists at Chaeronea in Boeotia in the year 338 B.C. The forces were equally matched, but Macedonia was victorious, thanks to the superior training of her army and the excellence of her cavalry. Sparta remained neutral in this contest; but she refused to recognize the leadership of Macedonia, even when that leadership was acknowledged at Corinth by a congress of representatives from the Greek states. At the same time a general alliance of Greeks was formed, in order to fight Persia under the direction of Macedonia.

The first Macedonian contingents had already reached the Asiatic shore of the Hellespont, when sudden death cut short the brilliant career of Philip, one of the world's greatest diplomatists and generals. In the autumn of 336 B.C. a marriage was to be celebrated at Aegae, the ancient capital of Macedonia— Pella became the capital later—between Philip's daughter, Cleopatra, and Alexander, King of Epirus; the purpose of this alliance was to strengthen the bond between the two countries. During the festival Philip fell by the hand of an assassin. He was only forty-seven years old. This accident had highly important political consequences. Who can tell what would have happened to Macedonia and Hellas if Persia had fallen a victim to the skilful diplomacy and ripe experience of Philip, and not to the assault of the young and romantic Alexander? The murderer was seized and killed on the spot by the king's guards. Whether the murder was merely a piece of personal revenge, or whether the injured and formidable figure of Olympias, Philip's rejected wife and mother of Alexander stood behind the murderer, was never cleared up; but tradition, even when hostile to Alexander, has never charged him with parricide.

The devotion of the army to the young prince, who had been associated with it from his childhood and had even commanded a division at the battle of Chaeronea, saved Macedonia from the strife that usually attended the succession. The army at once acknowledged Alexander as king. His rivals were removed, and the danger of disturbance vanished. But Philip's death forced Alexander to postpone the campaign against Asia. The king was almost a boy, and no one believed in the capacity of this boy to continue his father's policy. The outskirts of his empire were in excitement; Greece was in a ferment, which rose to the highest pitch of intensity when Alexander disappeared from view in the mountains of Illyria and a rumour of his death spread abroad. Thebes, and then Athens for the second time, headed a movement of hostility to Macedonia. But Alexander, after a successful march to the Danube, and after assuring the safety of his rear, made a sudden appearance under the walls of Thebes. He took the city by assault and destroyed it; the inhabitants were either slain or sold into slavery. Greece calmed down after the settlement with Thebes. Alexander was acknowledged as leader in place of his father, and Corinth was again the place where the acknowledgement was made. He started at once for Asia, to continue the design planned by Philip. The fate of Greece was no longer to be decided in Greece itself, but in Asia Minor, Syria, Babylonia, and Persia. Greece was a spectator of the drama that followed, and there were Greeks fighting on either side.

During the two years from 336 to 334 B.C. Persia had done nothing to anticipate the Macedonian attack. The fate of Philip had fallen also on Artaxerxes Ochus, and Persia's hands were tied until the usual palace intrigues came to an end. In this way Alexander's antagonist was not the able and experienced monarch, Artaxerxes, but his successor, Darius III, surnamed Codomannus, who had given no proof of his quality before this conflict.

Alexander's task was not easy. The war, nominally waged by Macedonia and Greece, was in fact waged by Macedonia single-handed. The Greek contingents in Alexander's army were negligible; it was impossible to rely upon them or upon the Greek fleet. In resources and especially in money Macedonia was decidedly inferior to Persia. But she possessed the same advantages which had once enabled Persia to become a world-empire—a young and vigorous nation of soldiers, the best weapons then attainable and all the military appliances devised by Greek science, well organized communications, and a young, bold, and able leader, backed by a number of generals who had gained experience in the service of his father.

Nevertheless, it was difficult for a contemporary to foresee the issue of the struggle. One of the chief advantages of Persia was her powerful fleet and command of the seas. The maritime power of Macedonia and Greece was not, indeed, inferior to that of Persia; but Athens, stronger at sea than any other Greek state, showed no enthusiasm in the cause, and, without her active assistance, Persia ruled the waves. Alexander's task was first to weaken and then to destroy this superiority of the enemy. To attain this object, he had to seize by land the bases of the Persian fleet one after another, beginning with Asia Minor and proceeding to Syria and Phoenicia. His victory on the Granicus in the north of the country gave him access to the harbours of Asia Minor, and he took them all in turn. A second victory at Issus, at the entrance into Syria from Asia Minor, put the Phoenician coast in his power. Tyre alone held out, but was taken after a long siege in which Alexander's engineers showed their ability to master the most difficult problems of siege warfare.

Alexander was now able to march against Babylonia and Persia without exposing his rear to danger. But he directed his steps first to Egypt and established his authority there. This expedition was indispensable, to supplement his conquest of Phoenicia; for thus he deprived the Persian fleet of their only remaining base. He needed Egypt also in order to supply Greece with food-stuffs and to secure by this means her friendly neutrality. The decisive conflict between Alexander and Darius was fought at Gaugamela in Babylonia (331 B.C.). The huge Persian army was destroyed, and Darius fled to his satrapies in central Asia, and was there put to death. Alexander's subsequent campaign in Turkestan and India was intended to complete the conquest of all the satrapies belonging to Persia. This romantic enterprise, though it produced an immense impression at the time, was not of great historical importance: Greek institutions could not find a home in the heart of Asia.

By the victories of Alexander it was decided that Greeks should take the place of Iranians as rulers of the East; and by them also the future destiny of Greece was settled. The Greek cities lost for ever their political independence: in spite of repeated attempts to recover it, the city-state was forced to submit to a monarchy. Ceasing to exist as an independent political unit, it became part of a great monarchical kingdom, while retaining only a shadow of self-government. The Greek city-state had played its part in the history of the world, and Greek monarchy now held the stage.

XIV

GREEK CIVILIZATION IN THE
FOURTH CENTURY B.C.

If the political development of Greece in the fourth century was based exclusively on the city-state, with its inherent belief in complete political independence, complete self-government, and, as far as possible, economic isolation from the rest of the world—and if this development was fundamentally hostile to any political union whatever to include all Greeks, yet Greek civilization tended more and more to transcend the narrow bounds of the city-state, until it became the common property first of all Hellas and then of all mankind. In the parts of Europe, Asia, and Africa which border on the Mediterranean, the conviction, which had long before been firmly held by the Greeks, now grew up in the minds of the majority, that there was only one civilization, that of the Greek city-state, and that everything outside of it was 'barbarism', i.e. a life under conditions which a Greek considered unworthy of a human being. It is interesting to note that modern historical thought has inherited this point of view from the Greeks. It is still a commonplace to contrast West with East—Greece, as the bearer of a true and unique civilization, with the East, as the possessor of a different civilization, lower than the first and not measurable by the same standards.

Nevertheless the Greeks, consciously in part and subconsciously in part, now impart to their production a more and more cosmopolitan character, leaving what is local and provincial and characteristic of a single city-state, and proceeding to a result accepted by all Greeks alike. This process is especially clear in art. The local schools, often referred to above, continue to exist; but local peculiarities become less important than the individual genius of the artist and his followers. In architecture, painting, and sculpture we cease to speak of the different schools, Peloponnesian or Ionian or Sicilian: we speak instead of Phidas, Praxiteles, Scopas, Lysippus, Polygnotus, Apelles, and so on. Their statues and paintings appealed to the Greek eye and mind; and every community was eager to adorn its temples, open spaces, and museums with their works.

Applied art adapted itself with special ease to this change in the manner of artistic production. The clients and customers, for whom this industry was carried on, were in many cases not Greeks themselves, though they set a high value on the productions of Greek art. Their taste influenced the work produced, and the Greek artist adapted himself successfully to it. The two chief centres for the sale of Greek articles illustrate most clearly this process: these are Italy and Sicily in the West (and to some extent Gaul and Spain), and Thrace and Scythia in the North and East. In Etruria, Samnium, Campania, and Apulia on the one hand, and at Panticapaeum in the Bosporan kingdom on the other, local schools of Greek art-workers are formed—potters, jewellers, and workers in wood, leather, and metal. These men, while remaining Greeks, add a trifle of local tang which makes their work attractive to their customers, while at the same time it Hellenizes their taste. Thus the Greeks enter on a new path of great historical importance: their civilization attracts men who are not Greeks, and so becomes the common property of the world.

In Asia Minor, and even in Phoenicia and Egypt, the Greeks carry on the same work with remarkable success. Such Anatolian political communities as Lycia and Caria, arising out of satrapies of the decaying Persian kingdom, become more and more Greek in the external manifestations of their civilization. It is sufficient to mention the Lycian tombs, covered with reliefs and reproducing, in some cases, paintings of Polygnotus, and the famous Mausoleum of Halicarnassus. This was the monument erected over the grave of Mausolus, King of Caria, at Halicarnassus, a half-Greek city and the capital of the kingdom. The best Greek artists of the century worked at the adornment of this monument. For the political future of Greece, however, this peaceful conquest of foreign nations was disastrous. In Italy, in Asia Minor, in south Russia, the native inhabitants became more and more prominent in political affairs, and many Greek cities, lying on the outskirts of the Greek world, lost their purely national aspect; many of them were unable to cope with the forces which they themselves had called forth. And so the foundations were laid for the Hellenistic kingdoms of the future with their hybrid civilization.

Her place in the life of the countries bordering on the Mediterranean Greece owed to her sublime intellectual triumphs in the fourth century B.C. In this period also, in spite of political degradation, in spite of the fact that she was only one of many Greek states, equally feeble and equally incapable of uniting Hellas into a single nation, Athens is still the foremost in the march of civilization. The dialect spoken and written by the Athenians of the fifth century becomes in the next century the language of every educated Greek, and banishes all other local dialects from literature and refined society. To speak Attic and to write Attic becomes obligatory for every man of education; and literature written in any other dialect has a merely local importance. The Attic dialect owed its position to the Athenian writers, who brought to perfection its expressiveness, its wealth of vocabulary, the pliancy of its syntax, and the harmony of its periods in prose and its strains in verse.

Some, indeed, of the literary forms invented by the Athenians had reached perfection in the fifth century. In these further development is impossible, and nothing is produced that can

1. PLATO

Plate XXIX   GREAT MEN OF 4th-CENTURY GREECE

1. Head of the great Athenian philosopher Plato. It is a copy, made in Roman times, of a contemporary or nearly contemporary bust. The portrait is no doubt idealized. Holkham Hall, England.

2. Head of the philosopher Aristotle. Copy, made in Roman times, of a contemporary portrait by a great sculptor of the late 4th century. There is no idealization in the head. It is a true realistic portrait of the greatest scholar of the world. Vienna Museum.

3. Head of the orator and statesman Demosthenes, the great rival of Philip and Alexander, the enthusiastic champion of the Greek city-state and the ardent Athenian patriot. It is a real portrait slightly idealized, part of a copy of the bronze statue by Polyeuctus set up in 280 B.C. The famous full-length statue of Demosthenes in the Vatican is a copy of the same original. Ashmolean Museum, Oxford.

2. ARISTOTLE

3. DEMOSTHENES

233

rival the past. This is the case of tragedy and, to some extent, of comedy. But, on the other hand, new forms of literary creation appear and run their dazzling race. The most conspicuous of these are philosophy and rhetoric. Both were created by the sophists of the fifth century. In the person of Plato Greek philosophy reaches its highest point, alike in form and in substance. This is not the place to speak of what Plato did to deepen and widen Greek speculative thought. His Theory of Ideas, and his doctrine that reason makes the world and himself intelligible to man, laid a foundation for the development of philosophic speculation not only in antiquity but at the present day. For the history of Greek civilization it is important to note that Plato was the first definitely to concentrate his attention, as student and thinker, on man and not on the external world, and that he gave to ethics and politics, regarded by him as inseparable from one another, the precedence over other sciences.

The power to discover truth and understand justice is the first step towards the realization of justice; and this realization is the basis for the moral life of the individual and for the right ordering of government and society. Plato's theory of the state, of which we have already spoken, is founded entirely upon the conception of justice. Criticism of existing constitutions and (to some extent) of Athenian democracy is not for Plato an end in itself: it serves merely as the introduction to an elaborate and detailed scheme for a new political and social system, based upon the realization of abstract justice. That scheme is visionary and Utopian: it takes no account of historical development or human nature; but it remains a true statement of the essential goal, at which all later social reformers have aimed, even when their opinions were diametrically opposed to Plato's.

It is quite possible that Plato himself, especially after his repeated attempts to convert to his philosophy the younger Dionysius, tyrant of Syracuse, realized the Utopian character of his scheme. For he followed up his visionary *Republic* with a second political treatise called *The Laws*, in which he not only tried to show how a Greek city-state might be founded on a rational basis, but also brought together all the scientific conclusions which had been attained by Greeks in law and politics. We have here the first codification of Greek law; and its influence upon the future has been very great.

Plato expounded his views to a scanty band of pupils in the form of lectures, which he delivered in the *Academeia*, a grove consecrated to the Attic hero, Academus. The lectures were not published, and we do not possess them. But, for the instruction of a wide circle of readers, Plato wrote and published his *Dialogues*, of which we possess a considerable part. Here in the form of conversations, carried on, as a rule, by Socrates, Plato's master, with some other person, Plato has expounded in a grand, brilliant, and copious style, his thoughts on various topics, and especially on ethics and politics. The *Dialogues* are admirable works of literature, in which the Greek language, while preserving all its simplicity and picturesqueness, was first adapted to express all the refinements of philosophic thought. Each dialogue is a finished work of art, and fascinates the reader from beginning to end.

Another pupil of Socrates and founder of a philosophic school was Antisthenes, an Athenian, who began his career as a rhetorician and sophist under the instruction of Gorgias. The business of this school was to define the relation of man to life, and to reconcile man with life and with himself. His preaching was founded on the conviction that earthly goods and the gains of civilization are vain. He called man to asceticism and the simple life; he bade them return to the laws of nature. The stability of mind thus acquired makes a man a king; he cares nothing for external things—food, drink, luxury, a fine dwelling, honour and glory; all such things are 'indifferent'. Social distinctions are meaningless: all men are brothers, and there is no difference between the slave and the freeman. He alone is free who is master of himself. Because Antisthenes taught in the gymnasium of Cynosarges, the name of Cynic was attached to the school.

The most famous pupil of Antisthenes was Diogenes of Sinope, who lived in the time of Alexander the Great. Cynicism gave birth eventually to Stoicism, so called because its founder, Zeno, taught in the *Stoa Poecile* or Painted Colonnade.

Yet another pupil of Socrates offered a different solution of the same fundamental question. This was Aristippus of Cyrene. He, too, seeks happiness for man. Starting from a purely materialistic standpoint, the standpoint of Democritus and Antiphon, and insisting on the relativity of our knowledge, he calls on men to trust their feelings. That which procures happiness and pleasure is good. But happiness and pleasure must not be our masters. To conquer them and thus gain true freedom, man has the power of reason. The truly happy man is he who has learned truth and conquered feeling, who is the master of pleasure and not its slave. In these precepts there is no place for religion. It is probable that the gods exist; but they are outside the world and have no concern with it. The chief disciple of Aristippus was Epicurus, always sick and always suffering, but a cheerful sage, who taught his pupils in his 'Garden'.

Aristotle, a pupil of Plato, differs in much from his master. His works have come down to us almost complete: immediately after their appearance they became the companions of every educated man and were used in schools. Aristotle was not an Athenian. He was born in Macedonia, but spent nearly all his life at Athens, first as Plato's disciple, and then as head of his own school, which was called the Peripatetic school, because he preferred to walk about and not to sit while delivering his discourses. Three years he spent in Macedonia at the court of Philip, supervising the education of his son Alexander. He wrote *Dialogues*, but they have been lost. His lectures, however, which deal with almost every department of contemporary knowledge, have been preserved. As literature these do not rank with the *Dialogues* of Plato: they show little attention to form, and many of the works which pass under his name were not actually written by him: some are notes of his lectures, taken by his pupils; others are the work of his pupils, written under his direction. In these lectures Aristotle and his pupils collected all that had been done previously in the different branches of knowledge, revised this matter, threw light upon it, and produced a finished picture of each separate science that was cultivated, more or less successfully, at the time. The sciences were divided by Aristotle into four groups: logic, metaphysics, natural history, and ethics. Rhetoric and politics he treated as a part of ethics; and poetics, or the philosophy of art, had a section to itself. For the history of civilization his works on natural history and ethics are especially important. Under natural history he included physics, astronomy, psychology, zoology, botany, and mineralogy. In all this field the reasoning is based upon experiment, as far as experiment was possible without instruments of precision. Aristotle's work in zoology and botany is especially remarkable: indeed he was the creator of both sciences.

This experimental method was applied by Aristotle to politics as well. Before proceeding to describe in the *Politics* the normal or preferable forms of government, he made a thorough study of the constitution in 158 Greek and foreign city-states. Other types of community he considered unworthy of attention. But each considerable city was studied historically and systematically by him or one of his pupils, relying upon the best accessible sources. One of these treatises has been preserved—his investigation of the Athenian constitution, and it is the main authority for the constitutional history of Athens. For this work Aristotle used a digest of Athenian history compiled by Androtion and other historical works and documents. Aristotle's *Politics*, dealing with the city-state in general and the ideal form of constitution, is the fullest and most searching examination we possess of political conditions in Greece, and there is no modern work on the same subject which surpasses it.

The development at Athens of rhetoric, i.e. the art of speaking and writing with grace and ease, was as vigorous as that of philosophy. Practice went hand in hand with theory. The fourth century produced a number of excellent orators and publicists, whose forensic and political speeches were published in their lifetime, sometimes immediately after delivery, and served as models to the next generation of orators and advocates. A political speech was generally delivered by the writer himself in the popular assembly; but most forensic speeches were written for others to deliver, since the Athenian courts required every defendant to conduct his own defence. Some political speeches were never spoken, but merely published as occasional pamphlets. Isocrates, already mentioned, published most of his political works in this way, and may truly be called the earliest of European journalists.

Lysias and Isaeus must be considered as the most brilliant forensic orators of the century. Demosthenes and Aeschines are not only brilliant advocates but admirable political orators. Many of the speeches of Demosthenes are extant. They were recognized by contemporaries, and have since been recognized by later generations as perfect models of rhetorical art. They combine loftiness and complete sincerity with faultless logical construction; and the marvellous beauty of each sentence and period often produces the impression of music itself. The speeches of Demosthenes show not only genius, but severe study and complete knowledge of the unalterable laws, laid down once for all by theorists of the subject, for musical speech. Apart from their artistic and literary merits, the speeches and political pamphlets of that age are priceless to the historian, because they are the chief source of information concerning the political events of the century, and also tell us of social and economic relations, of civil and criminal law. The first system of Greek law was compiled at Athens; and by degrees Athenian law became the law of all Greeks.

Rhetoric, or the art of speech, spread its influence outside the domain of forensic and political oratory. Every branch of prose literature was affected by it, and history first of all and more than all. History in the fourth century loses the scientific character which Thucydides tried to impart to it, and becomes little more than a department of artistic prose. The chief business of the historian is not so much to collect, verify, and explain historical facts, as to set them forth in a beautiful and attractive form. This is the main object of Xenophon, the only historian of the time whose works have been preserved. Something has been said above of Xenophon. His *Hellenica* or Greek history is a continuation of Thucydides, brought down to the battle of Mantinea in 362 B.C. His *Anabasis* describes admirably the retreat of the Greek mercenaries from Babylonia to the Black Sea and thence to Greece; the author himself took part in this retreat and was one of the leaders. The *Education of Cyrus* is partly a romance and partly a study of national characteristics, in which the writer has set forth his ideas about education, and has also communicated some interesting notices of contemporary life in Persia. In his *Recollections* he has drawn for us a portrait of his master, Socrates. Ephorus and Theopompus, whose works have been lost, were younger contemporaries of Xenophon. The former wrote a continuous history of Greece from the Dorian invasion to the end of his own life in 340 B.C.—the earliest attempt to write the history of a whole people; the latter, like Xenophon, wrote contemporary history in two works—a *History of Greece* and a *History of Philip*.

The development of science and some kinds of literature during this century was rivalled by the development of the plastic arts and sculpture in particular. The great sculptors of the time make it their chief aim to study man in every phase of his bodily and spiritual life. Scopas, one of the greatest sculptors of antiquity, endeavours in his single figures and groups to convey the intense emotions felt by men or gods at a crisis in their lives—the intense exertion of all their physical powers in conflict, their sufferings of mind and body. We do not possess a single statue from his hand in the original; but we have a number of reproductions and a few figures, carved by him or his pupils, which adorned the pediments of Athena's temple at Tegea. The extant sculptures, also, which came from the monument of Mausolus at Halicarnassus, are strongly influenced by the dramatic and passionate quality imported into the art by Scopas. The scenes of battle between the Greeks and Amazons depicted on the walls of the Mausoleum are full of passion and movement.

Praxiteles, a younger contemporary of Scopas, took a different line. He enjoyed great fame in his lifetime, and had a strong influence upon the later development of sculpture. Our museums are crowded with reproductions and imitations of his work. And one of his works has survived in the original—a statue of Hermes carrying the infant Dionysus in his arms. It was made for the temple of Hera at Olympia. In all the statues of Praxiteles we note the endeavour to convey in marble the beauty of the human form, male and female—not the ideal superhuman beauty which the statues of Phidias represent, but a purely human beauty in its highest perfection. When one looks at his Hermes, one does not recognize a god in that nude figure, but one admires the perfection of form in the youthful body and the harmonious nobility of the face. His Aphrodite, made for the city of Cnidus, impresses the spectator by the harmonious lines of a faultlessly beautiful female form; and his Satyr conveys that careless enjoyment of life which is natural to a being that is half-man and half-beast.

The same love for the beauty of form in the human body gives life to all the works of Lysippus, a younger contemporary of Praxiteles, who devoted himself entirely to the figures of young athletes. He was also the creator of portrait sculpture. Tradition reports that Alexander allowed no others than Lysippus and Apelles to carve and paint his likeness.

The same features are observable in painting. Large schemes of decoration give place by degrees to the production of single easel-pictures, intended for the adornment of public buildings or private houses. It is difficult, however, for us to judge of the painting, because not a single example from the hand of the great masters has been preserved even in a copy, while some specimens of the art, dating from this period, are the work of second-rate painters. In vase-painting, as the demand for Attic vases increased, the artistic quality fell off; and the vases do not convey, as precisely as they once did, the style and peculiar features of painting on a larger scale.

On the whole, the fourth century was a worthy successor of the fifth. The creative power of the Greek people was as strong as ever. It grew and flourished, conquering one new domain after another and attaining in some of them the same perfection that stamps the literature and art of the preceding century.

XV

THE WORLD-MONARCHY OF ALEXANDER THE GREAT, AND THE POLITICAL HISTORY OF THE GRAECO-ORIENTAL WORLD IN THE THIRD CENTURY B.C.

When Alexander had conquered the Persian monarchy, he was faced by a further problem. What was to become of the huge empire, of which he found himself the supreme and absolute ruler? How he intended to organize these vast dominions, we do not know. Indeed, it is possible that he had no clear notions himself on the subject. Death came upon him at Babylon in 323 B.C., at a time when he considered his military problem, the problem of conquest, as still unfinished. On the eve of his sickness and death, which took him entirely by surprise, he was planning an expedition to Arabia. Perhaps the conquest of Arabia seemed to him necessary, partly to protect the frontier of his empire in Hither Asia, and partly that he might be able to continue the task of conquering India. And another scheme may have appealed to his adventurous nature, the scheme which had attracted Themistocles and Alcibiades and became later the object of Pyrrhus, King of Epirus. This was the annexation of the western Greeks to his empire. Had he done this, he must infallibly have come into collision with Carthage and with the Italian tribes, who had by this time formed more than one powerful state.

Hence it is not surprising that Alexander gave less attention to organization than to purely military problems and matters affecting the basis of his own personal power. He governed his empire partly in accordance with the traditions of the Persian monarchy, and partly by means of temporary and purely military instruments—the generals commanding divisions of his army: it became their business to control the conquered countries and supply Alexander with the means for carrying out his further military enterprises.

He attached more importance to two questions. How was he to replenish the strength of his armies? And what source would supply him with additional staff-officers and coadjutors in the task of ruling the empire? As at the beginning of his campaigns, he placed little reliance upon the Greeks, whose political ideals were unchanged, and to whom Alexander and his power were an object of hatred rather than of attraction. There remained the Macedonians. But the resources of Macedonia were not inexhaustible, and a country of her size could only supply a limited number of men. The power of direction must, no doubt, be reserved for the Macedonians; but they must have help, and for this purpose other men must be found, as fit instruments as the Macedonians to carry out military and administrative business for their master.

It seemed to Alexander that the Iranians would answer his purpose. They were still a warlike and powerful nation, with the habit of war and the power to govern. He had learnt on the battle-field to respect their military capacity; and while governing the East he had seen their administrative powers and come to value their efficiency in organizing the Persian satrapies conquered by him. Thus impressed, Alexander set himself to bring together the Macedonians and Iranians, as the two most efficient elements of his empire; he even wished to blend them into one, at least in the army and in administration. The conversion of the army into a joint force of Macedonians and Iranians, the appointment of Iranians as military governors of provinces, his

1. ALEXANDER AND DARIUS III: MOSAIC FOUND AT POMPEII IN THE HOUSE OF THE FAUN

2. HEAD OF ALEXANDER

Plate XXX   ALEXANDER AND DARIUS III

1. Alexander and Darius III. Mosaic found at Pompeii at the House of the Faun. It reproduces an early Hellenistic painting. The artist shows one of the decisive moments in the war between Alexander and Darius (the battle of Issus or that of Gaugamela). He shows the fierce determination of Alexander and his army to conquer, as contrasted with the distress, fright, and bewilderment of the Persians.

2. Head of Alexander. (Detail.)

marriage with the Persian princess Roxana, and a number of similar mixed marriages between Persian women and generals, officers, and men of the Macedonian army—such were the first steps in that direction.

Alexander was anxious to be at once the Great King of Persia and the king of a small European people. This endeavour I should be inclined to regard as chimerical. To unite the dynasties of Macedonia and Persia was easy enough; but to establish the new dynasty upon an aristocracy and an army, which should be half Macedonian and half Iranian, was probably beyond the limits of what is possible for man. The difference was too great between the historical traditions of the two nations; and their mental attitude, the growth of ages, was too unlike. Yet the project itself is quite in keeping with Greek ideas of that time, and is entirely in the spirit of Plato's political fancies. To the speculative Greek mind no scheme seemed impossible, provided that the purely logical structure was harmonious and pleasing.

The second point that troubled Alexander was the nature of his own power. Philip, his father, had felt no anxiety about his position: he was the lawful King of Macedonia, inheriting his power from his ancestors and acknowledged by his people, while he ruled the Greeks because they had chosen him as their commander-in-chief. But for Alexander, a king of kings and ruler of a world-empire, more was needed. In the East kingly power was closely connected with religion, and to break that connexion would be a serious mistake. But there were many religions in Alexander's empire, and each had its own way of deciding whether kings were divine beings. How Alexander himself regarded this question, we do not know. He may, as a pupil of Aristotle, have taken the rationalistic view and treated it as a mere matter of politics; or the mystical side of the Greek mind, which saw no absolute distinction between the divine and the human and fully accepted the possibility of a divine incarnation, may have made itself audible in the conqueror's breast. We have no certain knowledge; but I am inclined to believe that Alexander ranked himself above ordinary mortals, not merely because he was a king and a distant descendant of Heracles. A man's thoughts are apt to take a mystical direction, when death threatens him every day, when his victories are checked by no limits, and when the flattery of those around him—flattery which in the ancient world, and especially in the East, took the shape of religious worship—went beyond all bounds.

The tendency of religious thought, both in the East and in the West, fell in with Alexander's own feeling. The conception of divinity became more and more spiritualized at this time, losing its local impress and breaking free from national limits. Religious bodies, unconnected with government and united only by a common belief and a common worship, came into existence again and again. The god of that period was not necessarily Zeus, or Ammon, or Ahuramazda, or Jehovah; often he was simply God. Hence it was not difficult for Alexander to believe the oracles of Apollo at Didyma and Ammon in Egypt, and at the same time to believe the priests of Babylon, when they assured him with one voice of his divine origin. It is certain that vast numbers of the people who inhabited his empire believed in his divinity. The legend of the 'divine Iskander' survives to this day in the Iranian world. The collapse of the Persian Monarchy at a single touch from the young King of Macedonia could not but seem a miracle to the mystical Oriental mind; and it could not fail to impress the Greeks also, especially the Anatolian Greeks, who had been inclined to pay divine honours even to Lysander and Agesilaus. To them Alexander's Indian campaign really seemed to be a repetition of the conquest of India by Dionysus. Thus it is natural enough that Alexander's power was formally pronounced to be divine; it became the custom everywhere to pay him divine honours, and this state of things was accepted by the inhabitants of his empire. Rationalists and sceptics in Greece might smile and return sarcastic answers when Alexander urged the recognition of his claim; but the divine nature of his power remained, for all that, a real and powerful factor in the life of his empire, even if we assume that he did not believe in it himself.

When Alexander died, leaving no legal heir of full age, it became an acute question whether the world-wide monarchy which he had left unfinished could still continue to exist. It was an artificial creation of a purely military kind, in which the disruptive forces were stronger than those which made for unity; and his personality was indispensable to its continuance. We have seen how strong a tendency there was in the Persian Monarchy, before the coming of Alexander, to dissolve into its component parts. Greece resented her submission as tantamount to slavery, and showed this feeling immediately after Alexander's death, till Macedonia was obliged once again to restore order by force. In fact, the only bond of union in the empire was the army, especially the Macedonian army with its hereditary devotion to the Macedonian dynasty. But this devotion of the soldiers to their lawful king could not maintain unity for ever, especially when the dynasty came to be represented by a feeble-minded youth and an infant.

Either Philip Aridaeus, Alexander's half-brother, or Alexander's posthumous son by Roxana, might be considered the lawful heir. But personal ambition and thirst for power prevailed over devotion to the dynasty in the minds of Alexander's generals. A prolonged conflict ensued, in which the question of supporting one or other of the heirs to the succession sank by degrees out of sight, and another question came to the front—whether Alexander's empire should hold together or split up into separate kingdoms, ruled by those who had been his closest companions and coadjutors. In this confused struggle for power all Alexander's heirs and all the members of the ruling house perished one after another; each of them was removed by one or other of the generals, who wished to secure the succession for themselves and to rule that vast empire without a rival.

Not one of them, however, had sufficient ability or sufficient influence over the soldiers, to compel the obedience of the whole army and to force the other generals to admit his supremacy. Each pretender to power had to meet a strong coalition of his rivals who commanded divisions of Alexander's army stationed in the different parts of the empire; and nearly all of them died a violent death. In this way Perdiccas, Antipater, and Polyperchon disappeared one after another. Antigonus, surnamed The One-eyed, one of the ablest generals, who also possessed a capable assistant in his son, Demetrius Poliorcetes, came nearest to realizing the conception of an undivided empire under his personal rule. But even his authority was not recognized by the other generals who ruled separate provinces—Lysimachus in Thrace, Seleucus in Babylonia, Ptolemy in Egypt, and Cassander in Macedonia. They united to inflict a decisive blow on Antigonus in a battle at Ipsus in Asia Minor in 301 B.C., which cost Antigonus his life.

The battle of Ipsus settled the question: the undivided monarchy of Alexander ceased to exist. It split up into a number of component parts, of which the three most important were these: Syria, including all the eastern parts of Alexander's kingdom and some of Asia Minor; Egypt; and Macedonia. The Seleucidae, or dynasty of Seleucus, established themselves in Syria; the Ptolemies or Lagidae, descendants of Ptolemy Lagus, ruled Egypt; while Macedonia, of which Greece was still a dependency, became, after much strife and bloodshed, the kingdom of the Antigonidae, or descendants of Antigonus the One-eyed. In Egypt and Syria the 'kings', as they styled themselves after 307 B.C.,based their power on the right of conquest, as successors of Alexander. Foreigners in the countries they ruled, they relied upon a mercenary army for support. The population submitted to them, as they had submitted to their predecessors, growing accustomed to them by degrees, until they settled down in the belief that it was impossible to resist their power and the power of the Greeks and Macedonians who came with them. In Macedonia the new dynasty of the Antigonidae considered themselves lawful successors of Philip's family, and acquired by degrees the confidence and support of the people. All three dynasties ruled over countries which had long been accustomed to absolute monarchy; and for this reason they were likely to last longer.

These powers are commonly called 'Hellenistic', a term which is applied also to the whole period between Alexander's death and the conquest of the East by Rome. Each of them, especially at the beginning of its independent existence, had aspirations to political supremacy and a restoration of the world-wide empire. But, apart from these pretensions, each had to face immediate problems, connected with the past history and economic needs of his realm. The situation led to constant wars between them; in consequence of war each was weakened, and a number of new independent kingdoms were formed by secession. These were mainly military monarchies, like the powers from which they seceded.

The first object of the Ptolemies was to secure the safety of Egypt, the country from which they derived all their political importance. Egypt was in constant danger, because the flat coast at the mouths of the Nile was at the mercy of any invader with a powerful fleet; and to conquer Egypt by land was easy for any enemy who controlled the Syrian and Phoenician coast. Thus to Egypt it was a matter of life and death, no less than in the age of the Pharaohs, to have a strong fleet and a good maritime base at home, and, as far as possible, to control the coast to the north. For the reasons that have been indicated, Alexandria, a Greek city founded by Alexander, became the key to Egypt and its capital. Alexandria had strong walls and a splendid harbour, partly artificial. Under Alexander and the Ptolemies Egypt turned definitely towards the sea and finally became one of the Mediterranean empires. Her wealth was based partly upon exports, and on the office discharged by the Nile as a cheap and convenient trade-route for Egypt and Central Africa. The wares of Arabia also were brought in caravans to the Nile from the Red Sea ports; and part of the trade between Hither Asia and India passed through the harbours of Arabia. Thus the chief anxiety of the Ptolemies was to develop and defend Alexandria, and to assure to Egyptian trade a free and wide market.

These objects brought Egypt in collision first of all with Syria, the empire of the Seleucidae, and formerly the Persian kingdom. It was as important to Syria as it had been to the Persian kings to command the coast-line of Palestine, Phoenicia, Syria, and Asia Minor: otherwise she would become an inland Asiatic power unconnected with the Greek world, and her kings would be unable to recruit her composite army with Greek and Macedonian mercenaries. The Iranian element in the population was never a support to the power of their new masters, and later seceded from Syria altogether. Hence the Seleucidae and the Ptolemies were constantly fighting for Palestine, Phoenicia, and south Syria; and the Anatolian coast was constantly passing from one rival to the other. The fortune of war was fickle, and neither combatant could claim a decisive victory. Their forces were approximately equal. The earlier Ptolemies—Soter, Philadelphus, Euergetes, and Philopator—succeeded in creating a great empire with a number of foreign possessions in Palestine, Phoenicia, south Syria, south and central Asia Minor, and on the coast of the Hellespont. But in the beginning of the second century B.C. the Seleucidae had the advantage of the later Ptolemies—Epiphanes, Philometor, and Euergetes II—till Egypt was in danger of becoming a province of an Asiatic kingdom. The former struggle of Egypt in the Eighteenth Dynasty against Hither Asia, and later against the Assyrian and Persian kingdoms, was repeated again in its main features. But eventually Syria's gradual disintegration left Egypt the sole and last heir to Alexander's Empire.

In fighting for supremacy at sea and control of the sea-routes, Egypt came into collision with the Greek city-states, especially Athens, and with the islands of the Archipelago. In disputing the command of the Aegean against Macedonia and Syria, the Ptolemies stuck to the former policy of Persia, which was afterwards adopted by the Romans also: they professed to defend the freedom of the Greek states, while within their own empire they demanded entire subservience from the Greek cities in Asia Minor and the islands. This policy brought against them the forces of the Macedonian kings. Antigonus Gonatas, son of Demetrius Poliorcetes, established himself as King of Macedonia in 276 B.C., and was followed by a line of active and able monarchs—Antigonus Doson, Demetrius, Philip V. To them control of Greece was highly important, because, without it, Macedonia would be exposed to attack by sea; and the master of Greece must also be master of the Aegean. Thus there was constant fighting between Macedonia and Egypt; the presidency over the league of Aegean islands was the prize for which they fought, and this presidency passed again and again from one rival to the other.

Constant warfare swallowed up the resources of the three great Hellenistic powers, drained their strength, and made them incapable of coping with the ever accelerating forces of internal disruption. Syria was the most heterogeneous of the three and suffered most from this cause. First to separate from her in 280 B.C. were Armenia, Cappadocia, Pontus, and Bithynia, formerly called satrapies of the Persian Empire, but, in fact, tributary kingdoms. Native kings with a veneer of Greek culture established themselves in all these countries, and tried to seize such Greek cities as lay within their domains; the form of government adopted was absolute monarchy of the type familiar in the East. The most civilized of these kingdoms was Bithynia, with its Thracian population and a whole row of ancient Greek cities on the Euxine and the Sea of Marmora.

The political life of Asia Minor was much complicated by the coming of the Celts (the Greeks called them Galatians), who crossed over about 278 B.C. from the Balkan peninsula, where the Macedonian Monarchy had been carrying on an obstinate struggle against them. They penetrated far into Asia Minor and established themselves on the plains of Phrygia, where they formed a strong alliance of several clans under the leadership of the clan-kings or princes. From this base they constantly threatened the peace of the country, bearing plunder, murder, and devastation in their train, and destroying the promising prospects of trade and industry. The Seleucidae were powerless to cope with the invaders, and therefore the inhabitants were forced themselves to undertake the task of defending their lands from these formidable barbarians. This state of affairs was the main reason which induced so large a part of Asia Minor to secede from the Seleucid monarchy and set up kingdoms of their own.

One of these independent powers was the kingdom of Pergamum. Pergamum was a fortified Greek city of moderate size which commanded the whole valley of the Caycus in Mysia; it had long been ruled by Greek tyrants who paid tribute to the Persian monarchy while it existed. When Alexander's generals were fighting against Antigonus the One-eyed, Lysimachus, who was one of them, adopted Pergamum as his base and entrusted the defence of it to one of his officers—Philetaerus, a Greek by one parent. The fort contained also a large sum of money, the general's war-chest. When Lysimachus fell in battle with Seleucus in 283 B.C., Philetaerus set up for himself and offered his aid to Seleucus. From that date Pergamum was a separate kingdom, at first tributary to Syria, but from the time of Eumenes I (263 B.C.) entirely independent.

This kingdom owed its stability to the bold and sagacious policy of Philetaerus and his successors, Eumenes I and Attalus I, who reigned from 241 to 197 B.C. They gained the attachment of the Greeks in the north-west of Asia Minor by their skill and courage in fighting the Galatians; they successfully defended against the invader not only their own domains but also the central and southern region of the country. At the same time they increased the prosperity of their kingdom by sensible and prudent management, and thus were able to maintain constantly a strong mercenary army and efficient fleet. This military strength made it possible to veer about at the right moment be-

tween Egypt, Syria, and Macedonia, and to increase their territory by degrees. They, too, were the first to realize the strength of
Rome, relying upon whom they became in the second century
B.C. masters of almost all central and southern Anatolia, by annexing the dominions which Syria and Egypt had held there.

Somewhat later than Asia Minor, central Asia also finally
severed its connexion with Syria. Bactria, a half-Greek country,
broke away c. 250 B.C.; and in 248 the territory of the old Medo-
Persian kingdom was invaded by the Parthians, a semi-nomadic
people of Iranian stock. By the middle of the second century
B.C. they had acquired Media, and at the death of their king
Mithridates I (138–7) they also dominated Mesopotamia and
Persia. The Parthians founded a strong state with a veneer of
Greek civilization, which lasted for many centuries, terrifying
the eastern provinces of Syria and proving itself later the most
powerful and formidable neighbour of the Roman Empire.

In Greece the forces of disruption never ceased working for a
single moment. Macedonia tried every means to consolidate her
authority and to convert the Greek city-states into administrative departments of the kingdom; but these attempts had no
lasting results. Fresh revolts were constantly stirred up by the
intrigues of Egypt and Syria. Sparta, which had never become a
part of the Macedonian monarchy, played a conspicuous part in
the struggle against Macedonia. Of special significance was her
political action during the short period when two of her kings—
Agis IV about 245–241 B.C., and then, with more success, Cleomenes from 227 to 222 B.C.—carried through a radical programme of economic and social reform. They divided up all the
land among a large number of Lacedaemonians, and thus restored for a time the military strength of Sparta. Antigonus
Doson, the Macedonian king, defeated Cleomenes in a decisive
battle at Sellasia in 222 B.C.; but Sparta, even under the successors of Cleomenes, still preserved her political independence.

Athens was less successful in her attempts to recover freedom.
During the Hellenistic Age she kept her democratic constitution

and some of her foreign possessions, and enjoyed periods of marked commercial prosperity; but all her endeavours to regain complete political independence miscarried. Her most considerable effort was the so-called Chremonidean war (267–263 B.C.), when, having Sparta and Egypt for allies, she sought to shake off the Macedonian yoke; but the yoke only became tighter because of her action. At a later time, in the reigns of Antigonus Doson and Demetrius, Macedonia was content with friendly neutrality on the part of Athens; but this neutrality was hardly distinguishable from tributary dependence.

Macedonia found stronger and more serious opponents in two leagues of city-states which were formed in Greece at this time—the Achaean League in the north of the Peloponnese, and the Aetolian League in north-west Greece. The constitution of both was federal; that is, each state included in the league had a vote on all matters of business which was proportionate to its own size and military strength. Though these leagues were tough and long-lived institutions, yet they were never able to unite under their banner any considerable part of Greece. Their endeavours to gain additional territory led to frequent wars against individual states and between the two leagues; and Macedonia made skilful use of these quarrels, interfering now on one side and now on the other.

As a result of the unceasing strife between governments the island of Rhodes now asserted itself as an entirely independent power in the Hellenistic world and the Archipelago. Her favourable situation on the main trade-routes from the East to Greece, and from Italy to Greece and the East, made Rhodes one of the largest seaport towns in Hellas, more important even than Athens. Her fleet became by degrees one of the strongest in the Hellenistic world; and at the end of the third century B.C. and throughout the second, it fell to her, with the tacit consent of the three great powers, to fight against piracy and secure the safety of navigation in the Aegean. In this task she was guided by a law devised by Rhodes herself and recognized by all Hellenistic powers, great and small, for regulating international trade and shipping. Cyzicus and Byzantium, large cities and ports, discharged the same office in the Hellespont and the Sea of Marmora, patrolling the seas in defence of commerce; while the Bosporan kingdom, which had now become powerful both by land and sea, maintained peace and order on the Black Sea from its capital Panticapaeum, the modern Kertch.

Thus by degrees there grew up in the Hellenistic world a very complicated and confused political situation. There were a large number of independent and partly independent powers, each jealously watching the movements of its neighbours. The attempt of any single community to extend its territory and its power at the expense of others met with vigorous opposition, for coalitions were constantly being formed to suppress such land-grabbers. Something like a balance of power was reached, which made it impossible for any of the powers to keep the lead for long. The members of this Hellenistic family were as follows: three great powers—Egypt, Macedonia, Syria; about a dozen petty Greek and half-Greek monarchies—Epirus in the Balkan peninsula; Pergamum, Bithynia, Pontus, Armenia, Cappadocia, and Galatia, in Asia Minor; the Bosporan kingdom on the Black Sea; Parthia and Bactria in central Asia, Cyrene and the Nubian kingdom in Africa; and also a number of independent Greek city-states, and the two Greek Leagues. Meanwhile, new states were growing up on the outskirts of the Greek world, and these began to pay some attention to Hellenistic affairs and the balance of power that ruled there. In the north of the Balkan peninsula a number of Thracian and Celtic states came into existence; in the steppes of south Russia a Scythian kingdom was followed by several kingdoms of Sarmatians. In the West the strongest powers were these: Carthage; the Sicilian Greeks, who had united again in the third century b.c. under the direction of Syracuse and her able ruler, Hiero II; various alliances of Italian clans, among which the league of Latin cities under the presidency of Rome was steadily growing in importance; and lastly, an alliance of Gallic or Celtic tribes in what is now France and in north Italy.

Thus the Greek world, even in the monarchical phase of its development, was reverting to the conditions of the fourth century B.C., that is, to extreme sub-division of political and military strength. Now, as then, war was the rule, not peace. Not a single one of the Hellenistic governments of this period possessed either a great extent of territory or a strong army. Egypt, under the weak and incompetent kings of the second century B.C., had lost nearly all her foreign possessions. Syria was crippled by constant internal commotions. Macedonia was perpetually at war with her Greek vassals and allies, especially with the Aetolian and Achaean Leagues. Nor did individual states enjoy peace at home. The strife of parties and classes was perhaps smothered in monarchies by the absolute power of the ruler, and came to the surface only in revolts of the natives against Greek rule; but it burned all the more fiercely in the Greek city-states. In most of them the same struggle of classes which marked the domestic politics of the fourth century B.C. was equally rife two centuries later.

XVI

THE GREEK WORLD AFTER ALEXANDER:
POLITICS, SOCIETY, AND ECONOMICS

After the death of Alexander the chief political powers in the
Greek world were the so-called Hellenistic monarchies, which,
with the exception of Macedonia, had once formed parts of the
ancient kingdom of Persia. All these were ruled by kings of
Macedonian birth and Greek culture, relying upon mercenary
troops, who were either Macedonians or Greeks or Hellenized
'barbarians'. These men were recruited by agents in the great
markets for mercenary soldiers in Greece and Macedonia, or
among the Thracian and Celtic tribes which inhabited Asia
Minor and the north of the Balkan peninsula. The kingdoms of
Asia and Egypt found support also in the numbers of foreign
settlers whom they attracted to their dominions. A medley of
races—Macedonians, Greeks, Jews, Syrians, Persians, and others
—the immigrants soon became Greek in their mode of life and
civilization. They formed a privileged class, comprising the well-
to-do citizens and the numerous officials of the kingdom.

Though these upstart Eastern dynasties were entirely strange
to the natives over whom they ruled, yet they had reason to believe that their position was secure. Their chief security was in
the economic prosperity of their subjects: they made it possible
to use the natural wealth of the country and the labour of the
inhabitants, both natives and settlers upon a wider scale and
with more system. This methodical exploitation of natural re-

sources increased the revenue and so made it possible for the king to maintain a large army and fleet, by means of which he could control his subjects at home and also stick fast to a foreign policy of his own. Hence, in the sphere of domestic affairs, the Hellenistic kings gave special attention to two points—the development of the country's resources and the taxable capacity of their subjects. In this matter they relied upon the tradition inherited by them from the Persian or native kings who had preceded them, and also upon the theory, created by themselves, of their own power.

This power they regarded as the power of a conqueror, to whom, by right of conquest, the country and its population belonged. As the heirs of Alexander they claimed divine origin also, and a supernatural sanction for their rule. They were assisted by finding a similar view of government and kingly power firmly believed by their subjects already. Throughout the East down to the time of the Macedonian conquest, government was based upon the unlimited and divine power of the king, who, in virtue of this power, had full right to dispose of the country and its inhabitants as he pleased. The Hellenistic kings of the different Eastern empires, following here also the example of Alexander, declared themselves the lawful successors of the native kings, and the heirs of their rights and privileges. Thus their power had a double aspect: to the Macedonians and Greeks they were successors of Alexander, but to the native populations they were the heirs of the extinct Eastern dynasties.

As master and owner of his kingdom the Hellenistic monarch exercised unlimited power in dealing with his own property, and considered the interests of the people as less important than those of the government, which he identified with his own personal interests and those of his dynasty. The prosperity of the people was a means, not an end, in his view. And this point of view concurs, in general, with the Greek feeling also about the state. That feeling required of the citizen complete submission to the state, unquestioning service, and sacrifice of his personal interests. The only difference was this—that in the monarchies the state was identified with a single person, whose will was law, whereas in a democracy a majority of the population belonging to a city-state were the government.

But in spite of this autocratic power, which was not contested by any one in the Hellenistic monarchies, the kings were forced to comply with tradition in their treatment both of the Hellenized settlers in their realms and of the native inhabitants. Their relations were different towards these two sections of the population. The latter section knew nothing of self-government and had no aspirations towards any form of it: they were accustomed to obey the officials appointed by the king. The Greeks, however, and other foreign settlers, such as the Jews, had their own idiosyncrasies and their own customs; and, above all, they were accustomed to a certain measure of self-government. This the monarchs were obliged to reckon with. For this reason, wherever a Hellenistic monarch, part of whose territory belonged to Greek city-states, was at the head of a government, he, like the Persian kings, respected the self-governing power of these communities; he merely deprived them of political independence and obliged them to pay part of their revenue into the royal treasury. Since a steady stream of Greek settlers quickened the economic life of the country and swelled the royal revenues, and since these settlers were a support to the power of the king, who secured to the Greeks financial prosperity in return, therefore the majority of the Hellenistic monarchs, especially the Seleucidae and the kings of Asia Minor, welcomed the appearance of new Greek cities in their dominions, and recognized their right of self-government.

The Ptolemies were an exception to this rule. Except Alexandria, founded by Alexander, and ancient Naucratis, and Ptolemais in south Egypt, founded by Ptolemy Soter, there were no cities in the whole kingdom which had Greek institutions and a predominantly Greek population. For the above-mentioned cities, however, the Ptolemies were forced to recognize the right of self-government; but this right was strictly controlled by the

1. A BRONZE BUST, PROBABLY
OF SELEUCUS I OF SYRIA

2. HEAD OF A MARBLE STATUE,
PRESUMABLY BERENICE II

Plate XXXI HELLENISTIC ROYAL PORTRAITS

1. A bronze bust, in all probability of Seleucus I of Syria. It is the best Hellenistic royal portrait in existence. This copy, probably made from an original by Lysippus, shows the indomitable will, intellectual power, and unlimited ambition of the king. Naples Museum.

2. Head of a marble statue, presumably Berenice II, wife of Ptolemy III Euergetes. Some extant traces of gold make it probable that the hair was gilded. The blonde hair of Berenice was celebrated by Callimachus in a poem (part of which has been rediscovered) which, in a Latin adaptation by Catullus (*The Hair of Berenice*), became a part of world literature. Museum, Bengasi, Libya.

261

sovereign, and no new Greek cities were permitted. The Greeks who came to settle were distributed among the larger and smaller centres of the population. But there also the Greeks and other foreigners, e.g. the Jews and Persians, formed small associations, within which they led their peculiar life. The Ptolemies were forced to concede certain rights to them, and to recognize them as corporations possessing elective representatives and a limited measure of internal self-government.

In all these matters Macedonia differed from the Eastern monarchies. The position of the king was still just what it had been in Philip's time: he was a national monarch, recognized as such by the nation. The army consisted of soldiers recruited within the kingdom. The kings laid no claim to divinity, and abstained from introducing worship of themselves as part of the official religion. The Greek cities situated in Macedonia and Thessaly, while politically subject to the kings, kept their self-government. The attitude of Macedonia to the cities of central Greece and the Peloponnese was determined from time to time by the actual strength of the rival parties; they were not permitted to have a foreign policy of their own, but their powers of self-government were seldom interfered with. Many of them, indeed, won by arms the power to pursue for a time their own foreign policy. In practice the Macedonian kings ruled only in those cities where they maintained a garrison of their own.

The economic conditions created by the Greek city-states were inherited by the Hellenistic monarchies. As early as the fifth century B.C. Greek trade predominated in the Mediterranean, and the Semitic traders of Carthage had to yield pride of place except to the west of Sicily. Even the Phoenician ports of Tyre and Sidon came by degrees under the influence of Greek traders, and dealt largely in wares produced in Greece. After the death of Alexander Greece is queen of the Mediterranean market and supplies nearly all the goods required by customers in the East and West in exchange for food-stuffs and raw material, and, to some extent, for luxuries, such as ivory, valuable woods, precious stones, and spices, imported from South Africa, Arabia, India, and China; but many of these luxuries were imported in the form of raw material to be manufactured in Greek workshops.

But Athens now loses her position as the chief market of the world; and Alexandria, as the port of transit for all Egyptian produce, such as grain, flax, glass, and papyrus, and for all produce exported from central Africa and the Red Sea harbours, becomes a centre, not only of trade on a great scale, but also of manufacture, where the native products and imported raw material are worked up with all the technical skill of the Egyptians. Alexandria becomes not only one of the chief markets which supply the world with grain, but also a great manufacturing centre, exporting throughout the Mediterranean a number of articles not produced elsewhere, such as paper, glass and flax, and also jewellery and cosmetics.

Side by side with Alexandria, some cities of Asia Minor are still important in commerce. Thus Miletus, Ephesus, and Pergamum take the lead in the production and exportation of woollen fabrics; while Cyzicus, Byzantium, Sinope, and especially Rhodes, become important as harbours of transit and vast exchanges, where the wares exposed are grain, hides, tar, hemp, building-wood, woollen materials, and slaves. These goods are supplied by the north coast of the Black Sea, with the Bosporan kingdom for a centre, by the Caucasus and Transcaucasia, by Asia Minor, Macedonia, Thrace, Syria, and Egypt. Delos, the island sacred to Apollo, rivals Rhodes as an international exchange. This importance of Rhodes and Delos is due to their geographical position: they lie on the routes which connect the north and south-east with Greece and Italy.

Phoenicia and the Syrian coast continue to be important centres of export and import, and admit to the sea the great caravan routes which connect the Mediterranean with central Asia, India, and Arabia. The caravan trade with Arabia finds an important centre in Petra, and the trade with Hither and central Asia centres at Palmyra. The sea-route from India goes either to

1. STONE BULLETS USED FOR ANCIENT ARTILLERY

Plate XXXII   WAR AND HUNTING

1. Stone bullets used for ancient artillery. They are of different sizes and weights. Similar stone bullets have been found in many ancient cities. The bullets were projected by catapults and attained velocities as high as 200 feet per second. The normal effective range was about 1,500 feet. This artillery was sometimes used on the battle field, but it was most effectively used as a weapon at the time of siege.

2. A FOREIGN SETTLER HUNTING IN PTOLEMAIC IDUMAEA

2. A hunting scene in Ptolemaic Palestine. The horseman is represented killing a leopardess with his long Macedonian lance. As the inscription says, the beast is already wounded by a dart. Two dogs are helping the hunter. The horse is covered by a saddle-cloth of Greek style. The hunter wears a short chiton and high-laced shoes, the Macedonian military dress. The painted inscription over his head is almost effaced. It seems that his (Semitic) name was Ananos. The horseman is followed by a trumpeter. The painting decorated a tomb, built in the 3rd century B.C. at Marissa in Idumaea.

1. MARBLE HEAD

2. BRONZE PORTRAIT HEAD

Plate XXXIII HELLENISTIC SCULPTURE

1. Marble head of a Galatian warrior. It belongs to the figure of the Galatian who, preferring death to captivity, killed himself after killing his wife. The original, a votive offering (in bronze) of Attalus I, once stood in the court of the temple of Athena at Pergamum. The so-called 'Dying Galatian' (see Pl. XXXVII) was probably a part of the same monument of Attalus, which celebrated his triumphs over the dreaded Gauls. A Roman copy is now in the Museo Nazionale delle Terme Diocleziane.

2. Bronze portrait head of one of the Levantine residents at Delos found in the ancient palaestra. The eyes are inlaid. The statue was probably made around 100 B.C. Both heads on this plate illustrate the emotional quality of Hellenistic art. National Museum, Athens.

the Arabian ports and thence to Egypt through the ports of the Red Sea, or through the Persian Gulf to the mouth of the Tigris, where stands the great commercial city of Seleucia, or Ctesiphon, the successor of Babylon in commercial importance. Antioch, on the river Orontes, becomes the capital of the Seleucidae, and attains the position of a great industrial city, where the raw material imported from Asia and India is worked up into the finished article.

In short, the Hellenistic world becomes one great market controlled by the Greek or Hellenized merchant and the Greek manufacturer. Most of the monarchies and cities retain Alexander's (that is, the Attic) standard of coinage (1 drachma = about 4.3 grams of silver). The Ptolemies, on the other hand, use the standard of their Phoenician cities (1 drachma = about 3.5 grams of silver) and, in this way, the Ptolemaic Empire forms an economically separate unit. The prevailing mood of the Eastern Greeks of early Hellenistic times is one of confidence in the unlimited capabilities of man and his reason. Aggressiveness and daring are evident. The Greeks in their new eastern homes are mainly concerned with securing for themselves a life of material prosperity and, if possible, of social prominence. To attain this they work hard and with enthusiasm. The manufacturer adopts and improves all the processes of skilled manufacture peculiar to the East, and adapts his wares to the taste of his customers. The Hellenistic trader becomes acquainted with the development of business life in the East, takes part in it, and elaborates it still further. Business methods are improved; credit and banking become increasingly important. All commercial transactions are based on credit and on abundance of coined metal. It is an immense convenience for exchange all the world over, when Greek, the universal language of civilization, also becomes by degrees the language for conducting business in the East. In all departments of life—in the form of the central government, in the system of administration, in the organization of the law courts, in taxation, and especially in business—local peculiarities fade away

Plate XXXIV   COINS OF THE HELLENISTIC PERIOD

(a) Tetradrachm of Ptolemy II Philadelphus of Egypt. Head of Ptolemy I r. *Rev.* Eagle on thunderbolt l. Name of the king. 284–247 B.C.

(b) Tetradrachm of Antiochus II Theos (the God). Head of the king r. *Rev.* Apollo seated on the 'omphalos' (the umbilicus, the centre of the earth) l. with arrow and bow. Name of the king. 261–246 B.C.

(c) Tetradrachm of Eumenes II of Pergamum. Head of the founder of the dynasty Philetaerus r. *Rev.* Athena seated l. Name of Philetaerus. 197–159 B.C.

(d) Tetradrachm of Prusias II of Bithynia. Head of the king r. *Rev.* Zeus standing l. Name of the king. 180–149 B.C.

(e) Tetradrachm of Perseus of Macedonia. Head of the king r. *Rev.* Eagle on thunderbolt in an oak-wreath r. Name of the king. 178–168 B.C.

(f) Tetradrachm of Euthydemus of Bactria. Head of the king r. *Rev.* Heracles seated on a rock l. Name of the king. About 220 B.C.

(g) Tetradrachm of Mithradates I of Parthia. Head of Arsaces, the founder of the dynasty r. *Rev.* Heracles walking l. Name of the king Arsaces. 171–138 B.C.

(h) Silver Cistophorus (¾ of an Attic tetradrachm) of Ephesus. The cistophori were first issued by Ephesus at about 200 B.C. as a kind of federal coin for Asia Minor; they were adopted and spread by the kingdom of Pergamum and later by the Romans. Cista mys-

tica (the mystic basket of the Dionysiac mysteries) with serpent issuing from it in an ivy wreath. *Rev.* Bow in bow-case between two serpents; r. the sacred stag of Artemis of Ephesus and l. the two first letters of the name of the city of Ephesus. 1st century B.C.

(i) Tetradrachm of Athens, struck by King Mithradates VI of Pontus and his factotum Aristion at Athens. Head of Athena r. *Rev.* Owl on an olive-oil amphora. Names of the city, of King Mithradates and of Aristion. In an olive wreath. 88 B.C.

All these coins are in the British Museum.

and acute angles become obtuse. Business life and life in general settle down everywhere on similar lines, familiar and customary all the world over, as free from local variations as the *koine*, the dialect spoken by all the Greeks of that age. Mobility becomes a salient characteristic of Greek life. Not only merchants but also artisans and technicians, physicians and artists are constantly moving. Royal officials easily pass into the service of another king. The Greek element is predominant in this new state of society and gives a unity and homogeneity to the entire Hellenistic world. The Eastern world is Hellenized by degrees. In many places, no doubt, this Hellenism is superficial, and Hellenic culture no more than a thin veneer.

The growth of the old Greek cities in Greece proper, Macedonia, Asia Minor, and Syria, the foundation by the Hellenistic monarchs of new Greek cities in Macedonia, Asia Minor, Syria, and even in Egypt, and the great development, founded mainly on slave labour, of trade and industry in these cities, led to an increase in the number of persons who were merely consumers, and not producers, of the means of subsistence. To these must be added the mercenary troops, the sailors who manned the fleets for war and commerce, and the steadily increasing swarm of government officials. Hence the problem of providing the cities with food, especially with bread, salt fish, cheese, wine, and vegetable oils, became more and more acute.

South Russia exported as before considerable quantities of corn, fish, hides, and other raw material, chiefly from part of the Crimea, the valley of the Kuban, the coast of the Sea of Azov, and the lower waters of the Don and Dnieper. In the first half of the third century B.C., the Scythian kingdom in the steppes of south Russia was broken up by the Sarmatians, a new Iranian stock coming from the East, and by Celtic and Thracian invaders from the West. But after a short period of decline and anarchy, the country was once more prosperous and engaged in active trade relations with Greece.

Elsewhere, Italy and Sicily were passing through a difficult period, full of wars and acute conflict, while Rome was unifying the country under her own supremacy; and this period was followed by the prolonged warfare between Rome and Carthage. Thus the economic life of the West was crippled for a time, and the export of food-stuffs and raw material ceased almost entirely. The Greek world depended more and more on Egypt and Asia Minor for sustenance. The prominence of Egypt in politics and her influence on other parts of the Hellenistic world were due to this, that she had the largest supplies of grain to dispose of. The kingdom of Pergamum also began to play the same part, and was one of the chief sources of corn-supply at the end of the third century B.C. Then and in the second century the African corn, grown in the territory of Carthage and the Nubian kingdom, came into the market. Such conditions as these in the production of food-stuffs led to fluctuating prices and financial instability in the Greek cities; they also opened a field for speculation, and a class of capitalists who speculated on a great scale was created. In many cases the Hellenistic kings themselves embarked on these speculations, making use of their economic advantages to gain political ends.

This state of things induced the kings of Egypt and Asia Minor and Hiero II in Sicily to give serious attention to the problem of increasing the productive powers of the lands over which they ruled. The systematic Greek genius came to their aid. Greek botany and Greek zoology now found a practical application in agriculture and stock-raising. Greek science collected the observations of practical farmers and breeders, combined them into a system, and made the first attempt to set the management of land on a scientific basis. Handbook after handbook on the subject appeared, dealing with the needs and peculiarities of different countries, and were regularly consulted by those landowners who managed their land on a capitalistic basis. It is a notable fact that among the authors of these manuals we find the kings of two of the monarchies mentioned above—Pergamum and Sicily. Another manual on the same subject written by Mago, a Carthaginian noble, was very famous.

This endeavour to increase the productiveness of the land shows itself also in new and improved methods applied to the cultivation of cereals; such were regular manuring of the soil, rotation of crops, and improvements in artificial irrigation. But special attention was paid to the scientific management of vineyards and olive trees; and novelties, in the way of fruit trees, vegetables, and grasses for fodder, were introduced into agriculture; while stock was improved by introducing new breeds and crossing them with the local strains. Improvements in agricultural science brought about a rapid transformation: primitive methods of tilling the soil gave place to a capitalistic system in which slave labour played a principal part. The same process is visible also in the domain of industry: here, too, kings set the example; here, too, slave labour and the large factory squeeze out more and more the independent artisan and domestic manufacture.

Connected with this is the extensive encouragement given by the kings to the enterprise of the Greeks settled in their dominions. We have seen already that trade was concentrated in Greek hands, and the same nation by degrees took the lead in agriculture and industry. The kings distributed large estates among their favourites, who were not owners but tenants under an obligation to introduce scientific methods of cultivation on these lands. A large amount of land belonging to the state was transferred to the hands of soldiers, who formed in Egypt a new class of foreign landholders, and created in Asia Minor and Syria new urban settlements. Great numbers of emigrants who were not soldiers were also attracted in order to develop the resources of the soil. Large territories in Asia Minor and Syria were allotted to settlers from Greece, and new Greek cities grew up there. In Egypt the settlers helped the king to organize the government of the country and its internal trade on the most satisfactory methods. The money which they gained these settlers invested chiefly in land.

In this way there grew up everywhere, both in town and country, a new middle class, containing both rich and poor. This class consisted, more often than not, of foreigners; and the native population were in general subservient to them and economically dependent upon them. Since all the territory of the realm belonged to the king, and the principle of private ownership applied only to districts bestowed upon Greeks and other settlers, and even in their case was limited, therefore the king could dispose of it all as he pleased. The native population, having cultivated the land from time immemorial, continued to cultivate it, not for themselves but for the king who owned it, and for those to whom the king had granted a part of it, together with its inhabitants, to enjoy for a term or in perpetuity. As before, the population remained bound to the soil, and their labour was exploited by the sovereign. Nor did the native population enjoy any more independence in their relation to the settlers. The latter seldom cultivated the lands bestowed on them: the usual practice was to leave the former tenants in possession and exact from them part of the produce. Wherever improvements in cultivation and reclamation of waste lands were undertaken by the king, or his favourites, or the settlers, this was carried out, almost invariably, by slaves or hirelings, and also by forced labour on the part of the native inhabitants.

Thus the immense majority of the natives in the Hellenistic monarchies were despised and impoverished; and this led to grave social and economic results. Wealth was concentrated in the cities. City dwellers, government officials, and the army, were almost the only customers for the products of industry. The rural population and the slaves, labouring for the benefit of others, have not the means to acquire anything whatever outside the limits of their most urgent needs. Whatever they must have, they try to produce for themselves. Hence industry is carried on to supply the needs of a comparatively small number;

workshops are not converted into regular factories; ingenuity is not employed to discover means of mass production; machinery does not take the place of manual labour. And this depressed condition of the people gives rise to hostile relations between the higher and lower classes, both in town and country. This hostility takes the form of strikes, and bursts forth from time to time in revolts of the native populations—revolts often headed by priests. Such revolts were especially common in Egypt, but were, of course, put down by means of the mercenary troops.

This system by which the native population was exploited and ground down was carried through with exceptional thoroughness in Egypt. All the economic life of the country was based upon government control, which embraced all agriculture, all industry, and all trade. The middlemen between the toiling millions and the government were sometimes officials and sometimes tax-farmers, but generally both together. The tax-farmers, who collected the taxes, also directed the labour of the workshops and even domestic manufacture, which produced goods for sale, not for purposes of the household; and the same class had a monopoly in the sale of certain commodities in specified parts of the kingdom. Of course, all this business was done under the supervision, and with the assistance, of the officials, who included the police.

The Hellenistic kings failed to establish a reasonable mode of co-existence between the Greeks, who were the associates of the ruler, and the natives, the economic backbone of the realm. They could not settle the conflict between the Greek and the Oriental forms of life, between the Greeks and the natives, between the Greek economic system, based on private initiative, and the state economy of the East. They were faced with the gulf between the 'haves' and the 'have-nots', the proprietors and the working classes. The co-operation of the powers was made impossible by the ceaseless struggles for political hegemony. The wars absorbed an enormous quantity of human energy, encouraged the destructive spirit, and created an ever-increasing sense of uncertainty, which induced apathy.

Greece, particularly Athens, rapidly recovered from the economic crisis of the late fourth century. Greece derived a great advance in prosperity from several sources—the immense booty thrown on the market by the conquest of the Persian Empire, new opportunities of employment in the armies and administration of Alexander and his successors, emigration to the newly founded Greek cities and settlements in Asia and Egypt, and the new markets for Greek products in the East. The rapid increase in the demand for Greek goods inflated the prices of all commodities and also raised the price of labour. The New Comedy illustrates the life of a new, powerful, and wealthy middle class.

However, after the period of large migration to the East came to an end, the economic difficulties and the social unrest increased. The constantly recurring wars and concomitant civil strike caused by the struggle of Hellenistic kings for Greece led to a gradual decline of the middle class. The slow but steady emancipation of the East from dependence on Greece for industrial goods which were made for mass consumption decreased the demand for these Greek manufactures. The importance of free labour rapidly declined. The bourgeoisie shaped the life of the city according to its own interests and ideas. But politically, workers enjoyed the rights of full citizens and the proletariate constantly strove, by using its political force, to realize the reforms it most coveted: cancellation of debts and redistribution of land.

In the end the conditions of life became burdensome and unstable in almost all Greek cities. The rift between rich and poor, the *bourgeoisie* and the proletariate, grew wider. The strife was carried on by political and social revolutions which ended in the victory of one class or the other and the extermination of their rivals, while the property of the vanquished was confiscated and distributed. The article which Athens inserted in the civic oath after the Peloponnesian war, providing that no citizen should propose division of land or cancellation of debt, appeared now in the constitutions of many city-states. The Corinthian League of Greek communities, founded by Philip and renewed subsequently by Alexander, Demetrius Poliorcetes, and Antigonus Gonatas, was partly political and partly social in its aims; and one of its main objects was to suppress social revolution. But the League was unsuccessful; and the Achaean and Aetolian Leagues, the two largest in Greece, failed also, in spite of their rigid and systematic principles in favour of property. Social revolution burst out repeatedly, now here and now there, and steadily undermined the prosperity of Greece and the islands. The Hellenistic kings were powerless to cure this cancer of Greek life, and no city ever seriously attempted to solve the social problem. The problem of wealth and poverty was regarded by philosophers as a question of personal morals.

One episode of the kind is especially well known to us—the prolonged war of classes at Sparta. There the social question was exceptionally acute. We have seen how the predominance of Sparta after the Peloponnesian war brought wealth to the country and to many individual Spartans. On the other hand, the loss of Messenia, which followed on the blows inflicted by Boeotia, ruined a number of the Spartiates, while their failures in foreign policy and heavy casualties in war reduced to a minimum the number of Spartiates enjoying full rights. Thus there grew up among the Spartiates themselves, to say nothing of the Perioeci and Helots, a sharp division between the aristocracy and the proletariate, the rich and the poor. The growth of communistic and socialistic ideas, the conviction that Sparta had once been a land where the ideal of communism had been fully realized, and also an ardent patriotism which refused to put up with the political insignificance of the country—such were the motives which drove the young king, Agis IV, to enter on the path of social and economic reform. About 244 B.C. circumstances happened to be favourable, and he endeavoured to carry out his plan. All debts were to be cancelled; the land was to be confiscated and divided up among 4,500 Spartiates and 15,000 Perioeci. Some of the large landholders, whose property was mortgaged, supported the first item of this programme, and it was carried; but the endeavour to realize the second proved fatal to Agis. His opponents, led by the other king, Leonidas, put him to death in 241 B.C.

Thirteen years later the attempt was renewed by Cleomenes III, the son of Leonidas. In order to carry out his designs Cleomenes did not stop short of violence. By banishing some and executing others he strengthened his personal position and apparently carried out the whole programme of Agis. Then at the head of a regenerated Sparta he tried to seize power in the Peloponnese and throughout Greece. At first he was supported by the proletariate in all the cities. But in the end, in order to preserve the existing system of society and to prevent the unification of Greece round Sparta, Antigonus Doson, king of Macedonia, declared war against Cleomenes and inflicted a decisive defeat on him at Sellasia. Thus the reforms of Cleomenes were brought to naught. The attempt was renewed once again in 207 B.C. by Nabis, who had seized power at Sparta. But by that time Rome was beginning to assert her authority in Greece. After the death of Nabis the Achaean League put an end, not only to his projects of social reform but also to the political importance of Sparta in general.

In consequence partly of the social disorder in Greece, from which Athens alone was free, and partly of the prosperity of the East, which had now become the centre of economic life, the marked progress which Greece had made at the beginning of the third century B.C. began to flag and fail more and more at the end of that century and in the next. Population and wealth began to leave Greece; and her ruin was completed by Rome.

XVII

GREEK CIVILIZATION IN THE THIRD
AND SECOND CENTURIES B.C.

It is usual to regard the period which followed the death of
Alexander as a period when the civilization of Greece mingled
with that of the East, to form a new civilization which became
the property of all men who were civilized at all. But this view
is not supported by the facts. Above all, there was no real fusion
of nationalities in the Graeco-Oriental monarchies ruled by
Alexander's successors. Considerable numbers of Greeks or Hellenized barbarians were diffused over the surface of the Eastern
world, collecting mainly in the cities, and admitted to their
ranks certain members of the native population, preferring those
who were highest in station. As I have pointed out already, these
Greeks and Hellenized barbarians formed the highest class in
the new Hellenistic kingdoms: they spoke Greek, and had a
common manner of life, and shared the same interests and the
same education and upbringing. But they remained merely a
minority and foreigners to the great mass of the inhabitants.
The latter continued to live their own life, to speak their native
tongues, and to believe in their own gods. Greek culture found
hardly any access to their midst. It remained an urban culture,
and these Eastern cities were a mere superstructure, independent
of the native population. The kings never wanted the Greeks to
become amalgamated with the natives. To say nothing of India,
central Asia, Syria, Palestine, and Arabia, even in Asia Minor

and Egypt, where the connexion with Greece had existed for many centuries, the process of Hellenization was extremely slow; and even in the period of Roman domination, we have the express evidence of Paul the Apostle that the natives of Asia Minor still spoke Phrygian and Galatian.

Under such conditions it is difficult to suppose that the civilization of the East could exercise any strong influence upon the genius of Greece; and in fact we find hardly any trace of such an influence. Greek literature, Greek art, and Greek science remained Greek even after the death of Alexander. Some kinds of literature—the fairy tale, the novel, and apocalyptic literature —were slightly affected; and Eastern influence may be seen also in some local peculiarities of Greek art and some offshoots of Greek science, such as astrology and, perhaps, alchemy; but especially in the sphere of religion, where many Oriental ideas were assimilated by the Greek part of the population.

Thus the civilization of the so-called Hellenistic Age is really Greek civilization. In what then did its power consist, and what were its distinguishing marks? First of all, we must altogether discard the once fashionable notion, that this was a decadent civilization. We shall see later that the facts lend no support to this theory. The Greek genius was just as creative as it had been in earlier times; and it still shaped forth treasures not less precious than those of the fifth and fourth centuries B.C. It is true that the form of this civilization was altered; but the alteration followed the lines laid down in the fourth century. Athens in the fourth century aimed at creating a single civilization for all Greece, and was able to go far in that direction. In the third century the task was accomplished: Greek civilization actually spread over the world, and was shared by every one who, within the limits of the ancient world, lived a civilized or, in other words, an urban life.

At this time these dwellers in cities all spoke Greek, and the language was tacitly accepted as the only language for civilized people. The external conditions of life were the same for them all. Their cities had paved streets and squares, an excellent system of water-supply and drainage, hygienic markets, extensive school-buildings and libraries, stone theatres, athletic grounds and race-courses, elaborate temples and altars, and public buildings corresponding to the size of the city, where the town council and popular assembly held their meetings. In the provincial towns there were comfortable detached houses of moderate size, and in the capitals palaces on one hand and large lodging-houses on the other. And just these external conditions were reckoned as indispensable to the life of a civilized being.

Throughout the whole extent of the Hellenistic world this class read the same books, admired the same plays on the stage, and listened to the same musicians and actors who travelled from city to city. They all received a similar training and education in the wrestling-schools and gymnasiums, which exercised the body and educated the mind by music and letters—a combination characteristic of Greece. And again, unless he had undergone this Greek education, unless he could read Homer, Plato, and Sophocles, and enjoy the comedies of Menander and the refined music of the age, no one was counted a man of culture. All who stood outside this common culture were reckoned as barbarians, whether they lived outside or inside the circle of Hellenistic kingdoms. It is remarkable also that the Greeks did not force their civilization upon any man. To make proselytes by force never occurred to their minds. Their culture owed its worldwide recognition mainly to its perfection, and partly to the fact that it belonged to the dominating and ruling class of the population. One of the few attempts made to carry on propaganda by force was made by Antiochus IV in Judaea; and it ended in utter failure; for it provoked a violent reaction of nationality among the Jews.

Under such conditions the creative genius of Greece finally lost its local limitations: it ceased to belong to separate Greek cities and became the common property of all Greeks. The poets of Alexandria or Athens no longer wrote for a restricted circle of fellow-citizens, but for every one, all the world over, who lived the Greek life and who thought and spoke in the Greek language. Long before, Greek philosophers had begun to speak of man in general; and now authors, musicians, savants, and artists worked for the sake of this audience. Access to Hellenic civilization was freely granted to all who were able and willing to take part in it. The conception of a certain quality peculiar to a civilized being—the conception embodied in the Latin word *humanitas*—dates from this age, and so does the idea of a civilized world. The famous relief of Archelaus, a native of Priene in Asia Minor, which represents the crowning of Homer by the World and Time, clearly emphasizes the fundamental idea of Hellenistic humanity: Homer, the father of that humanity or, in other words, of Greek civilization, had created it for the sake of the whole world and to last for ever. The future proved that the pride of that age in its past and present was justified.

The power of the Greek genius did not show itself only in the creation of Greek civilization. It is manifest also in its infectious quality—in the fact that its influence extended far beyond the limits to which the Greek nation expanded. Hellenistic culture, though it was scarcely affected by Eastern influence, had a strong effect itself upon the future development of the East. It is true that this effect was not visible at once—the Greek leaven was slow in working—but it contributed largely to the renascence of Eastern civilization which took place under the Roman Empire and in the early Middle Ages: witness the Persian culture of the Sassanian era, the culture of north India at the beginning of the Roman Empire, and the renewal of culture in Armenia, Georgia, and finally Arabia in the early Middle Ages.

The infectious character of Greek civilization had also a powerful influence on the creation of Western European civilization, chiefly in Italy and, to some extent, in Gaul and Spain. The Latin culture of Italy and the West is one branch of the Greek culture of the third and later centuries—not a slavish copy, nor an imitation, but an independent national development of Greek ideas, Greek art, and Greek literature in the Latin West, a participation by the West in the city-life of the Hellenic East with all its external characteristics.

What new element did the Hellenistic Age add to the acquisitions of Greek civilization? What gives us the right to call this age creative? Let us, first of all, turn our attention to religion. What strikes us is the close connexion between religion and morality in this period. This was partly due to philosophy, especially Stoicism, to literature which discussed eagerly problems of public and private morals, and to the contact with the religions of the East. All this, taken together, prepared a soil for the growth of Christianity with its high moral and religious teaching. It is notable that at the same time the most prominent question in the sphere of religion concerns death and a future life; and with this is bound up another question—a man's conduct in his lifetime in point of morality as well as of religion. The Eleusinian mysteries of Demeter, which, in combination with Orphism, had given a central position to these matters in their divine revelation, after the death of Alexander spread over the entire Greek world, penetrating Egypt, Italy, Sicily, and the remote colonies on the shores of the Black Sea. Gold plates inscribed with Orphic texts, which tell of what awaits man after death, have been found in south Italian graves belonging to the early Hellenistic Age, and also in Cretan tombs. Alexandria had an Eleusis of its own and a shrine of Demeter constructed on the Athenian pattern. An interesting document was lately found in Egypt—a roll, containing certain prayers commonly used in the mysteries, and an indication of what the believer may expect in a life beyond the grave. With these tendencies we may connect the diffusion over the whole Greek world of the cult of Sarapis, founded originally by the Ptolemies in Egypt and combining Greek and Egyptian beliefs, the Greek notions of a future life, and the ideas of Thracians and Anatolians concerning the same fundamental question.

This growing interest in the problem of a future life led to the gradual introduction of Eastern forms of worship into the Greek world. These cults were carried on by independent communities, which were not connected with any distinct country or nation. The Greeks were attracted by their mysterious and magnificent rites and the mystic meaning that they concealed, by the deep religious feeling of the worshippers, and by that opportunity of allegorical and philosophical interpretation which their tragical and edifying myths freely afforded. But at the same time the Greeks were repelled by the coarseness and sensuality of the Eastern mysteries. They sought, therefore, while accepting these forms of worship, to import into them their own religious and moral conceptions, and to mitigate the primitive rudeness of the ritual—in a word, to Hellenize them. In this connexion we may notice the rules of some Anatolian religious bodies, whose members united to celebrate the mysteries of the Great Goddess, and included in their requirements purity of heart as well as of body. These moral ideas they personified in a number of new divine figures, male and female, including Justice, Purity, and Virtuous Actions.

Greek religion thus becomes more and more spiritual and abstract, and at the same time loses its connexion with special city-states. In the mind of an educated Greek the idea of God in general, the idea of the divine, begins to take the place of particular deities; and the latter survive only in poetry and art and in the creeds of the uneducated. In the light of these new tendencies, which became more and more prevalent both in Greece itself and among the Greeks of the Hellenistic monarchies, it is easier to understand the attempt of the Hellenistic kings to combine politics and religion in worship paid to the sovereign, to which we have referred in the preceding chapter. This worship, in so far as it entered into the life of their Greek or Hellenized subjects, had no connexion with the old Eastern king-worship which still persisted in its ancient forms among the native population of these countries. The worship of kings which became established by degrees in the Greek cities was quite

1. MARBLE STATUETTE

Plate XXXV   THE SELEUCID EMPIRE
AND ITS PROTECTORS

1. Marble statuette of the Tyche (Fortune) of Antioch, the capital
of the Seleucids. This late reproduction of the statue was made in
bronze by one of the pupils of Lysippus, Eutychides. The 'Good
Fortune' of the city is seated on a rock. Under her feet is the river
Orontes, represented as a swimming boy; on her head she wears a
mural crown; in her right hand she holds stalks of grain. The type
of city goddess created by Eutychides became popular in the ancient
world. The head and some other parts are restored after other repli-
cas of the original. Vatican, Rome.

2. A CULT IMAGE FROM DURA-EUROPOS

2. A cult image from Dura-Europos. The bas-relief dedicated in
A.D. 158–9 in a temple at Dura shows, as the Palmyrene inscription
on the base states: 'The god-patron (*Gad*) of Dura'. He is represented as Zeus, seated on an eagle throne, wearing the royal diadem,
and holding stalks of wheat in his right hand and a sceptre in his left.
He is being crowned by Seleucus Nicator who, the inscription tells
us, is founder of the city. Seleucus Nicator, attired in Macedonian
battle dress, wears a diadem and ear-rings, and holds a lance. The
dedicant in Palmyrene priestly dress is burning incense on an altar.
Yale Gallery of Fine Arts.

different: it was intimately bound up with that conception of divinity mentioned above. To a Greek it was not at all astonishing that this divine element should, from time to time or continuously, be incarnated in leaders, saviours, and benefactors of mankind. Hence are derived the names under which the Hellenistic kings were worshipped—Soter, 'Saviour'; Theos, 'God'; Epiphanes, 'The Revealed One'; Euergetes, 'Benefactor'; New Dionysus, and New Heracles.

Side by side with religious mysticism, we find rationalism and materialism widely diffused in the society of the age. Agnosticism, which denies that man can know anything about God; atheism, which disbelieves in God; scepticism, and euhemerism, which explains away the supernatural part of religion—all these had plenty of partisans and followers, for whom religion was merely an artificial invention of the human mind. An instance of this tendency is the deification of Luck and Fortune—Tyché, *Fortuna*—powers whose worship was widely diffused throughout the whole Hellenistic world.

The inexhaustible power of Greek genius, even after the death of Alexander, is clearly shown in the domain of art and letters. New kinds of literature come to the front, created by the requirements and changed character of the age. Some of the old forms, tragedy for instance, die out by degrees, while others, such as epic poetry, change their aspect; and new forms, closely allied to the old, flourish luxuriantly. Dramatic poetry is chiefly represented by the New Comedy, a comedy of character and idea and, in a less degree, of intrigue. It proceeds from the tragedy of Euripides and the philosophic study of human character in all its variety—a subject on which Theophrastus, the pupil of Aristotle, wrote a book. An Athenian, Menander, was the most famous writer of these comedies; and some manuscripts of his plays have recently been discovered in the ruins of Egyptian towns and villages.

Akin to comedy are a number of new literary types, half realistic and half philosophical. Such are the mimes—scenes from common life, a distorting mirror which reproduces the low life of Greek cities. Sophron in the fifth century B.C. had been a skilful writer of mimes, and he was now followed by Herondas, a native of Cos. Together with the literary mime there were popular forms of it, full of lively humour and often frankly obscene. Partly sung and partly spoken, they parodied both comedy and tragedy; they turned chiefly on love and the adventures of lovers. Very few specimens of this latter kind have been preserved: it did not reckon itself as literature and made no claim to permanence.

Another popular form of composition is the Diatribe, mainly Cynic in its origin. Written both in prose and verse, it fights a fierce battle against the conventionality, hypocrisy, frivolity, immorality, and injustice of the time. The most famous writer of Diatribe in prose was Bion, a native of Olbia on the Black Sea; but from recent discoveries we know more of the Diatribes in verse, written by Crates of Thebes, Menippus of Gadara, Cercidas of Megalopolis, Phoenix of Colophon, and Timon of Phlius. The work of Cercidas is specially interesting, because it pictures so clearly the stormy politics and social life of the time.

In contrast with ludicrous and trifling scenes of town life, the Idyll, in which Theocritus, a Sicilian, reached the summit of perfection, depicts the life of shepherds and husbandmen—a life so remote and so desirable to the dwellers in great cities with their bustle and noise and pursuit of gain. The same idyllic note is imported into miniature epics, in which ancient legends are retold, and which, like the idyll, combine romantic description of the past with fine writing about lovers and, in some cases, delicate delineation of character. Callimachus is the chief writer of the little epic.

The wider horizon of the Hellenistic Greeks, their greater knowledge of other nations, and the stress laid by philosophers on humanity as distinct from nationality, made society take an interest in the so-called barbaric peoples—Scythians, Thracians,

1. AN ON-STAGE SCENE FROM ONE OF THE 'NEW' COMEDIES

Plate XXXVI   NEW COMEDY

1. A bas-relief showing an on-stage scene from one of the 'new' comedies. A young man of respectable family comes home after a banquet. He is in high spirits, hardly able to walk, and is shouting and brandishing the filet worn at the banquet. His slave has to support him. A girl-flutist accompanies him. The infuriated father is rushing toward the young man, prepared to give him a thrashing with his stick. His friend tries to stop him. Roman copy of a Greek work. Naples Museum.

2. BAS-RELIEF OF MENANDER

2. Bas-relief of Menander. The most popular author of the New
Comedy, here shown in the heroic dress which symbolizes his blessed
after-life, is seated on a chair contemplating a comic mask of a youth,
representing one of the chief characters of his plays. The mask of a
girl and of a father, other stock types in his comedies, are on the
table before him. Behind the table stands the majestic figure of a
woman who is probably a Muse. It is likely that the relief dates from
the 1st century B.C. Lateran, Rome.

and Celts. The philosophers, followed by such historians as Ephorus, approach the study of these races from the moral point of view: their souls are vexed by the corruption of contemporary society, and they paint a somewhat imaginary picture of the noble savage, combining reality with fancy, and representing his life as an embodiment of personal and social morality. From the same sources the Romance of travel and adventure is developed after Eastern models; the author carries his hero and heroine from one unknown country to another, and finally unites them in the bonds of marriage. Of Eastern origin is the fairy tale also, which now, when written in Greek by Aesop, becomes a favourite both with adults and children.

Another highly popular form of literature is the Epigram—a brief rendering in verse of the most various impressions, a terse and witty summary of whatever excited the poet's interest. To the same category belong metrical epitaphs, which describe in brief the character of the dead man and the feelings of surviving relations and friends; and also inscriptions on consecrated objects. Hellenistic poetry lays more stress on love than on any other emotion. An infinite number of elegiac poems, with mortal men or immortal gods for heroes, were written at this time. As most of these poets had patrons among the powerful of this world and many of them were dependants of the kings, their verse often ministers to the pride of these personages—proclaiming the luxury of their palaces and parks, the splendour of their festivals, and the glory of their military exploits. Nevertheless, the poets are not blind to the seamy side of life. For instance, Lycophron in his *Alexandra* (another name for Cassandra, who declaims the whole tragedy as a monologue) in mysterious language, full of mystical and mythical presentiment, foretells the speedy ruin and destruction of those great Hellenistic monarchies which seemed so firmly established.

Finally, that local patriotism which, in spite of the dispersion of the Greeks, never ceased to burn in their hearts, and the consciousness that the city-state and its past glory were dying out by degrees, created a romantic interest in that half-legendary past not only among savants, but also among poets who were themselves savants and antiquarians. Thus there were produced such works as the *Aitia* of Callimachus, partly ethical and partly scientific, in which the learned poet parades before the reader's eyes a succession of far-fetched myths and forgotten legends, often dealing with unimportant and depopulated places. The same combination of science and poetry is found in attempts to expound in verse a treatise on some technical subject: Nicander's *Antidotes to Poisons* and *Snake-Bites*, and the versified Astronomy of Aratus are familiar instances.

In all the literary production of the Hellenistic Age one common feature is observable: apart from the interest of the subject, the reader demanded of the author excellence of form. And this excellence has been carried to the highest point in the best work. The vocabulary is copious, varied, and elegant; the style is refined and highly flexible, varying with the subject; the metres are handled with the utmost care on strictly scientific methods. Authorship had become a speciality requiring a long and laborious apprenticeship. A special class of writers by profession was now seen for the first time in Greek society.

These men did more than create a new literature: they guarded jealously and studied attentively all that had been done before their time. Most of them, whether poets or prose-writers, were scholars also, who gave a considerable part of their time to the study of the best productions belonging to that period which they also regarded as classical in the history of Greek literature; they published critical editions and commentaries on those productions. This interest in the past has borne fruit of the highest importance. For these learned authors first introduced past literature into schools, as an indispensable study for every educated man. They, too, saved for posterity the meagre information which we possess concerning the writers from the seventh to the third centuries B.C. They created literary biography and based on it the history of literature. Under their influence the first great public libraries were formed.

Under their influence also books made their way into private houses and families; and this promoted the trade in books and laid a foundation for the publishing business. The ubiquity of books in the life of the Hellenistic Greeks is clearly proved by the discoveries of books or scattered leaves in the private houses and tombs of Greeks who lived in the cities and even villages of Egypt. If a considerable part of Greek literature, and especially the classical, pre-Hellenistic part, has been preserved, we owe this to the scholars of the Hellenistic Age.

To study the past is the special province of history, which is partly literature and partly science; and it goes without saying that the historians of this age took a lively interest in the past, whether immediate or remote, of the Greeks themselves and of so-called 'barbarians'; nor did they neglect the history of their own times. A number of writers, some of whom had taken part in the incidents they described, wrote the history of Alexander's reign. The Hellenistic monarchies and individual Greek cities had also their own historiographers. Others studied the history of the East. Recent archaeological discovery has thrown much light on the history of Egypt and Babylonia; our previous knowledge, except that gained from Herodotus, was almost all derived from two Hellenized priests of this period, Manetho and Berosus, an Egyptian and a Babylonian. And other historians, notably Timaeus, undertook a new task, by collecting and arranging facts referring to the history of the West, especially of Italy. I may notice also that the religious books of the East were first translated at this time: the first translation of the Old Testament into Greek was made at Alexandria under the Ptolemies.

While the historian in literary form either described a single period in the development of the past or wrote a general history from the earliest times, there were also many historical specialists in the Hellenistic Age who collected materials for history in monographs or threw light upon disputed points. It should also be noticed that men were interested, not only in the records of political events, but also in the history of human civilization. The first general outline of civilization and its development in Greece was written by Dicaearchus, a pupil of Aristotle, and called *The Life of Hellas*. Unfortunately, hardly anything has been preserved out of the immense historical production of the Hellenistic Age. The Romans, who guarded jealously the classical literature of Greece, took little interest in Hellenistic history. So most of the historical works belonging to this period disappeared gradually from circulation and found no place in medieval libraries. And, indeed, the same fate befell the other writers and savants of the age: our knowledge of them is derived from sorry fragments or extracts preserved by later writers, under the Roman Republic or the Roman Empire.

Art in the Hellenistic Age, whether architecture or sculpture or painting, was still Greek. Architects gave their attention chiefly to buildings for secular purposes. Temples, indeed, were still built in large numbers, remarkable for vast proportions and increasing elegance of detail; and immense altars surrounded by colonnades, like the altar of Zeus at Pergamum, were constructed; but no new architectural ideas or forms were employed in these works. Secular architecture, on the other hand, was rich in invention. Royal palaces, parks and gardens to surround them, pavilions and lakes in the parks, royal country residences—all these were planned and built in rapid succession at Alexandria, Antioch, Pergamum, and Pella. Construction of this kind offered new problems to the architects of the day. Though they could learn much from their Eastern predecessors, it is certain that they solved many of their difficulties independently; for one thing, they employed for their new objects the colonnades and pillars which had been first freely used for Greek temples. Unfortunately, not a single Hellenistic palace has been preserved, except that of Pergamum, which was built in Roman times. But it is very probable that the Palatine residence and Italian villas of the Roman emperors were copied from the palaces and villas of the Hellenistic monarchs.

About their methods of town-building we have much fuller information. A number of cities, which were either founded or entirely rebuilt in this age, have been investigated in recent times: such are Pergamum, Miletus, Priene, Assus, Magnesia on the Maeander, in Asia Minor; Pompeii in Italy; and others in Sicily, Syria, and Egypt. Everywhere we see the skill with which the town has been planned, the regularity with which the separate districts have been laid out, the care with which the sites for public buildings and open spaces were chosen. The haphazard arrangement of houses which had before been normal now gave place to a regular system. Types of public buildings were definitely fixed for the first time and constantly repeated—halls for the city council, the civil courts, and the body of citizens; theatres and concert-rooms; markets and exchanges; lighthouses; gymnasiums and wrestling-grounds; fields for athletics and racecourses. Lastly, now and not till now, architecture stoops to the construction of convenient and beautiful private houses, with entrances, courts, and enclosed gardens.

Another architectural novelty which belongs to this period is the rapid erection of temporary buildings, purely decorative, and large and beautiful, for the festivals and gaieties of the Hellenistic kings. Thus an immense pavilion was constructed in a few days at Babylon by Alexander's orders, on the occasion of a splendid banquet given to his soldiers when by his command they were marrying Persian brides; and another pavilion, of great size and richly adorned, was put up at Alexandria by the architects of Ptolemy Philadelphus as a banqueting-room on a great occasion. Among the triumphs of architecture some Hellenistic writers mention huge floating palaces built for the kings of Egypt, and a luxurious vessel for passengers and cargo built in Sicily by the orders of Hiero II.

In sculpture and painting Hellenistic art repeats the subjects of the classical period, or imitates the simplicity and severity of the ancients in what are called archaistic statues and pictures; and also it seeks new paths of its own. The novelties of their art resemble the novelties of their literature. Some attempt to realize the colossal and the grandiose, as in the statue of Helios at Rhodes; or, as in the altar of Pergamum, to represent superhuman suffering and the limits of bodily and mental effort; other delight in the idyllic and romantic, or in realism carried to the point of caricature and oddity. The altar of Pergamum shows an accumulation of contending figures in the battle of gods and giants; the Laocoon depicts the suffering of a man dying in ineffable torments; and the mosaic found at Pompeii represents Alexander and his Macedonians fighting Darius and his Persians. But sculpture and painting depict other scenes as well—the noble knight saving a tender maid from a terrible dragon; Dionysus, finding Ariadne sleeping, when she was deserted by her faithless lover, Theseus; the young and old Centaurs in the power of mischievous Eros; a group of shepherds with their sheep and goats beside a rustic shrine; a peasant driving his cow to market; a fisherman returning from his toil; a lioness with her cubs, a ewe with her lambs, a flock of pigeons on the edge of a vessel of water; a tipsy old woman holding a bottle; a little slave asleep beside a lantern; scenes from the life of barbarian nations. In fact, there is no limit to the subjects chosen by painters and sculptors.

Apart from this variety of subject and treatment, the Hellenistic sculptors, led by Lysimachus, attacked and finally solved one of the hardest problems of sculpture in general—the problem of movement. In the Hellenistic statues movement is expressed, not only by the position of the separate limbs, but by every muscle of the body: each muscle is affected by the violent or slow motion of the figure.

Painting now attained absolute mastery of technique. Perspective was carefully studied, and foreshortening correctly practised; the problem of representing bodies in space was dealt with; serious attention was paid for the first time to landscape, which

1. MODEL OF THE RESTORED 'ACRA' OF PERGAMUM

Plate XXXVII ART OF PERGAMUM

1. Model of the restored 'acra' of Pergamum as seen from the west, made by H. Schleif. Pergamum Museum, Berlin.

2. A marble copy of one of a group of bronze statues dedicated by King Attalus I (241–197 B.C.) in the courtyard of the temple of Athena at Pergamum in memory of his brilliant victories over the Galatians (see Pl. XXXIII). The statue represents a wounded Galatian dying. The pathos of death is rendered with mastery. The sculptor is not rejoicing over the death of a barbarian: he is full of sympathy with the brave fighter. 3rd century B.C. Capitoline Museum, Rome.

3. Portrait of Attalus I, the ruler of Pergamum. From Pergamum. 3rd century B.C. Berlin Museum.

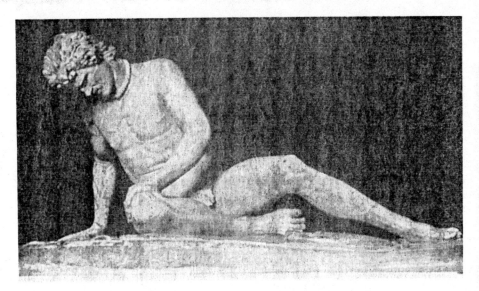

2. THE DYING GALATIAN

3. PORTRAIT OF ATTALUS I

involved such difficulties as the grouping of figures and the conveying of light and shade.

Perhaps the most remarkable achievements of the Alexandrian Age were performed in the domain of science. Philosophy at this time became detached from science and occupied a special position of its own. It was entirely devoted to the study of humanity, and preferred the psychological point of view to the physiological. The Academy, founded by Plato, continued to discuss the theory of knowledge which their master had been the first to open up; but the final result of inquiry was to convert Plato's idealism into a dull and barren scepticism. Far greater influence was enjoyed by other Socratic schools founded in the fourth century B.C. The Peripatetics, or followers of Aristotle, now definitely devoted themselves to the exact sciences and the social sciences. The Cynics, Stoics, and Epicureans take just the opposite view: they assert their complete independence of science. And all three schools have a further point in common. When the civic ideal set by the city-state had collapsed, the more reflective inhabitants of the Hellenistic states sought feverishly for a meaning of life, an ideal, and rules of conduct. A few could draw consolation from religion; but the purely rationalistic education given by philosophy in the past had produced its effect, and the majority sought an answer to their doubts, not from God but from reason. And that answer came from the Cynics, Stoics, and Epicureans. The schools all start with the same idea: a man can find satisfaction nowhere but in himself and his own inner world. Tranquillity of mind (*ataraxia*) is a thing inside us; to the sage the external world is a matter of indifference. 'It is possible', said the Stoic, 'to adapt yourself to that world, and to work in it and for it honestly and actively; but you must not sacrifice your own peace of mind.' 'You may fight with it and show it up', said the Cynics, 'and put on a warlike aspect in relation to it.' 'You may look at it with a pitying sneer', said the Epicureans, 'and take from it the best it has to give; but this is of small account compared with that peace of mind which turns a slave into a free man and a king.' A man has duties towards his fellow men, but his chief duty is towards himself; and that alone can save him from a life of petty anxiety and moral insignificance.

This theory of indifference, however, had little practical effect upon men's actions. They continued to work and to create, especially in the domain of science. Of the social sciences I have already spoken. Still more was accomplished in what are called the exact or experimental sciences. We are still quite unable to estimate the progress made in these by the Greeks of the third and second centuries B.C. Their treatises are lost, and we have to piece them together from selections or later work in the same field. This is a difficult and complicated process, for which a knowledge of languages and ancient history is needed, and also a knowledge of the stage reached at a given period by this or that branch of exact science. But even now it is becoming clear that many capital discoveries of modern times were, in principle, anticipated by the savants of the Hellenistic Age. By a series of experiments Herophilus explained the functions of the brain, studied the nervous system, and mastered the main principles of the circulation of the blood. Aristarchus of Samos, a contemporary of Ptolemy II, came to the conclusion that the earth moves around the sun, and measured the distances of the sun and of the moon. The attainments of Archimedes in mathematics and mechanics were extraordinary, and mathematical astronomy remained dependent on the Greeks up to Newton. Manuals of geometry used in our schools go back to Euclid's *Elements*, just as all our grammars proceed from the textbook of Dionysius, an Alexandrian scholar of the second century B.C. What Euclid did for geometry was done for trigonometry by Apollonius of Perga. The foundations of mathematical geography were laid by Eratosthenes. Nor would it be difficult to add many more names to this list.

At least in some fields, including for instance architecture and engineering, pure science began to help practice. Archimedes is also famous for his machines, such as the water-pump and the military engines used against the Romans during the siege of Syracuse (212 B.C.). The Hellenistic astronomers needed and built very complex computers which indicated the moon phenomena and the movements of the planets.

It is typical also of the Hellentistic Age that learning and the importance of learning were then for the first time recognized and appreciated by the state. The private philosophic schools still went on; but side by side with them rose the first public establishments for the encouragement of literature and science. The Museum (or 'Home of the Muses') at Alexandria was the first learned society maintained by the state. It was a society of savants and men of letters who devoted their whole lives to science and literature. A great library was placed at their service, and also other appliances for study, for instance, a zoological garden. Pergamum could boast of a similar institution, and so sought to rival Alexandria in this field also.

CHRONOLOGY

All dates before 776 are hypothetical and approximative with a margin of error of 100-200 years, before 2000, and 50-100 years, afterwards.

Earliest settlements in the Greek World	?
First pottery	6th millennium
The earliest datable agricultural settlement in Greek lands (at Khirokitia, Cyprus)	about 5600
First settlements at Athens and Troy	about 3000
Bronze Age	about 2500
First palaces in Crete	about 2000
Shaft-and-vault graves at Mycenae	XVIII–XVII cent.
Prosperity of Crete	about 1600–1400
The Linear Script B	about 1450
Destruction of Cnossus	about 1400
The predominance of Mycenae	about 1400–1200
'Homeric' Troy	about 1275–1225
Destruction of Mycenae	about 1100
Colonization of Asia Minor	X–IX cent.
Greek colonization	VIII–VI cent.
Unification of Attica	VIII cent.
The first Olympic games	776
List of Spartan Ephors begins	754
List of Athenian Archons begins	683
The earliest coinage	VII cent.
Social revolutions in Greece (Age of Tyrants)	about 650–500
Solon elected Archon	595
Pisistratus tyrant	561
Restoration of Pisistratus	540

BIBLIOGRAPHY

Cambridge Ancient History, vols. II–IX (London: Cambridge University Press; New York: The Macmillan Company, 1924–32) offers a full-scale survey of Greek history and full bibliographical listings. Hence, the following suggestions for further reading mention, for most of the divisions, only a few recent books, generally in English. Current scholarly output is listed yearly in *L'Année philologique*.

I. REFERENCE BOOKS

Oxford Classical Dictionary (Oxford: The Clarendon Press, 1949).
J. Warrington, *Everyman's Classical Dictionary* (E. P. Dutton & Co., 1961).
Catherine B. Avery, ed., *The New Century Classical Handbook* (Appleton-Century-Crofts, 1962).

II. SOURCES (SELECTIONS IN TRANSLATION AND HISTORIOGRAPHY)

G. W. Botsford and E. G. Sihler, eds., *Hellenic Civilization* (Columbia University Press, 1915).
A. Momigliano, *Studies in Historiography* (Harper Torchbooks paperback, 1966).
For archaeological illustrative material see *Cambridge Ancient History, Plates*, vols. I–III (1927–34).

III. GEOGRAPHY

M. Cary, *The Geographic Background of Greek and Roman History* (Oxford University Press, 1949).
J. Myres, *Geographical History in Greek Lands* (Oxford University Press, 1952).
J. O. Thomson, *History of Ancient Geography* (Cambridge University Press, 1949).
M. Cary, E. H. Warmington, *Ancient Explorers* (1929; Penguin revised paperback, 1967).

C. McEvedy, *The Penguin Atlas of Ancient History* (Penguin paperback, 1967).

A. A. M. van der Heyden and H. H. Scullard, *Shorter Atlas of the Classical World* (Thomas Nelson & Sons, 1962).

J. O. Thomson, *Everyman's Classical Atlas*, 2nd ed. (E. P. Dutton & Co., 1963).

H. Bengtson, *Grosser historischer Weltatlas*, vol. I, 4th ed. (Munich: Bayerischer Schulbuch-Verlag, 1962).

IV. SURVEYS OF GREEK HISTORY
A. General Works

G. Grote, *History of Greece*, vols. I–XII (first published London, 1846–56; reprint, E. P. Dutton & Co., 1934).

H. Bengtson, *Griechische Geschichte*, 2nd ed. (Munich: C. H. Beck, 1960).

J. Hatzfeld, *History of Ancient Greece*, rev. ed. by A. Aymard; tr. by A. C. Harrison (Norton, 1966).

B. Textbooks

J. B. Bury, *History of Greece*, 3rd ed. (London: Macmillan & Co., 1951).

N. G. L. Hammond, *A History of Greece to 322 B.C.*, 2nd ed. (Oxford University Press, 1967).

C. Auxiliary Disciplines

E. J. Bickerman, *Chronology of the Ancient World* (Thames & Hudson, 1967).

C. T. Seltman, *Greek Coins*, 2nd ed. (London: Methuen and Co., 1955).

L. Robert, 'Epigraphie' (in *L'Histoire et ses méthodes*, C. Samaran, ed., Paris: Gallimard, 1961).

V. THE AEGEAN WORLD

The Cambridge Ancient History, new edition, vol. II, to be published shortly. The chapters on the Stone Age in the Aegean (by S. S. Weinberg), the Middle Bronze Age (by J. L. Caskey), Cyprus (by H. W. Cattling), Troy (by C. W. Blegen), the Minoan civilization (by F. Matz) and the chapters on the Mycenean civilization (by F. H. Stubbings, V. R. d'A. Desborough and N. G. L. Hammond) have already been published separately.

R. W. Hutchinson, *Prehistoric Crete* (Penguin original paperback, 1962).

G. E. Mylonas, *Mycenae and the Mycenaean Age* (Princeton University Press, 1966).

S. Hood, *The Aegean Before the Greeks* (Thames & Hudson, 1967).

C. W. Blegen, *Troy and the Troyans* (Thames & Hudson, 1963).

J. Chadwick, *The Prehistory of Greek Language* (Cambridge University Press paperback, 1965).

G. Thomson, *The Greek Language* (Cambridge: Heffer & Sons, 1961).

306

VI. HOMER AND HISTORY

G. Murray, *The Rise of the Greek Epic*, 4th ed. (Oxford University Press paperback, 1960).

G. Steiner and R. Fagles, eds., *Homer* (Prentice-Hall paperback, 1962) [critical essays].

D. L. Page, *History and the Homeric Iliad* (University of California Press paperback, 1959).

M. I. Finley, *The World of Odysseus*, rev. ed. (1956; Meridian Book paperback reprint, World Publishing Co., 1959).

J. B. Wace and F. H. Stubbings, eds., *A Companion to Homer* (London: Macmillan & Co., 1962).

G. S. Kirk, *The Homeric Poems as History* (separately published chapter of the new edition of *The Cambridge Ancient History*, 1965).

VII. ARCHAIC GREECE

C. G. Starr, *The Origins of Greek Civilization: 1100–650 B.C.* (Alfred A. Knopf, 1961).

A. R. Burn, *The Lyric Age of Greece* (St. Martin's Press, 1960).

P. Walcot, *Hesiod and the Near East* (University of Wales Press, 1966).

A. Andrews, *The Greek Tyrants* (Harper Torchbooks paperback, 1963).

G. L. Huxley, *Early Ionian* (Humanities Press, 1966).

M. I. Rostovtzeff, *Iranians and Greeks in South Russia* (Oxford University Press, 1922).

J. Boardman, *The Greeks Overseas* (Penguin original paperback, 1964).

VIII. CLASSICAL GREECE

A. R. Burn, *Persia and the Greeks* (St. Martin's Press, 1962).

A. T. Olmstead, *History of the Persian Empire* (1948; Phoenix paperback reprint, University of Chicago Press, 1959).

I. T. Hill, *The Ancient City of Athens* (Harvard University Press, 1953).

Aristotle, *Constitution of Athens*, tr. and ed. by K. v. Fritz and E. Kapp (Hafner Publishing Co. paperback, 1950).

C. Hignett, *History of the Athenian Constitution* (New York, Oxford University Press, 1953).

A. E. Zimmern, *The Greek Commonwealth*, 5th ed. (1931; Galaxy Books paperback reprint, Oxford University Press, 1961).

J. de Romilly, *Thucydides and the Athenian Imperialism* (Barnes & Noble, 1963).

A. H. M. Jones, *Athenian Democracy* (Frederick A. Praeger, 1958).

——, *History of Sparta* (Blackwell, 1967).

A. R. Burn, *Pericles and Athens* (Collier paperback, 1962).

V. Ehrenberg, *The People of Aristophanes*, 3rd ed. (Schocken paperback, 1962).

P. E. Corbett, *The Sculpture of the Parthenon* (King Penguin paperback original, 1959).

P. Roussel, *Sparte* (Paris: Boccard, 1939).

IX. CONSTITUTIONAL HISTORY AND LAW

N. Fustel de Coulanges, *Ancient City* (1st French edition, 1864; Anchor Books paperback, Doubleday & Co., Inc., 1956).

P. Vinogradoff, *Outlines of Historical Jurisprudence*, vol. II: *The Jurisprudence of the Greek City* (Oxford University Press, 1920).

J. W. Jones, *The Law and Legal Theory of the Greeks* (Oxford University Press, 1956).

R. J. Bonner and G. E. Smith, *The Administration of Justice from Homer to Aristotle*, vols. I and II (University of Chicago Press, 1930–38).

V. Ehrenberg, *The Greek State* (Norton paperback, 1964).

K. Freeman, *Greek City-States* (Norton paperback, 1963).

M. Lang, *The Athenian Citizen* (American School of Classical Studies at Athens paperback, 1963).

Aristotle, *Constitution of Athens*, tr. and ed. by K. v. Fritz and E. Kapp (Hafner Publishing Co. paperback, 1950).

C. Hignett, *History of the Athenian Constitution* (New York, Oxford University Press, 1953).

J. A. O. Larsen, *Representative Government in Greek Roman History* (University of California Press paperback, 1955).

V. Martin, *La Vie internationale dans la Grèce des cités* (Paris: Recueil Sirey, 1940).

H. Frish, *Might and Right in Antiquity* (Hafner Publishing Co., 1949).

X. SOCIAL AND ECONOMIC LIFE

A. Sources (Selections in Translation)

M. L. W. Laistner, tr. and ed., *Greek Economics* (London: J. M. Dent & Sons, 1923).

B. Monographs

G. Glotz, *Ancient Greece at Work* (Alfred A. Knopf, 1926).

W. L. Westermann, *The Slave Systems of Greek and Roman Antiquity* (American Philosophical Society, 1955).

F. Heichelheim, *Ancient Economic History*, vol. I (Gregory Lounz, 1959).

A. W. Andreadès, *A History of Greek Public Finance* (Harvard University Press, 1933).

H. Bolkestein, *Economic Life in Greece's Golden Age* (W. S. Heinman, 1958).

C. General Works: Technology

C. Singer, ed., *Oxford History of Technology*, vols. I & II (Oxford University Press, 1954 and 1956).

L. Casson, *The Ancient Mariners* (The Macmillan Company, 1959).

F. E. Adcock, *The Greek and Macedonian Art of War* (University of California paperback, 1962).

A. M. Snodgrass, *Arms and Armour of the Greeks* (Thames & Hudson, 1966).

XI. GREEK CIVILIZATION
A. General Works

A. Aymard and J. Auboyer, *L'Orient et la Grèce antique*, 4th ed. (Paris: Les Presses Universitaires de France, 1959) [vol. I of *Histoire générale des civilisations*].

W. Jaeger, *Paideia: The Ideals of Greek Culture*, vols. I–III (Oxford University Press, 1943–45; vol. I—Galaxy paperback, 1965).

G. Murray, *Greek Studies* (Oxford University Press, 1946).

L. Pearson, *Popular Ethics in Ancient Greece* (Stanford University Press, 1961).

A. W. H. Adkins, *Merit and Responsibility: A Study in Greek Values* (Oxford University Press, 1960).

U. E. Paoli, *Cane del popolo* (Florence, Felice de Monnier, 1958).

M. Smith, *The Ancient Greeks* (Cornell University Press paperback, 1961).

H. Marrou, *A History of Education in Antiquity* (New American Library, Mentor Books paperback, 1964).

B. Literature

H. J. Rose, *A Handbook of Greek Literature* (Dutton Everyman paperback, 1961).

C. M. Bowra, *Ancient Greek Literature* (1933; Galaxy Books paperback reprint, Oxford University Press, 1960).

A. Lesky, *History of Greek Literature* (Barnes & Noble, 1966).

H. C. Baldry, *Ancient Greek Literature in its Living Context* (Thames & Hudson, 1967).

A. W. Gomme, *The Greek Attitude to Poetry and History* (University of California Press, 1954).

B. Snell, *Poetry and Society: The Role of Poetry in Ancient Greece* (Indiana University Press, 1961).

C. W. Bowra, *Greek Lyric Poetry*, 2nd ed. (Oxford University Press, 1961).

P. W. Harsh, *A Handbook of Classical Drama* (Stanford University Press paperback, 1944).

T. Woodward, ed., *Sophocles: A Collection of Critical Essays* (Prentice-Hall paperback, 1966).

G. Murray, *Euripides and His Age* (Oxford University Press paperback, 1965).

R. Lattimore, *The Poetry of Greek Tragedy* (Harper Torchbooks paperback, 1966).

G. F. Else, *The Origin and Early Form of Greek Tragedy* (Harvard University Press, 1965).

G. Murray, *Aristophanes* (Oxford University Press, 1933).

T. B. L. Webster, *Greek Theatre Production* (London: Methuen & Co., 1956).

M. Bieber, *History of the Greek and Roman Theater*, 2nd rev. ed. (Princeton University Press, 1961).

J. B. Bury, *Ancient Greek Historians* (Dover Publications paperback, 1957).

F. E. Adcock, *Thucydides and his History* (Cambridge University Press, 1963).

G. Kennedy, *The Art of Persuasion in Greece* (Princeton, 1963).

J. D. Denniston, *Greek Literary Criticism* (London: J. M. Dent & Sons, 1924) [Selection of texts in translation].

M. Platnauer, ed., *Fifty Years of Classical Scholarship* (London: Basil Blackwell & Mott, 1955) [monographs and papers on individual Greek authors].

C. Art

P. MacKendrick, *The Greek Stones Speak* (New American Library, Mentor Books paperback, 1966).

G. M. A. Richter, *Handbook of Greek Art* (Doubleday & Co., Inc., 1960).

C. T. Seltman, *Approach to Greek Art* (Dutton Everyman paperback, 1960).

R. L. Scranton, *Greek Architecture* (Braziller paperback, 1962).

G. M. A. Richter, *The Sculpture and Sculptors of the Greeks*, 3rd ed. (Yale University Press, 1950).

E. Pfuhl, *Masterpieces of Greek Drawing and Painting* (The Macmillan Company, 1926).

R. M. Cook, *Greek Painted Pottery* (Quadrangle Books, 1960).

M. Robertson, *Greek Painting* (World Publishing Co., 1959).

J. D. Beazley, *The Development of Attic Black-Figure* (University of California Press, 1951).

J. J. Pollitt, *The Art of Greece: 1400–31 B. C.: Sources and Documents* (Prentice-Hall paperback, 1965).

D. Philosophy and Science
1. Sources (Selections in Translation)

T. V. Smith, *Philosophers Speak for Themselves*, vols. I & II (Phoenix Books paperback, University of Chicago Press, 1956).

G. S. Kirk and J. E. Raven, *Presocratic Philosophers* (1957; Cambridge University Press paperback reprint, 1960).

K. Freeman, *Ancilla to the Pre-Socratic Philosophers* (Harvard University Press, 1948).

H. D. Oakley, *Greek Ethical Thought* (London: J. M. Dent & Sons, 1950).

A. J. Brock, *Greek Medicine* (E. P. Dutton & Co., 1929).

T. L. Heath, *Greek Astronomy* (London: J. M. Dent & Sons, 1932).

M. R. Cohen and I. E. Drabkin, *A Source Book in Greek Science* (Harvard University Press, 1959).

2. Philosophy

E. Zeller, *Outlines of the History of Greek Philosophy* (Meridian Books paperback, World Publishing Co., 1955).

W. K. C. Guthrie, *A History of Greek Philosophy*, 5 vols. (Cambridge University Press, vols. I & II, 1962, vols. III–V in preparation).

Th. Gomperz, *Greek Thinkers*, 4 vols. (Humanities, 1901).

J. Burnet, *Early Greek Philosophy*, 4th ed. (Meridian Books paperback, World Publishing Co., 1957).

F. M. Cornford, *From Religion to Philosophy* (Harper Torchbooks paperback, 1957).

——, *Before and After Socrates* (Cambridge University Press paperback, 1960).

A. E. Taylor, *Socrates* (Anchor Books paperback, Doubleday & Co., Inc., 1959).

A. Koyré, *Discovering Plato* (Columbia University Press paperback, 1960).

G. M. A. Grube, *Plato's Thought* (Beacon Press paperback, 1958).

A. E. Taylor, *Plato* (Meridian Books paperback, World Publishing Co., 1956).

W. Jaeger, *Aristotle* (Oxford University Press paperback, 1962).

W. D. Ross, *Aristotle* (1955; Meridian Books paperback reprint, World Publishing Co., 1959).

W. K. C. Guthrie, *In the Beginning: Some Greek Views on the Origins of Life and the Early State of Man* (Cornell University Press Paperback, 1958).

3. Political Philosophy

T. A. Sinclair, *History of Greek Political Thought* (London: Routledge & Kegan Paul paperback, 1961).

E. Barker, *Greek Political Theory: Plato and His Predecessors*, 4th ed. (Barnes & Noble paperback, 1951).

——, *Political Philosophy of Plato and Aristotle* (Dover Publications paperback, 1959).

4. Science

B. Farrington, *Greek Science* (Pelican Books paperback reissue, Penguin Books, 1961).

M. Clagett, *Greek Science in Antiquity* (Collier paperback, 1956).

B. L. Van der Waerden, *Science Awakening* (Wiley paperback, 1963).

O. Neugebauer, *The Exact Sciences in Antiquity*, 2nd ed. (Harper paperback, 1962).

S. Sambursky, *The Physical World of the Greeks* (Collier paperback, 1962).

R. Taton, ed., *Ancient and Medieval Science* (Basic Books, 1964).

G. Sarton, *Ancient Science and Modern Civilization* (1954; Harper Torchbooks paperback reprint, 1959).

E. Religion

F. M. Cornford, *Greek Religious Thought from Homer to the Age of Alexander* (London: J. M. Dent & Sons, 1923) [source book].

G. Murray, *Five Stages of Greek Religion* (Anchor Books paperback, Doubleday & Co., Inc., 1955).

W. K. C. Guthrie, *The Greeks and Their Gods* (Beacon Press paperback, 1955).

W. K. C. Guthrie, *Orpheus and Greek Religion* (Norton paperback, 1966).

M. P. Nilsson, *Greek Folk Religion* (Harper Torchbooks original paperback, 1961).

——, *Greek Piety* (Oxford University Press, 1948).

M. P. Nilsson, *History of Greek Religion* (Norton paperback, 1964).

A. J. Festugière, *Personal Religion Among the Greeks* (University of California Press paperback, 1954).

A. D. Nock, *Conversion* (1933; Oxford Paperback reprint, 1961).

E. R. Dodds, *The Greeks and the Irrational* (Beacon Press paperback, 1957).

F. Cumont, *Astrology and Religion Among the Greeks and Romans* (Dover Publications paperback, 1960).

E. Rohde, *Psyche: The Cult of Souls and Belief in Immortality Among the Greeks*, vols. I and II (Harper Torchbooks paperback, 1965).

M. P. Nilsson, *Cults, Myths, Oracles and Politics in Ancient Greece* (Copenhagen: Einar Munksgaard Ferlag, 1951).

H. J. Rose, *Handbook of Greek Mythology* (Dutton Everyman paperback, 1959).

W. C. Greene, *Moira: Fate, Good, and Evil in Greek Thought* (Harper Torchbooks paperback, 1963).

Richmond, Lattimore, *Themes in Greek and Latin Epitaphs* (University of Illinois Press paperback, 1962).

M. Hadas and M. Smith, *Heroes and Gods* (Harper, 1965).

F. Family Life

R. Flacelière, *Love in Ancient Greece* (Macfadden paperback, 1964).

C. Seltman, *Women in Antiquity*, new ed. (Collier paperback, 1962).

W. K. Lacey, *The Family in Classical Greece* (Thames and Hudson, 1967).

H. A. Harris, *Greek Athletes and Athletics* (Indiana University Press, 1966).

XII. HELLENISTIC PERIOD
A. Sources (Selections in Translation)

C. C. Edgar and A. S. Hunt, eds. and trs., *Papyri*, vols. I & II (Harvard University Press, 1960).

E. Barker, *From Alexander to Constantine* (Oxford University Press, 1956).

E. Bevan, *Later Greek Religion* (Beacon Press, 1950).

F. C. Grant, *Hellenistic Religions* (Liberal Arts paperback, Bobbs-Merrill Co., 1953).

B. General Surveys

M. Rostovtzeff, *Social and Economic History of the Hellenistic World*, vols. I–III (Oxford University Press, 1941).

W. W. Tarn, *Hellenistic Civilization* (Meridian Books paperback, World Publishing Co., 1961).

E. Will, *Histoire politique du monde hellenistique* (Belles Lettres, Paris, 1966).

C. Monographs

U. Wilcken, *Alexander the Great*, ed. by Eugene N. Borza (Norton paperback, 1967).

W. W. Tarn, *Alexander the Great* (Beacon Press paperback, 1956).

G. T. Griffith, ed., *Alexander the Great: The Main Problems* (Barnes & Noble, 1966).

F. W. Walbank, *Philip V of Macedon* (Cambridge University Press, 1940).

H. I. Bell, *Egypt from Alexander the Great to the Arab Conquest* (Oxford University Press, 1948).

R. Taubenschlag, *The Law of Graeco-Roman Egypt*, 2nd ed. (Warsaw: Państwowe wydawnictwo naukowe, 1955).

V. Tcherikover, *Hellenistic Civilization and the Jews* (Jewish Publication Society, 1959).

H. I. Bell, *Cults and Creeds in Graeco-Roman Egypt* (Philosophical Library, 1953).

A.-J.Festugière, *Epicurus and His Gods* (Harvard University Press, 1956).

L. Edelstein, *The Meaning of Stoicism* (Harvard University Press, 1966).

E. Bevan, *Stoics and Sceptics* (Oxford University Press, 1913).

D. Dudley, *History of Cynicism* (London: Methuen & Co., 1937).

S. K. Eddy, *The King Is Dead: Studies in the Near Eastern Resistance to Hellenism 334–31 B. C.* (University of Nebraska Press, 1961).

B. E. Perry, *The Ancient Romances* (University of California Press, 1967).

M. Bieber, *The Sculpture of the Hellenistic Age*, rev. ed. (Columbia University Press, 1961).

T. B. L. Webster, *The Art of Greece: The Age of Hellenism* (Crown, 1966).

INDEX

Athena Promachos, 167.

Athens, earliest history, 22, 29, 41, 52, 65, 74, 75; from 800 to 600 B.C., 81–97, 106; during the Persian Wars, 121, 125–35; the Athenian Empire, 136–50, 167, 207; The Peloponnesian War, 151–61; from 500 to 400 B.C., 162–202; in fourth century, 203, 204, 205, 206, 219, 220, 231, 275; and Macedonia, 216, 222, 223, 224, 225, 226, 227, 254–5.
—art, 138, 163–7, 190–202; drama, 179–84, 275, 286–7; government, 208–11; learning, 178–9, 184–90, 237–9, 280–81; trade and industry, 167, 177, 208–9, 213, 214, 263.
—Acropolis, 16, 113, 162, 163–7.
—Erechtheum, 167, 168, 214.
—Parthenon, 166–8, 170, 191, 195, 214; statue of Athena, 166, 194.
—Phalerum harbour, 82.
—Piraeus harbour, 82, 141, 161, 167, 185, 211.
—Pnyx, 167.
—Propylaea, 163–6, 167.
—*Stoa Poecile*, 163–236.
—Temple of Athena, 106, 162–3.
—Temple of Athena Nike, 166, 168.
—Temple of Athena Parthenos, 166.
—Temple of Athena Polias, 167.

Athos, Mount, *see* peninsula of Chalcidice.

Atreus, Treasury of, 43.

Attalus I, 253, 266, 296.

Attica, 22, 29, 111; language, 40, 41, 231; social conditions from 800 to 600 B.C., 41, 45, 64, 81–97, 106, 176, 177, 211; during Persian Wars, 127, 132, 133, 134, 140; and the Peloponnesian War, 156.

Augustus, 15.

Axius (Vardar) river, 220.

Ayia Irini, 50.

Azov, Sea of, 270.

Babylon, 242, 267, 294.

Babylonia, 11, 12, 17, 20, 21, 29, 239, 249, 292.
—and Persia, 123–4, 204.
—Alexander in, 226, 228, 242, 247.
—Herodotus in, 187, 188.

Bacchylides, 138.

Bactria, 254, 256.

Balkan peninsula, 11, 12, 16, 34, 63, 70, 92, 124, 125, 126, 136, 140, 219, 222, 252, 256, 258.

Berenice II, 261.

Berosus, 292.

Bion, 287.

Bistritza, *see* Haliacmon.

Bithynia, 252, 256.

Biton, 102.

Black Sea, 53, 111, 157, 160; coast of, 34, 41, 47, 59, 63, 70, 124, 125, 139, 146, 148, 202, 212, 214, 256, 263, 282, 287.

Boeotia, 22, 29, 41, 45, 61, 64, 73, 74, 81, 82, 92, 106, 110, 127, 132, 133, 134, 147, 207, 216, 223, 225, 276.

Bosphorus, 70, 93, 219; the Straits, 53, 63, 70, 220.

Bosporan kingdom, 230, 256, 263.

Bryaxis, 197.

Brygos, 154.

Busiris, 68–9.

Bug, river, 63, 70, 187.

Byblos, 55.

Byzantine Empire, 12.

Byzantium, 70, 148, 256, 263.

Cadmea, 206.

Caere, 68–9, 138.

Caicus, river, 49.

Calauria, temple of Poseidon, 106.

Callimachus, 287; *Aitia*, 290.

Campania, 230.

Canusium, 142.

Cappadocia, 252, 256.

Caria, 81, 230, 231.

Carians, 59.

Carthage, 62, 67, 121, 134–5, 159, 207, 218, 242, 256, 262, 271, 272.

Catullus, *The Hair of Berenice*, 261.

Cassander, 249.

Cassandra, *see* Lycophron.
Caucasus, 13, 34, 139, 263; Caucasian coast, 70.
Caycus, 253.
Celtic states, 256.
Celtic tribes, 257, 258.
Celts, 13, 67, 70, 252, 270, 290; *see also* Galatians.
Centaurs, 166, 193, 197, 295.
Ceos, 110.
Cephissus, river, 81.
Cercidas, 287.
Cercinites, 70.
Chaeronea, 225, 226.
Chalcedon, 70.
Chalcidice, 66, 93, 158, 222, 223.
—peninsula of (Mount Athos), 70, 126, 153, 221.
Chalcis, 66, 74, 121.
Chalybes, 59.
Charon, 200–201.
Chersonesus, 70.
Chersonnese, Thracian, 93.
China, 263.
Chios, 41, 58, 148.
Chremonidean War, 255.
Christ, 6, 15.
Christianity, 282.
Chrysafa, 116.
Cilicia, 22.
Cimmerian Bosphorus, 70.
—Empire, 70.
Cimmerians, 57, 122.
Cimon, 141, 145, 146, 163, 176.
Clazomenae, 178.
Cleisthenes, 93–7, 140.
Cleobis, 102.
Cleomenes, 254, 277.
Cleon, 158.
Cleopatra (of Macedonia), 225.
Cnidus, statue of Aphrodite at, 240.
Cnossus, 17, 20, 21, 29, 30.
—Palace of, 25, 26, 27, 37, 55.
Codomannus, *see* Darius III.
Colchis, 139.
Colophon, 287.
Corcyra, 153, 156, 216.
Corinth, 16, 41, 65, 66. 68, 74, 80, 82, 88, 105, 121, 147, 152, 153, 161, 225, 226.

—Gulf of, 81, 157.
—Isthmus of, 41, 66, 74, 81, 88, 91, 132, 133, 147.
—Temple of Poseidon, 105.
Corinthian League, 276.
Cos, 287.
Crates, 287.
Cratinus, 183.
Cretans, 22–3, 29, 45.
Crete, 17, 20, 21, 22, 29, 30, 37, 41, 64, 74, 75, 282.
Crimea, 70, 148, 212, 270.
Critias, 161.
Croesus, 123, 143.
Croton, 66, 105, 121.
Ctesiphon, *see* Seleucia.
Cumae, 66.
Curium, 33.
Cyclopes, 43.
Cynics, 235–6, 298.
Cynosarges, 235.
Cynuria, 80.
Cyprus, 16, 17, 33, 34, 41, 50, 55, 146.
Cyrene, 114, 118, 236, 256.
Cyrus, 57, 123, 143, 160, 203, 204, 212.
Cythera, 157.
Cyzicus, 70, 160, 213, 256, 263.

Daedalus, 107.
Dalmatia, 67.
Danube, river, 63, 125, 226.
Darius, 125, 126–30, 142.
Darius II, 160.
Darius III (Codomannus), 227, 228, 295.
Delos, 140, 263.
—Temple of Apollo, 101, 105, 106.
Delphi, *frontis.*, 41, 74, 93, 102, 188, 194, 223.
—Temple of Apollo, 101, 105, 117, 123, 223.
Demeter, 101, 104, 112, 174, 282; *see also* Great Goddess.
Demetrius, 252, 255.
Demetrius Poliorcetes, 249, 252, 276.
Democritus, 185.

Demosthenes, 224–5, 232, 238.
Dexilaos, 196.
Dicaearchus, *The Life of Hellas*, 293.
Didyma, 247.
—Temple of Apollo, 101, 105.
Diogenes, 236.
Dionysius (of Syracuse), 208, 218, 234.
Dionysius (of Alexandria), 299.
Dionysus, 104, 112, 193, 199, 247, 295.
—Festival of, 111–12, 179.
Dioscurias, 70.
Dnieper, river, 63, 70, 187, 270.
Dniester, river, 63, 70, 125.
Dodona, temple of Zeus, 105.
Don, river, 63, 70, 270.
Dorian colonies, 157.
Dorians, 36, 40, 41, 75, 76, 81, 82, 106, 158, 239.
Draco, 88.
Dura-Europos, 285.
Duris, 139, 154, 198.

Egypt, earliest history, 11, 13, 16, 17, 20, 21, 29, 34, 36, 47, 58.
—4th cent. B.C., 214, 217, 230.
—and Persia, 123–5, 141, 146, 217.
—and Athenian Empire, 146, 147, 202.
—Herodotus in, 187, 188.
—Alexander in, 228, 247.
—and the Ptolemies, 249, 250–51, 260.
—and Macedonia, 252, 255.
—and Pergamum, 254.
—after Alexander, 250, 256, 257, 258, 263, 267, 270, 271, 274, 275, 279, 282, 292, 294.
Elea, 66, 108.
—Eleatic philosophy, 108, 178.
Eleusinian mysteries, 174, 179, 284.
Eleusis, 81, 174.
—Temple of Demeter, 101.
Elis, 80, 148; coins of, 202.
Elpinice, 176.
Empedocles, 178.
Epaminondas, 222.

Ephesus, 41, 50, 56, 121, 263, 268–9.
—Temple of Artemis, 117.
Ephialtes, 144–5.
Ephorus, 136, 239, 290.
Epicureans, 298.
Epicurus, 236.
Epiphanes, *see* Ptolemy V.
Epirus, 72, 219, 220, 242, 256.
Eratosthenes, 299.
Eretria, 74, 121, 125, 126.
Eros, 295.
Etruria, 68, 121, 214, 218, 230.
Etruscan cities, 121.
Etruscans, 62, 67, 70.
Euboea, 41, 66, 74, 126, 127.
Euclid, *Elements*, 299.
Euergetes, *see* Ptolemy III.
Euergetes II, *see* Ptolemy VII.
Eumenes I, 253.
Eumenes II, 268.
Euphronios, 138.
Eupolis, 183.
Euridice, 175.
Euripides, 180, 182, 210, 286.
Europe, 5, 12, 13, 125, 142, 229, 281.
Eurotas, river, 74–5, 78.
Eurymedon, river, 141.
Eurypontidae, 76.
Euthydemus, 268.
Eutychides, 284.
Euxine, 93, 252.
Evans, Sir Arthur, 17, 26, 27.
Flamininus, 205.
France, 202, 215, 257.

Gad, 285.
Gadara, 287.
Galatia, 256.
Galatians (Celts, q. v.), 252, 253; language, 279; statues of, 266, 296.
Ganymede, 164.
Gaugamela, 228, 245.
Gaul, 67, 135, 146, 214, 230, 281.
Ge, 99.
Gela, 66, 121, 135, 192.
Gelon, 135, 192.

Georgia, 281.
German tribes, 12.
Gorgias, 235.
Graeco-Roman civilization, 13.
Granicus, river, 49, 227.
Great Goddess (Great Mother), 24, 27, 29, 32, 50, 53, 54, 55, 56, 283; *see also* Demeter.
Greece, art, 15, 105–6, 111–20, 279, 293–8; religion, 99–106, 279, 283–6; philosophy, 15, 105, 178–9, 184–7, 234–7.
—Civilization, 12, 13, 15.
—2nd and 1st mill. B.C., 17, 22.
—and Aegean kingdoms, 16–48, 49–53, 74, 76, 82, 100.
—Anatolian, 49–71.
—7th and 6th cents. B.C., 98–120.
—6th and 5th cents. B.C., 162–202.
—4th cent. B.C., 203–15, 229–41.
—and Alexander, 216–28.
—after Alexander, 258–79.
—3rd and 2nd cents. B.C., 280–300.
Greeks
—Anatolian, 123, 124, 187, 247.
—Ionian, 125, 134, 162.
—Italian, 159, 162, 207.
—Sicilian, 121, 134, 159, 162, 207, 218, 256.

Hagia Triada, 30, 32, 55.
Haliacmon (Bistritza), river, 220.
Halicarnassus, 187.
—Mausoleum at, 231, 240.
Harmodius, 93.
Hectaeus, 111.
Hector, 35.
Hegeso, 196.
Helen, 74.
Helios, 295.
Hellas, 49, 56, 100, 121, 162, 206, 225, 229, 231, 255.
Hellespont, 92–3, 126, 141, 160–61, 225, 251, 256.
Hephaestus, 100.
Hera, 100, 142.
Heraclea, 70.

Heracles, 68–9, 101, 154, 199, 247, 268.
Heraclitus, 178.
Hermes, 175, 193, 240; Psychopompus, 200–201.
Hermus, river, 49.
Herodotus, 102, 111, 143, 187–9, 190, 292; *Histories*, 142; *Persian Wars*, 188.
Herondas, 287.
Herophilus, 299.
Hesiod, 61, 64.
Hiero II, 256, 271, 294.
Hieron, 192.
Himera, 135.
Hipparchus, 91, 93.
Hippias, 91, 93, 127.
Hippodamus, 185.
Hittite Empire, 17, 36, 53, 56, 57, 59, 122.
Homer, *frontis.*, 44, 53, 100, 109–110, 280, 281; *Iliad*, *frontis.*, 22, 34, 35, 41, 44, 74, 100; *Odyssey*, *frontis.*, 22, 41, 44, 100.
Homeric poems, 39, 41, 45, 100, 109, 172, 176.

Iberians, 67.
Ictinus, 163, 168.
Ida, Mount, 219.
Ilissus, river, 81.
Illyria, 220, 226.
Illyrians, 67, 219, 220.
Imbros, 41, 205.
India, 125, 250, 263, 267, 281; Alexander in, 228, 242, 247.
Indo-Europeans, 220; language, 16; *see also* Aryans, Iranians, Parthians, Persians, Sarmatians, and Scythians.
Ionia, 22, 68, 81, 126, 127, 176.
Ionian art, 113, 194, 230; cities, 126, 147; dialect, 40, 41, 106; islands, 66.
—Ionian philosophy, 108, 187.
Ionians, 41, 81, 82, 88, 187.
Ipsus, 249.
Iranians, 13, 70, 125, 228, 243–6, 247, 251, 254, 270.
Isaeus, 238.

Isis, 32.
Isocrates, 207, 217, 224.
Isopata, 30.
Issus, 227, 245.
Ister, 70.
Italy, 11, 12, 13, 34, 36, 47, 62, 63,
    66, 67, 88, 104, 105, 108, 117,
    121, 135, 142, 146, 147, 152, 157,
    158, 191, 195, 202, 205, 214, 215,
    218, 230, 231, 242, 255, 257, 271,
    281, 292, 294.
—Italian clans, 256.
—Italian temples, 194.

Jason, 202.
Jehovah, 247.
Jewish religion, 15.
Jews, 258, 260, 262, 280.
Judaea, 280.

Kertch, 256; straits of, 212, 219.
Kore, 103, 174.
Kuban, 270.

Lacedaemon, 75, 80; Lacedaemonian
    League, 161.
Lacedaemonians, 254.
Laconia, 74, 75, 76.
Laertes, 46.
Lampsacus, 213.
Laocoon, 295.
Lapithae, 166, 193, 197.
Larissa, 41.
Laureium silver mines, 130.
Leleges, 16.
Lemnos, 41, 205.
Leochares, 197.
Leonidas, 279.
Lerna, see Argolis.
Lesbos, 58, 110, 121, 148.
Leto, 99, 172.
Leucippus, 178.
Leuctra, 206.
Ligurians, 67.
Locri, Epizephyrian, 66.
Lycia, 22, 122, 230; tombs, 231.
Lycophron, *Alexandra*, 290.
Lycurgus, 75, 82.
Lydia, 57, 59, 82, 122.

Lydian Empire, 62, 123; kings, 123.
Lysander, 160, 161, 204, 247.
Lysias, 238.
Lysimachus, 249, 253, 295.
Lysippus, 230, 240, 284.

Macedonia, 92, 93, 146, 158, 236,
    249, 252, 254, 255, 256, 257, 258,
    259, 262, 263, 270, 277.
—and Persia, 126, 216–28, 243–6,
    248.
Macedonians, 258, 259, 295.
Maeander, river, 49, 294.
Magnesia, 294.
Mago, 272.
Mallia, 20.
Manetho, 292.
Marathon, 127, 130, 134, 138, 140,
    163, 182, 204.
Mardonius, 127, 133–4.
Marmora, Sea of, 53, 59, 63, 70, 141.
    252, 256.
Massilia, 67.
Mausolus, 197, 231; *see also* Halicar-
    nassus.
Medes, 123.
—Medo-Persian kingdom, 254.
Media, 254.
'Mediterranean civilization', 250.
Mediterranean Sea, 62, 70, 144, 146,
    221, 229, 262, 263.
Megalopolis, 287.
Megara, 41, 66, 74, 82, 88, 91, 110,
    147, 152, 153, 161.
Menander, 280, 286, 289.
Menelaus, 74.
Menippus, 287.
Merenpta, 34.
Mesembria, 70.
Mesopotamia, 11, 16, 58, 254.
Messana, 66.
Messene, 74, 75.
Messenia, 76, 80, 276.
Messenian Wars, 206.
Midas, 57.
Miletus, 29, 41, 66, 71, 101, 111,
    121, 126, 212, 263, 294.
—Milesian philosophy, 108, 178,
    185.
Miltiades, 130, 141.

Tegea, temple of Athena, 239.
Tempe, vale of, 131.
Teos, 110.
Terpander, 110.
Thales, 108.
Thebes (Greece), 22, 29, 34, 41, 61, 74, 106, 206, 222, 226, 287.
Themistocles, 114, 130–31, 132, 141, 242.
Theocritus, 287.
Theodosia, 70.
Theognis, 71, 110.
Theophrastus, 286.
Theopompus, 136, 239; *History of Greece*, 239; *History of Philip*, 239.
Theozotos, 64.
Therma (Thessalonica, now Salonica), 221.
Therma, gulf of, 221.
Thermopylae, 131, 132.
Theseus, 83, 87, 138, 202, 193, 295.
Thessalians, 45.
Thessalonica, *see* Therma.
Thessaly, 16, 40, 41, 44, 64, 74, 92, 131, 133, 134, 166, 222, 223, 262.
Thetis, palace of, 84.
Thisbe, 22.
Thrace, 93, 104, 125, 126, 137, 146, 148, 158, 219, 220, 230, 249, 263.
Thracian states, 256.
Thracian tribes, 70, 125, 130, 220, 258.
Thracians, 222, 270, 282, 287.
Thrasybulus, 161.
Thrasymachus, 185.
Thucydides, 156, 181, 189–90, 239.
Thurii, 187.
Tiberius, 15.

Tigris, 267.
Timaeus, 292.
Timotheus, 197.
Timon, 287.
Tiryns, 22, 25, 40, 42, 43.
Titans, 104.
Tityos, 99.
Tomi, 70.
Transcaucasia, 59, 263.
Trapezus, 70.
Triptolemus, 174.
Triton, 138.
Trojan War, 74.
Troy, 16, 21–2, 29, 34, 42, 53, 154.
Turkestan, Alexander in, 228.
Turkish powers, 12.
Tyché (Fortuna), 284, 286.
Tylissus, 20.
Tyrants, Thirty, 161.
Tyras, 70.
Tyre (Phoenicia), 227, 262.
Tyrtaeus, 68, 75, 100.

Ural, mountains, 219.
Utica, 62.

Van, 59.
Ventris, Michael, 17.
Vulci, 191.
Xenophanes, 108.
Xenophon, 186, 204, 207, 212, 239; *Anabasis*, 50, 239; *Education of Cyrus*, 239; *Hellenica*, 239; *Memorabilia*, 186; *Recollections*, 239.
Xerxes, 130–32.

Zeno, 236.
Zeus, *frontis.*, 48, 56, 100, 101, 112, 113, 142, 166, 164, 247, 268.

GREECE
AND
ASIA MINOR

MILES

0   40   80   120

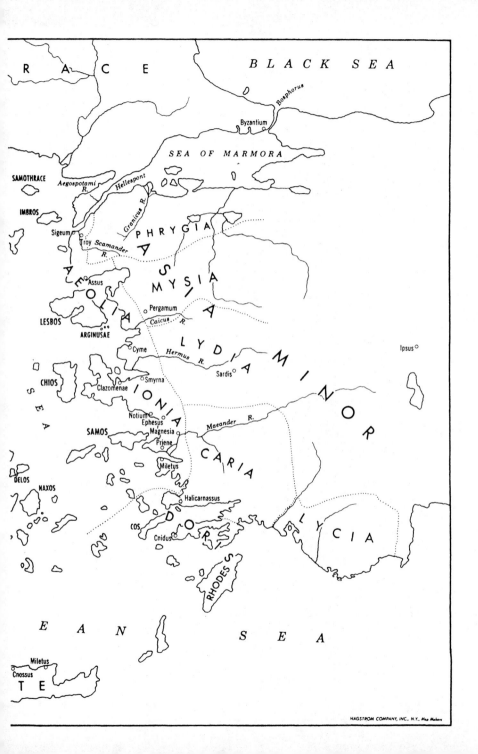

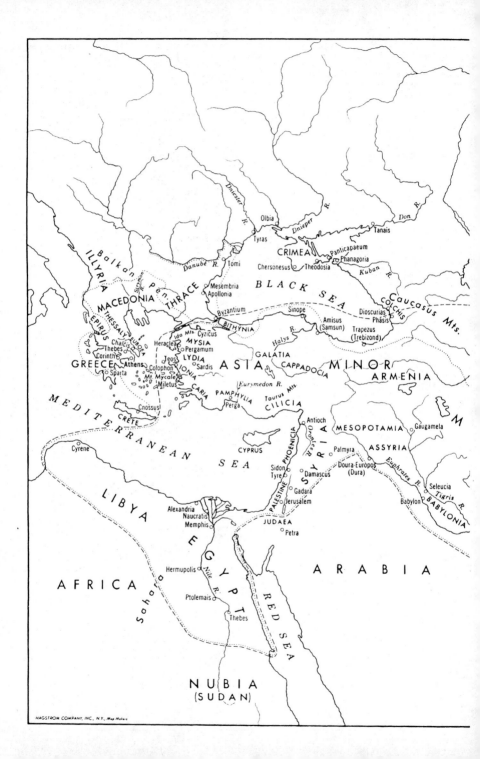

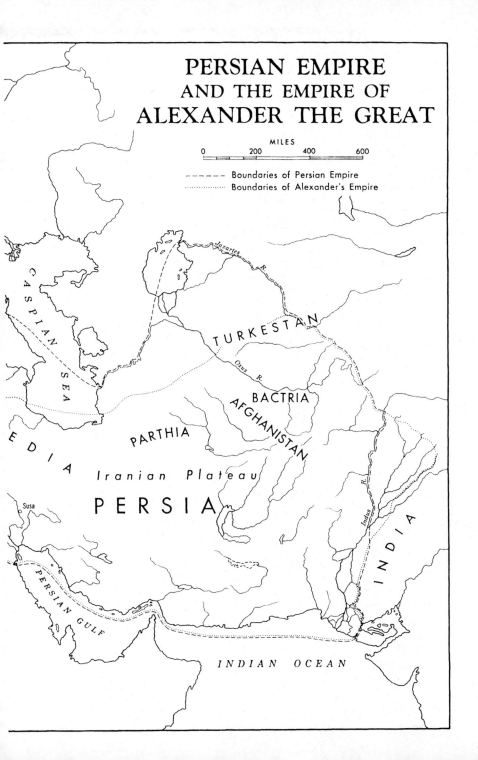

PERSIAN EMPIRE
AND THE EMPIRE OF
ALEXANDER THE GREAT

MILES

0   200   400   600

– – – – – Boundaries of Persian Empire
·············· Boundaries of Alexander's Empire

Jaxartes R.

CASPIAN SEA

TURKESTAN

Oxus R.

BACTRIA

AFGHANISTAN

PARTHIA

EDIA

Iranian Plateau

PERSIA

Susa

Indus R.

INDIA

PERSIAN GULF

INDIAN OCEAN

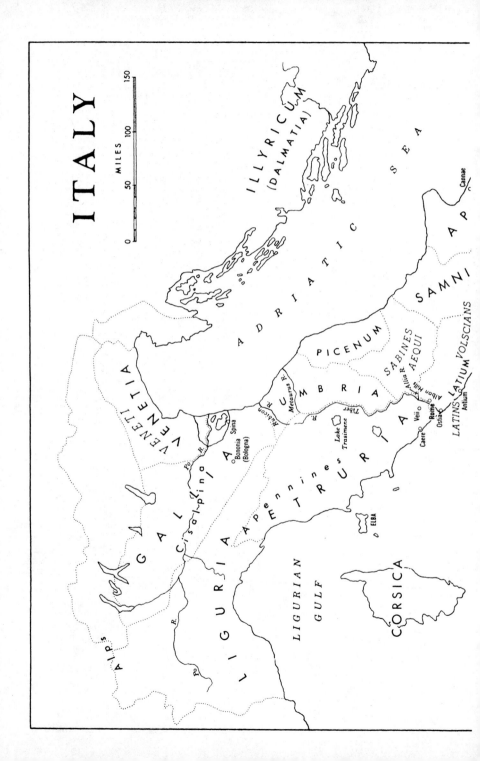

ITALY

MILES

0   50   100   150

ALPS

GALLIA

Cisalpina

VENETIA

Po R.

LIGURIA

Spina

Bononia
(Bologna)

Rubicon R.

Metaurus R.

UMBRIA

Apennines

TRURIA

PICENUM

ADRIATIC

SEA

ILLYRICUM
(DALMATIA)

Lake
Trasimene

Tiber

Veii

Caere

Rome

Ostia

Antium

Albon Hills

Allia R.

SABINES

AEQUI

VOLSCIANS

LATINS LATIUM

SAMNI

AP

Cannae

ELBA

LIGURIAN

GULF

CORSICA

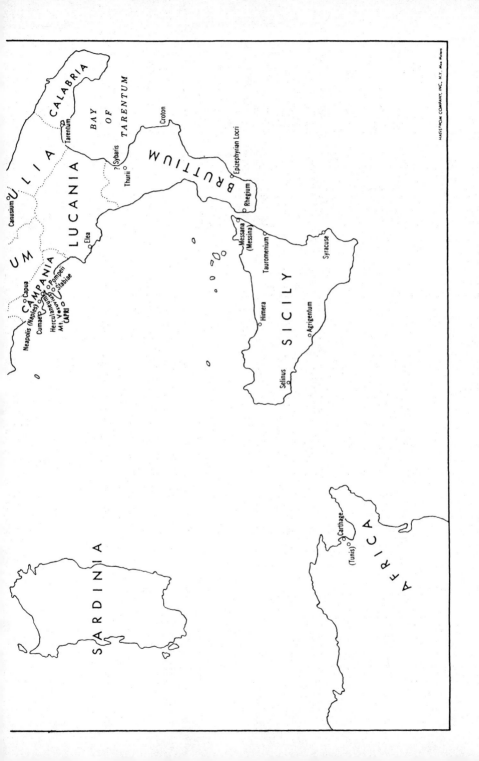